# GENESIS

## A Commentary for Bible Students

# WILBUR GLENN WILLIAMS

General Publisher:  Donald D. Cady
General Editor:  Ray E. Barnwell
Senior Editor:  David A. Higle
Theological Editor:  Philip A. Bence
Managing Editor:  Darlene Teague
Editor:  Kelly Trennepohl
        Laura Peterson
        Bobbie Sease

# CONTENTS

# EDITOR'S PREFACE

This book is part of a series of commentaries seeking to interpret the books of the Bible from a Wesleyan perspective. It is designed primarily for laypeople, especially teachers of Sunday school and leaders of Bible studies. Pastors also will find this series very helpful. In addition, this series is for people who want to read and study on their own for spiritual edification.

Each book of the Bible will be explained paragraph by paragraph. This "wide-angle lens" approach helps the reader to follow the primary flow of thought in each passage. This, in turn, will help the reader to avoid "missing the forest because of the trees," a problem many people encounter when reading commentaries.

At the same time, the authors slow down often to examine particular details and concepts that are important for understanding the bigger picture. Where there are alternative understandings of key passages, the authors acknowledge these so the reader will experience a broader knowledge of the various theological traditions and how the Wesleyan perspective relates to them.

These commentaries follow the New International Version and are intended to be read with your Bible open. With this in mind, the biblical text is not reproduced in full, but appears in bold type throughout the discussion of each passage. Greater insight will be gained by reading along in your Bible as you read the commentaries.

These volumes do not replace the valuable technical commentaries that offer in-depth grammatical and textual analysis. What they do offer is an interpretation of the Bible that we hope will lead to a greater understanding of what the Bible says, its significance for our lives today, and further transformation into the image of Christ.

David A. Higle
Senior Editor

# AUTHOR'S PREFACE

For thirty-three years, I have taught an introductory course in Old Testament to beginning university students. Of the thousands that have taken the course, all have taken on a semester project of some type. Most have chosen to write an appraisal paper on "What I thought about the Old Testament, and what I now think about it." For this assignment, they have been expected to write the first half at the beginning of their study, and the remainder a week before the end of the course.

Most of the papers have begun something like this: "I set my mind to read the entire Old Testament, but soon got bogged down with all the genealogies of Genesis 10 and 11. I gave up the project, going back to the New Testament." Some students testified that they made it through Genesis, but could not get past the antiquated laws and ordinances beginning in Exodus 21, followed by all the tedious descriptions of the Tabernacle and its fittings and furniture.

Admittedly, casual readers struggle to read the Old Testament and find connections between all its books. Casual readers do not quite grasp why a prophet wrote what he did, since they do not know how to connect those writings to historical information given in the books of Kings and Chronicles. Even when reading Genesis, people cannot understand why God would allow His people to participate in what appear to be pagan practices by people of faith.

To make the Old Testament a more approachable book has been part of my lifelong quest. But of all the Old Testament books, the most difficult book to grasp fully in significant ways has been the book of Genesis. Why?

First, there are great differences between the cultural practices of the times of the patriarchs and those of our time. These differences involve multiple wives (29:21-30), marriage to close relatives (20:12), favoritism within the family causing deception and rivalry (25:28; 27:2-40), servitude that bordered on slavery (29:24, 29), and the almost absolute exploitation of women (19:8).

Second, Genesis is a book that compressed the most amount of time in its coverage. And great gaps of time exist between chapters and verses. For example, thirteen years transpire between the events of chapters 16 and 17. Twenty years occur between verses 20 and 26 of chapter 25. Hundreds of years pass between the end of Genesis and the beginning of Exodus. But the greatest span of time is encompassed in the first eleven chapters, chronicling the period from the Creation to the life of Abraham. Unfortunately for us, God did not reveal definitively the amount of time involved in this period. God gave only a skeletal outline of the world's history to the time of the patriarchs. From there, relatively speaking, He allowed events to slow to a crawl so all could see how He worked to make salvation possible for all the world.

In graduate school, I chose to study under Jewish professors. I hoped that these descendants of those to whom God chose to give the truth could help me glean additional nuances of meaning from Hebrew thought and expression. I am grateful for their teaching. I hope some of what I learned comes through to the reader of this book. I have not attempted to be overly technical but have sought to clarify the depth of meaning in and behind the text.

I have tried to discover the heart of God as He expresses it in the pages of Genesis. He patiently worked with people prone to influence from pagan customs, those who gave in to the pull to sin, those who repeatedly moved away from Him. With undying love and faithful leadership, God worked so steadily to bring Abraham to a level of faith that could be reckoned **to him as righteousness** (15:6). God enabled Isaac to live a sufficiently peaceful life through the unfaltering obedience of Abraham (25:11). Jacob, ever more crafty and more prone to deception, finally quit trying to manipulate others when, in anticipation of meeting Esau, he met the Lord instead. God changed his grasping inner nature. I prayerfully hope that readers of this commentary will also meet the Lord and be changed by the experience.

In appreciation for assistance in the composition of this book, my deepest gratitude goes to Dr. Phil Bence, who often challenged my assumptions, gave invaluable advice, made constructive suggestions, and helped me to give a more cohesive presentation of the truth. My gratitude also goes to Darlene Teague and Kelly Trennepohl, who unfailingly read the manuscript with patient, word-by-word scrutiny to improve expressions and keep verb tenses uniform, thereby greatly improving the readability of the book. Above all, though, no small part of this work has come from God's help in the thoughts, ideas, and expressions that have been prayerfully presented. I pray you approve; more yet, I pray He approves.

Wilbur G. Williams
Marion, Indiana

# INTRODUCTION

W hat makes the Bible unique? Documents from Old Testament times, written over a period of hundreds of years and in numerous countries, have now been unearthed. In them are found accounts of the creation of the world and its people, a fall, a world flood, and codes of laws and conduct. All these accounts relate in different ways to similar accounts in the Bible. Why were these other accounts lost? Why did they have to be unearthed? In contrast, why, despite the efforts of many to destroy the Bible, does it still live? Why would men like William Tyndale, the father of the English Bible, at the cost of his life, translate the Scripture so English-speaking people could have access to it? Why is it that the most-read book in the world is the Bible? Why is it that more than one hundred million new copies of the Bible, in whole or in part, are printed every year?[1]

Three key words help people grasp the uniqueness of the Bible.

The first word is *revelation:* truth and information that God himself has disclosed. Not everything in the Bible is truth, but every word is true. Some of its content, material in the narrative parts of Genesis for example, appears merely as information. Genesis describes the practice of multiple wives not as an example God's people should follow but merely to make them aware of the ancient practice.

The second key word to understanding the Bible is *inspiration:* the supernatural process by which revelation found its way to the written page. The actual meaning of the Greek word *inspired* (see 2 Timothy 3:16) is "God breathed." Picture God breathing His truth through the minds of selected humans so they could write it onto the pages of Scripture. Peter speaks of men being "carried along by the Holy Spirit" (2 Peter 1:21). While the Lord used the vocabulary of each writer in Scripture, the ideas were God's ideas. We call the writer of the book of Job the "Shakespeare of the Old Testament" because the vocabulary used in Job supercedes that used by all other biblical writers. However, the words of other writers are no less God's words. Note these phrases that appear throughout the Bible: "And God said . . ." and "This is what the Lord says." They let us know that God speaks through the pages of the Bible. He wished His people to read all that those pages contain.

God chose the authors through whom He gave His revelation. Over the years, most people have agreed that Moses wrote Genesis, though the book itself does not mention him. God inspired the author's words and the writer seems to have counted carefully the words used. Though it does not show in the English translation, in the original Hebrew the author often used groups of words divisible by the number seven. In 1:1, there are seven words, while in 1:2 there are fourteen words. In 2:1-3, there are thirty-five words. The name for God—"Elohim"—is found thirty-five times; "earth" and "firmament" are both used twenty-one times. Two phrases—"and it was so" and "God saw that it was good"— are each used seven times. Also in 2:1-3, "the seventh day" is mentioned three times in sentences that each have seven words. Since seven represents perfection, the author and God made the account as perfect as they could using specific numbers. The author tried to communicate that God was inspiring the words.

The third key word to the Bible's uniqueness is *illumination*. When believers read the inspired revelation, God spiritually illuminates their minds. While God does speak to nonbelievers as they read or hear the Word, 1 Corinthians 2:14 states that "the man who isn't a Christian can't understand and can't accept these thoughts from God. . . . They sound foolish to him, because only those who have the Holy Spirit within them can understand what the Holy Spirit means. Others just can't take it in" (LB). While good books can edify, only the Bible can illuminate.

For want of a better way of titling the books of the Old Testament, the Jews picked the first word of the text. For the book of Genesis, that first word was *Bereshith,* most often translated "In the beginning." After the close of the Old Testament period, but before the birth of Jesus, Jews called this book "The Book of the Creation of the World." The name English Bibles use to designate this book ("Genesis") came from verse 4 of chapter 2 of the book in the Septuagint[2]: "This is the book of the 'geneseos' of heaven and earth."

What are the overarching truths of Genesis? The fifty chapters of Genesis present these paramount truths:

- God is the source of all life.
- God is holy.
- God wants obedience from people.
- Every person is born a sinner and needs salvation.
- God judges sin.
- God in love wants sinners to confess their sin to Him.

- God wants a special relationship with people.
- Faith and works are necessary components of salvation.

What are the other truths of Genesis? The book starts with the creation of the universe, after which God created the human pair from whom all peoples of the world have come (see Genesis 1–11). The focus narrows to the patriarchs of the Hebrew people whom God chose as primary recipients of His revelation. While Genesis is a part of the Pentateuch (the Bible's first five books), it varies significantly from the Pentateuch's other four books in its time span. The other four books cover a mere one hundred twenty years, while Genesis covers thousands of years. Genesis provides helpful background information for the remaining four books. Without Genesis, readers would be left to guess where and how the nation of Israel emerged and under what circumstances the people of Israel became God's covenant people. Genesis informs readers that the God who led the Hebrews out of Egypt was not just a tribal god tied to some geographical locality. In fact, there was no geography until He created it. To emphasize His bigness, God began His creation with the cosmos. Then He put in that cosmos a mere speck, our world, so He could give humankind a habitat in which to live and develop. He created everything with Adam and Eve and all their descendants in mind. He provided all they needed to exist.

While Genesis describes how humanity got its beginning, it provides many other important revelations. How sin entered the world is confined to one chapter (chapter 3), while the lives of the patriarchs encompass thirty-eight times that much space (chapters 12–50). God did not provide more definitive information as to when He began all things. He undoubtedly knew this subject would spawn many heated debates, and yet He did not consider it important enough to enlarge on it. Other important truths God did want to reveal appear in nearly every chapter.

One revelation God gave is that He wanted His creatures to know more about Him as a person. Accordingly, He revealed himself as vibrantly alive and intensely personal. Before He created His star players, Adam and Eve, He spent five times as much time to prepare a world for them. Then He took a piece of himself (His image) and put it in them (see 1:26), which made them at once a far greater threat, but also a far higher promise than anything else He had made.

A second important revelation in Genesis is that God wanted fellowship with His creation. He desired a give-and-take friendship. "One of the most significant differences between the God of Israel and the other ancient Near Eastern gods was that Yahweh chose to reveal himself to his people—who he is and how to please him."[3] God revealed His desire for intimate relationship when He engaged in conversation with Adam and Eve after their sin (3:9-13) and with Cain after his murder of Abel (4:9-10). God knew human beings would rise higher and achieve more if they continually sought Him and His holiness. But, rather than force himself on His creation, He continually came down to make himself available. Genesis shows God seeking His people, at times even more intently when they strayed, and always wanting a response. God gave life to Cain (4:1). Cain took life from Abel (4:8). God punished Cain but at the same time protected his life (4:15).

Rites and ceremonies were not the focus of religion during the time of the patriarchs. And pagan-influenced social customs made life difficult. The slow and hard lessons of character building had to be pounded out on the anvil of experience every day. Abraham showed his character when he allowed the younger Lot the choice of land for grazing (13:8-18), when he prayed an intercessory prayer for Sodom and Gomorrah (18:22-32), and when he refused personal profit that he could have gained from booty taken from invading kings (14:22-24). Isaac revealed his character when, while able to overcome the contentious Philistines who were stopping up his newly dug wells, he simply moved on and dug new ones (26:17-24). Jacob reached a new level of character when, while wrestling with God, he refused to stop his struggle until God blessed him (32:26). Joseph exhibited his character when he refused to get even with his brothers, instead seeing what they had done as God's working for good (50:20). In each of these men's lives, God met them where they were and helped them know more about who He is.

A third revelation is that no matter how far humans strayed from God's plan, He went to where they were to help them turn from their errant ways. God went to Abraham in Egypt and plagued Pharaoh for having taken Sarah (12:17). God went to Abraham in his errant ways again by appearing to Abimelech in a dream in order to hinder Abraham's plan (20:3-7). When Jacob made poor decisions, causing him added problems, God went to Jacob and revealed himself in an unforgettable dream (28:12-15; 35:1-15). God was always at the next crossroads, ready to pick up the pieces and carry on.

A fourth revelation is that God does not make a treaty with sin (12:17) and that sin carries with it a punishment (3:24; 6:13; 19:15). God is perfect and His ways are perfect. Though His creatures may be a great distance from His perfection, His standard for them has been a relative perfection that would decrease life's struggle against sin. This lesson came especially hard for Jacob. He began life grasping to take something that was really not his (25:26). As opportunity allowed, he took advantage of Esau (25:29-34), he deceived his own father Isaac (27:5-35), and he outwitted his father-in-law, Laban (30:25-43). Because of his own actions, Jacob was often pursued by sorrow and added struggles.

A fifth revelation is that God is a covenant God. He emphasized His desire of making covenants by giving himself selflessly, always making the first move. His desire for a close and binding relationship is encompassed in the word "covenant." When speaking to Noah, God used the word seven times in nine verses (9:9-17). Again God used this word ten times with Abraham in twenty verses (17:2-21). God also made a covenant with Abraham's son and grandson, Isaac and Jacob. God remembered this single covenant (made with Abraham, Isaac, and Jacob) when He helped their descendants escape from Egypt (see Exodus 2:24). God took the initiative. God wanted Abraham to know that, though He was planning to destroy Sodom, the patriarch's intercessory prayer was important and God could be influenced by it (see Genesis 18). At the times Jacob needed God most, it seemed God was not near, but He was. If God did not reveal himself, there was an overriding purpose. With Abraham, God seemed to be silent for thirteen years, apparently waiting until Abraham knew he had no other recourse in having a child but by trusting in God (see 16:16; 17:1). But God honored the covenant He made with Abraham.

## MODERN BIBLE CRITICISM

The opening book of God's holy Word was held by nearly all biblical scholars to be divinely inspired and inerrant in its expression until nineteenth-century scholars looked at the Old Testament with a skeptical eye and dubious detachment. Influenced greatly by the idea of the evolutionary development of Hebrew history, they discarded the thought that the biblical record presented reliable history. They conjectured that the people written about in the Book had a rather rudimentary, pagan-influenced origin to their faith and only slowly came to the belief in one God. It was thought that God's people had borrowed heavily from other literature, there finding myths and legends based on sordid ideas of numerous gods and goddesses, and that they only gradually purified their literature of its polytheism. The scholars further believed that much of the Old Testament was actually written many years later than what was commonly thought.

The consensus of critical scholarship today is that the use of two different names for God—"Yahweh" (written in Hebrew as "Jehovah" and in English as LORD) and "Elohim"—indicates that two different sources were combined by someone who lived much later than the events recorded in Genesis and the other four books of the Pentateuch. The work of the writer who used "Jehovah" for God's name is called the "J" document. He is thought to have lived about 850 B.C. The work of the writer who used "Elohim" for God's name is called the "E" document. He is said to have lived about 100 years later. Over a century later, during Josiah's reform in 621 B.C., when the Temple was being refurbished, the book of Deuteronomy was discovered. It is termed the "D" document. Finally, the origin of a writing called the "Priestly" work—labeled the "P" document—has been traced to the days of Ezra in the fifth century. I reject the theory of multiple sources for the following reasons:

- Moses' authority is denied.
- These ideas suggest that the patriarchs probably did not exist.
- Myths are entwined with facts.
- The belief in only one God is assumed to have come very late.
- Nearly all of the Old Testament was orally transmitted until the ninth century.
- It is thought that the Exodus probably did not occur.
- It is assumed that the miraculous and supernatural events recorded were invented.
- It is suggested that there was no worship center called the Tabernacle.
- The views are based on the idea of spiritual and physical evolution.
- The Old Testament as we have it is presumed to have been the work of pious forgerers.
- The Bible is taken as the word of men and not the word of God.

The words of Edward Young apply here:

There have been those who . . . have considered it [Scripture] nothing more than the national literature of the Hebrews, a purely human literary production upon a level with other similar productions of antiquity. This position is unsatisfactory because it is in basic error. It regards the Bible as a book of only human origin, whereas, as a matter of fact, the Bible is basically a book of divine origin.[4]

Many archaeological discoveries in the past century have rendered invalid many of the claims of this documentary approach to the study of God's Word. For example, thousands of clay tablets have been found at various sites in present-day Egypt, Iraq, Syria, Lebanon, and Turkey which reveal the cultural milieu that existed in the time of the patriarchs. These revelations squelch the idea that the patriarchal narratives are mythical. However, nothing as yet has come to light that can be related directly to the patriarchs, and it is highly unlikely that anything will. Roaming Bedouins who did not live in walled towns, who preferred tents for homes, who followed sheep and goat grazing patterns, and who used very little pottery left few remains that can be found.

"Genesis has not been compiled from several sources by one redactor or by several redactors, but is the work of one author, who has recorded the traditions of his people with due reverence but *independently* and according to a uniform plan. And that uniform plan was God's plan."[5]

## WHO WROTE GENESIS?

While Moses is the best candidate to have written Genesis,[6] there are some parts that were probably added by later editors. For example, many towns in Genesis 14 have names listed that were not known in Moses' day.[7] There are several notations that refer also to a later time such as "to this day" or "of today" that would have been written after Moses died.[8] It is not likely that Moses would have written the words "before any Israelite king reigned."[9] Moses is not likely to have described the Holy Land from the perspective of looking east ("beyond the Jordan" [Deuteronomy 1:1 RSV]) since he did not cross the Jordan. One can understand how later copyists, trying to assist readers in comprehending the text, would have added these notations with that in mind.

If Moses is the author of Genesis, it seems reasonable that he used previously compiled genealogy lists (see, for example, chapter 5). Names tied to certain places may well have come to him by oral traditions, such as the naming of wells (16:13-14; 26:18-33), the treaty arrangements (21:27-31), sacred spots (22:14; 28:16-22; 33:20), and covenant locations (31:45-52). But Moses needed divine revelation to write chapters 1 and 2.

While no one can know who wrote all parts of Genesis in its present structure, it is inspired of God. Otherwise it would not be part of divine Scripture. No arbitrary committee selected books for inclusion in the Old

Testament. The thirty-nine books came to be included because each played a decisive role in formulating personal faith and stimulating private and public worship. If any had been excluded, surely there would have been a demand that the oversight be corrected. Those who compiled the final edition of the Old Testament did little more than "rubber-stamp" what the people had come to value. One of my former professors expressed it best when he wrote, "Like a growth of a tree, which passes imperceptibly from the stage of a sapling that might be transplanted, to the stage where it is impossible to remove it, save by felling, canonicity grew imperceptibly."[10]

## ENDNOTES

[1]Peter Hicks, "A Very Special Book" in *The Complete Bible Study Tool Kit,* J.F. Balchin, D.H. Field and T. Longman III, eds. (Downers Grove, Illinois: InterVarsity Press, 1991), p. 236.

[2]The Septuagint is the Greek translation of the Old Testament from the third century B.C.

[3]Paul D. Wegner, *The Journey from Texts to Translations* (Grand Rapids, Michigan: BridgePoint Books, 1999), p. 21.

[4]Edward J. Young, *An Introduction to the Old Testament* (Grand Rapids, Michigan: Wm. B. Eerdmans Publishing Co., 1960), p. 27.

[5]*Jewish Encyclopedia,* p. 609.

[6]*For* arguments in support of this view, see *A Survey of Old Testament Introduction,* revised and enlarged, by G.L. Archer (Chicago: Moody Press, 1994), pp. 108–9.

[7]See Genesis 14:7-8, 14; 23:2; 28:19; 31:21; 35:6, 19, 27; 36:31.

[8]See Genesis 19:37-38; 22:14; 32:32; 35:20.

[9]See Genesis 36:31.

[10]Harold H. Rowley, *The Growth of the Old Testament* (New York: Harper and Row, 1963), p. 173.

# GENESIS OUTLINE

**I. FOCUS ON THE WORLD 1:1–2:3**
  A. The Setting 1:1-13
    1. Heavens and Earth Appear 1:1-2
    2. First Day 1:3-5
    3. Second Day 1:6-8
    4. Third Day 1:9-13
  B. The Development 1:14–2:3
    1. Fourth Day 1:14-19
    2. Fifth Day 1:20-23
    3. Sixth Day 1:24-31
    4. Seventh Day 2:1-3

**II. FOCUS ON HUMANITY 2:4-25**
  A. Adam's Commencement 2:4-7
  B. Adam's Containment 2:8-17
  C. Man's Counterpart 2:18-25

**III. FOCUS ON THE FALL 3:1–4:26**
  A. Sin's Coronation 3:1-6
  B. Sin's Curse 3:7-21
  C. Sin's Consequences 3:22-25
  D. Sin's Contamination 4:1-26

**IV. FOCUS ON JUDGMENT 5:1–11:9**
  A. From Adam to Noah 5:1-32
  B. Judgment Nears 6:1-22
    1. Corruption Growing 6:1-12
    2. Compensation in Sight 6:13-22
  C. Judgment Now 7:1–8:14
    1. Command: Enter the Ark 7:1-10
    2. The Flood Begins 7:11-16
    3. The Flood Covers All 7:17-24
    4. The Flood Concludes 8:1-14
  D. Judgment Past 8:15–11:9
    1. The Command to Leave the Ark 8:15-22
    2. The Charge Given 9:1-7

**VIII. FOCUS ON ISAAC 24:1–27:46**
  A. For Isaac: A Wife 24:1–25:18
    1. The Right Mate Desired 24:1-49
    2. The Right Mate Chosen 24:50-67
    3. Abraham: Death 25:1-11
    4. Ishmael and Family 25:12-18
  B. For Isaac: Twins and Trouble 25:19–27:46
    1. The Struggle Begins 25:19-26
    2. Birthright Bargained Away 25:27-34
    3. The Famine Begins 26:1-6
    4. Isaac Deceives Abimelech 26:7-11
    5. Isaac Prospers 26:12-25
    6. Isaac's Peace Pact 26:26-33
    7. Isaac's Grief 26:34-35
    8. Isaac Deceived 27:1-40
    9. Esau's Grudge 27:41-46

**IX. FOCUS ON JACOB 28:1–31:55**
  A. From Deceiver to Deceived 28:1–30:43
    1. Jacob Meets God 28:1-22
    2. Jacob Meets Rachel 29:1-12
    3. Jacob Meets His Match 29:13-30
    4. Jacob Has His Family 29:31–30:24
    5. Jacob and His "Bargain" 30:25-43
  B. The Great Escape 31:1-55
    1. Jacob Decides to Leave 31:1-21
    2. Laban Pursues His "Gods" 31:22-32
    3. Jacob and Laban Argue 31:33-42
    4. Jacob and Laban Make a Covenant 31:43-55

**X. FOCUS ON THE NEW JACOB 32:1–37:1**
  A. Jacob's New Nature 32:1–33:17
    1. Jacob With God 32:1-32
    2. Jacob With Esau 33:1-17
  B. Jacob's New Problems 33:18–37:1
    1. Jacob at Shechem 33:18–34:31
    2. Jacob at Bethel Again 35:1-15
    3. Jacob Suffers Loss 35:16-29
    4. The Family of Esau 36:1–37:1

**XI. FOCUS ON JOSEPH  37:2–39:23**
    A.  Joseph: From Status to Slavery  37:2-36
        1.  Jealousy of the Brothers  37:2-11
        2.  Joseph's Death Plotted  37:12-24
        3.  Joseph Sold Into Slavery  37:25-36
    B.  Joseph and Judah Compared  38:1–39:23
        1.  Judah in Canaanite Land  38:1-30
        2.  Joseph in Potiphar's House  39:1-23

**XII. JOSEPH: FROM PRISON TO PALACE  40:1–45:28**
    A.  Joseph: From Slavery to Status  40:1–41:57
        1.  Joseph Interprets Dreams  40:1–41:36
        2.  Joseph Made Prime Minister  41:37-57
    B.  Joseph: Reunion With His Brothers  42:1–43:34
        1.  The Brothers Visit Egypt  42:1-38
        2.  The Brothers Return  43:1-34
    C.  Joseph: Identity Revealed  44:1–45:28
        1.  Joseph's Final Check of His Brothers  44:1-34
        2.  Joseph Identifies Himself  45:1-28

**XIII. FROM CANAAN TO EGYPT  46:1–50:26**
    A.  Jacob's Family Reunited  46:1–47:26
        1.  Jacob Moves to Egypt  46:1–47:12
        2.  Joseph Eases the Famine  47:13-26
    B.  Final Days  47:27–50:26
        1.  Jacob's Final Wish  47:27-31
        2.  Jacob's Final Blessing  48:1-22
        3.  Jacob's Final Prophecy  49:1-28
        4.  Jacob's Burial  49:29–50:14
        5.  Joseph's Total Forgiveness  50:14-21
        6.  Joseph's Final Days  50:22-26

# Part One

# FOCUS
# ON THE WORLD

## Genesis 1:1–2:3

Genesis, of course, is the first book of the Bible. It answers such questions as these: How did this world begin? How did it come to be populated? From where did people come? Was there some purpose to it all? The answers are quite briefly stated in Genesis and the rest of the Word: God made the earth; from it He made Adam; from Adam eventually came Abraham, who then became the ancestor of Jesus the Messiah. One needs only to read the first few chapters to realize that what Victor Hamilton calls "the arithmetic of Genesis" is striking. In his words, "Only two chapters are devoted to the subject of creation and one to the entrance of sin into the human race." Yet "thirteen chapters are given to Abraham, ten chapters to Jacob, twelve chapters to Joseph." Then he asks, "Can one man be six times more important than the world?"[1]

It appears that God, through humanity, wanted to present the record of Creation, the development of sin in the world, and the spread of humankind throughout the world in the briefest manner so as to get to the patriarchal period as quickly as possible. So the divine report moves from ages to years, even months, and sometimes it slows to days.

One feels inclined to ask why God disregards the rest of humanity, while focusing intently on only four men and their descendants. Were there not other people somewhere in the world at that time who were just as interested in finding answers to their sinful dilemmas? It was out of concern for the whole world that God singled out the patriarchs. Of all the races of the world, there had to be just one that would be especially equipped and dedicated to receive and transmit God's eternal Word to the sacred page, so that through it He could reach the rest of humanity. It was a process slowed not by God's hesitation or delay but by humankind's slowness to accept and assimilate the truth.

Jews have an interesting legend that God went one by one to representatives of all the peoples of the world in Abraham's day, seeking to find a person who would take responsibility to father a race who would be God's special recipients of the revelation. One after another, they all refused the task because of the harassment, persecution, and abuse it would entail. Finally, Abraham agreed.

Tolstoy once observed, "The Jew is that sacred being who has brought down from heaven the everlasting fire, and has illumined with it the entire world. He is the religious source, spring, and fountain out of which all the rest of the peoples have drawn their beliefs and religions."[2]

## ENDNOTES

[1]Victor P. Hamilton, *Handbook of the Pentateuch* (Grand Rapids, Michigan: Baker Book House, 1982), p. 18.

[2]Dr. J.H. Hertz, *The Pentateuch and Haftorahs,* vol. 1 (New York: Oxford University Press, 1936), p. 45.

# 1

# THE SETTING

## Genesis 1:1-13

The great curtain of time opens with nothing but God, who pre-dates it and transcends it. He never began. In Scripture, He is always assumed. No space is given to prove His being, but He is the origin and fountain of all things. While He was the author of all, there was no stage for Him to begin His creative work. He set that stage to begin His work.

## 1. HEAVENS AND EARTH APPEAR (1:1-2)

The account of the creation of the world by God is stated in the most brief, most complete, or most exalted way. The opening words in Genesis have caused much discussion: **In the beginning God created . . .** (Gen. 1:1). This traditional translation makes the phrase an independent clause. It affirms that everything that came into being afterwards was entirely God's work.

Many scholars have noted the same arrangement of words in many other ancient documents that use a similar phrase as is found in Genesis 1:1, and it is translated as a dependent clause.[1] These scholars insist the more correct translation is "When God began to create the heavens and the earth. . . ." But this makes the second verse read, "The earth [already] was formless and void." This would suggest that when God began His creative task, He started with matter that already existed. This view has pagan origins, for in early literature, things like salt water, fresh water, silt, and sky were gods that brought all things into being. Nothing was indicated about their origin. Nor should one expect such insight, for the gods were created in man's image. This reverses the biblical account where man was created in God's image.

The biblical record did not come *from* the mind of a human author, but came *through* it. God used each writer's vocabulary, typical expressions, and writing style, but the Lord of all inspired what was written. So it is not a matter of what man thinks; it is rather what God intended the translation to be.

If one translates Genesis 1:1 as a dependent clause, then the truth that God predated everything is not supported. That God alone existed when He decided to create the world is a truth found throughout the Bible. For example, "By faith we understand that the universe was formed at God's command, so that what is seen was not made out of what was visible" (Hebrews 11:3; see also Psalm 33:6, 9; John 1:3; Hebrews 1:2; 6:5; 2 Peter 3:5; Romans 4:17). If the beginning phrase of Genesis 1:2 was intended to be a dependent clause, then, in order to blend with the truth elsewhere in the Bible, we must translate it "By way of beginning, God created the heavens and the earth."

The Hebrew verb that describes God's activity at this time is *bara*. Never is this word used in Scripture to express man's action. It is always used to describe God's work in creating, since He is the only one who can bring something out of nothing. Additionally, if He starts with something He has at that moment already created, the verb is changed to **formed** as with Adam, or **built** as with Eve.

This opening verse lifts us to heaven and allows us to observe God in His initial act of speaking the universe into existence, for in the expression of **the heavens and the earth,** the universe as we know it today is intended.

Did God create other worlds with intelligent life on them? It could be, but if He did, each had its own revelation, like the Bible God gave people on earth. Our sacred Word is intended exclusively for us so that we can know how God prepared the way for both our first parents and, ultimately, for our own births. Indeed, we were in God's mind as much as were Adam and Eve.

The **earth** at that time was in a state of formlessness, emptiness, and darkness. It had the appearance of a trackless waste where nothing lived, nothing roamed, nothing grew, and nothing could happen by itself. As Job observed, God had suspended the mass of "the earth over nothing" (Job 26:7).

When did all God's creative activity take place? Had He yet set the clock? The Bible does not say. Many people claim God created the world only six thousand years ago. But much evidence continues to emerge that argues for a much earlier creation. Archaeologists confirm that pottery, formed by hand, sometimes painted by hand and baked in a kiln, strongly suggests the existence of a sixth millennium B.C. period.

While anything God created would have had the appearance of age,[2] it does seem unlikely that He would have created such things as fired pottery, put it in a buried context to make it appear older than it really was, so that people who would declare the numerous time measuring devices which operate by laws He created are all in error, and by so doing express great faith by affirming, without any supporting evidence, that the pottery was really made and used at a much later period of time.

One theory as to how God could have created our world much earlier than six thousand years ago takes Genesis 1:1 as separated in time from the remainder of the chapter by a gap of undetermined length. This view is strengthened by the description that God's **first day** did not end at 1:5, where the Hebrew, translated literally, has "One Day," or "Day One." It rather ends at 1:1, where we are told that **God created the heavens and the earth** in a completed, orderly form. While the original Hebrew describes all the other days with ordinal numbers—such as **second day** (1:8), **third day** (1:13), and **fourth day** (1:19)—the writer described only Day One differently. Further, this view calls for a translation of 1:2 to read, **Now the earth [became].** Though **was** is the more common translation of the Hebrew word used here, on occasion the word correctly means *became*.

Those who hold this view find evidence of it in Jeremiah 4:23-26, where the prophet Jeremiah spoke of a vision he had in which he "looked at the earth, and it was formless and empty. . . . [He looked] at the heavens and their light was gone. . . ." While Jeremiah wrote this in the context of the coming devastation on Judah, the view is that he saw, as a result of the disobedience of the people, a return to the state that occurred after God's perfect creation of **the heavens and the earth** (Gen. 1:1).

If God created a perfect heaven and earth on the first day (Gen. 1:1), then was Satan, after failing to take over heaven, "hurled to the earth, and his angels with him" (Revelation 12:7-9)? And did this cause a destructive disorder to occur? One theory holds that after a great gap of undetermined time God reconstituted the world, as described in Genesis 1:2 through 2:1-2, which had been caused by Satan's fall to become **formless and empty.**[3] If this was so, the first earth could have been where dinosaurs and even a prehistoric human-like animal (all now extinct) once lived. Note also, Isaiah 45:18 declares that God "did not create it [the earth] to be empty, but formed it to be inhabited." Further, this theory speculates that Satan caused the earth to be void. If we translate Genesis 1:1 traditionally, we get a picture of God creating chaos first, out of which He later brought order. Those who hold this view believe a gap of undetermined duration occurred, after which God returned the **heavens and earth** to their original condition.

29

In Genesis 1:2, God intentionally narrowed the focus to **the earth,** for the word **earth** has more significant emphasis by being placed at the beginning of the sentence. Perhaps God knew man would eventually have an inclination to worship heavenly bodies, so nothing more was said about the **heavens** after 1:1.

We read that **earth,** at the time of 1:2, was **formless.** Isaiah used the same word in Isaiah 34:11, where it was translated "desolation." This indicated that the earth lacked any orderly definition. It was in a chaotic state.

Next we read that the **earth** was **empty** (Gen. 1:2) or void of anything that grew. It had the barrenness of a moonscape. The same Hebrew word used here is found in Job's description of God's spreading "out the northern skies over empty space" and hanging "the earth on nothing" (Job 26:7). The **earth** was bleak, barren, and devoid of any living thing (Gen. 1:2).

The third Hebrew word describes the earth as having **darkness . . . over the surface of the deep** (1:2). While **the deep** was not defined, it was somehow *related* to **the earth.** It was liquid mass of tremendous volume without any illumination whatsoever.

**Hovering over the waters** was **the Spirit of God.** We call rivers and seas "waters," but in this instance it was yet another way of designating the earth's fluid consistency. **Water** was used this way in Scripture to designate something that was normally solid becoming soft (see Joshua 7:5; Ezekiel 21:7). The phrase **the Spirit of God** is understood as the third person of the Trinity.[4]

Just what was intended by the activity of **the Spirit of God hovering over the waters** (Gen. 1:2) is clarified by the use of the word in other instances, such as Deuteronomy 32:11 where Moses described "an eagle . . . [hovering] over its young." We can imagine a mother bird nurturing, training, protecting, and looking after every aspect of the life of her offspring. This helps us to understand how the Holy Spirit was relating to this fluid, moving substance that God had created.

One might ask, "But why did **God** need the **Spirit** to function this way? Could God not do this nurturing by himself?" Such a question does not help us to understand what was occurring here. For God was and is the Holy Spirit, and the Holy Spirit was and is God! They are not separated, yet they sometimes appear that way to the human mind. The **Spirit of God** was actively maintaining this creative substance called **earth,** doing everything needed to prepare it for God's next stage in its development.

## 2. FIRST DAY (1:3-5)

In Genesis 1:3, **God** spoke **light** into being. While God could, and often did, communicate in sounds clearly understood by man, He did not speak with vocal cords as we know them. God's speaking creation into being was a far more profound activity than simply opening a mouth and uttering sounds. John said God created by His Word which was "in the beginning . . . with God . . . and the Word was God" (John 1:1). The apostle emphatically informed us Jesus was that Word of God which brought into being "all things" (Gen. 1:2) at the time of creation.

Could not God the Father have created alone? Again a moot question. For God was and is Jesus, and Jesus was and is God. The way we can understand the relationship of God and His Son, both very active at the Creation, is by understanding the inseparability of the sounds one makes from the person who makes those sounds. So here, in the first three verses of the Bible, we see the Trinity at work collectively and individually.

God created the **light** (1:3). There had been none before that time. All that existed earlier was a formless, empty, stirring mass covered with darkness. While God did not need to have **light** to do His work, we learn that everything He did was to prepare for the creation of Adam and Eve and all humankind that would follow.

What was the consistency of this **light** God created? We are not told. While it was possible to have light without a light bearer (for example, lightning), it might be that the light came from the burning mass from which God made **the greater light to govern the day** on the fourth day (1:16). This might explain how the vegetation—seed-bearing **plants and trees** (1:11)—could grow after God created them on the **third day** (1:13). God does not give a complete explanation that eliminates all questions about His procedures and techniques. Probably the human mind simply cannot fathom all the ingredients of God's recipe for His own activity. We can only comprehend God's work from the completed project.

God, at this time, **saw that it** [the light] **was good** (Gen. 1:18). There was not even a remote possibility that anything God did was other than *good*. This biblical account was meant to give us a grasp of what occurred during this time of creation, so God used what are called anthropormorphisms—that is, human expressions to explain divine activity and assessment. When a person accomplishes something through his own activity, it would be natural for him to look at it afterwards to determine if it has met his expectations. If

31

he is satisfied with the results, he calls it "good." In this sense, the word was used here and in verses 10, 12, 18, 21, 25, and 31 to describe God's evaluation of His own creative work.

The second half of 1:4 reveals that God did not eliminate all darkness when He created light. The darkness simply gave way to the light when God separated them. Darkness must always give way to light when light comes, not vice versa. God created our world this way. Remember that Jesus would in time refer to himself as "the light of the world." He said, "Whoever follows me will never walk in darkness, but will have the light of life" (John 8:12). It was in this sense that He told His disciples, "You are the light of the world" (Matthew 5:14). David wrote in his psalm of deliverance, "the LORD turns my darkness into light" (2 Samuel 22:29).

As Jesus made light symbolic of himself, so darkness was made symbolic of one that does not have the light of Christ. In the Gospel of Matthew, we read the parable Jesus told of a marriage feast. The king in that parable described hell as " the darkness, where there will be weeping and gnashing of teeth" (Matt. 22:13). If God is light, then darkness, the opposite of light, is everything that He is not. Isaiah 9:2 speaks about "the people walking in darkness, [seeing] a great light," and compared it to those "living in the land of the shadow of death."

God named the **light "day,"** and the **darkness "night."** The use of the word **day** here stood for more than just the daylight hours when the sun illuminated the earth. This was not possible until the **fourth day.** The word **day** was God's day. And since "with the Lord a day is like a thousand years, and a thousand years are like a day" (2 Peter 3:8; Psalm 90:4), we cannot know the precise length of that day.

Was it twelve hours long, as many argue, or twenty-four, or forty-eight? Or was the word used in the sense of a day-age of unknown length? The first day began when God caused the first light to appear, and it concluded when He caused that light to disappear. Clearly God did not need a long duration in which to create the world. He could have created everything in six twenty-four-hour periods, as many think He did. For that matter, God could have spoken the whole universe into existence with only one command, such as "Let it all come forth now!" But for whatever purpose, He did not choose that way.

God's first full day of creative (or re-creative) activity was concluded with the words **and there was evening, and there was morning.** One is immediately made aware of the order of these two parts of the day— **evening** comes before **morning** (1:5). We might expect that order to have been reversed, with **morning** being the introduction of light, and **evening** signaling the withdrawal of it. But, as stated here, darkness existed before God made light appear. Since this was the order given, in Jewish reckoning the night precedes the day. The seventh day, their "Sabbath," begins at sunset on Friday evening. It ends at evening dusk on Saturday.

Because of the arrangement of **evening** before **morning,** some have argued for another theory of Creation called the *intermittent day* theory. This theory holds that each of the creative days were started by God and, while His creative activity lasted for twenty-four hours, He did not start the creative activity of the next day until a period of time had elapsed. He did this to allow all that He had created on that day to develop and multiply. In other words, the oaks He created continued their assigned work, to produce acorns, to grow more oaks, to produce more acorns, to grow more oaks. These growth periods for each day ceased when the **evening** of the next day of God's creative activity began.

## 3. SECOND DAY (1:6-8)

God's **second day** in Genesis 1 involved creating an **expanse** to separate the water **under** it from the water **above it** (Gen. 1:7). The point of reference is the expanse itself, for the Hebrew literally designates "the under side" and "the upper side." The difference seems to be between water as water at the bottom of the **expanse** and water as humidity above it. We again see God's orderly preparation for humankind by making it possible for water to escape being continuously contaminated with "salts," in order for plants and animals to grow and also to allow humans and animals to consume it.

The expanse God created is named **sky** (1:8). The same word in Hebrew appears in 1:1 where it is translated "heavens." In the earlier usage of the word, it referred to our whole universe. Here it described only that part of the whole we can grasp when we view it with our human eyes. When we look up into the **sky** (1:8), we can see humidified water in the form of clouds. And when this water accumulates in volume, it descends in the form of rain, sleet, or snow.

The **second day** concluded with a second **evening** and **morning** (1:8).

## 4. THIRD DAY (1:9-13)

On the **third day** (Gen. 1:9-13), God made the fluid mass He had created on Day One to separate into **water** and **dry ground.** These now emerge for the first time by themselves. God then proceeded to name them **land** and **seas** (1:10). Again, when God observed this segment of His creative activity, He recognized that it fully complied with His total creative plan; therefore, **it [too] was good** (1:10).

When water and land had been given their assigned locations, God put in place what people would need to survive—all types of vegetation. Again He did this with His Word. He created not only the first **plants and trees** but also the **seeds** to insure their continued survival after the death of the original Creation. Those seeds produced only what was related to **their various kinds.**

According to the text here, there is no possibility of evolution, where one **kind** (1:11-12, 21, 24-25) of thing after thousands of years evolves into another **kind** of thing.[5] The word **kind** here must stand for "species." Every specific kind of plant or tree had within its seed an abundance of varieties that would need only the guidance of a gardener to develop. For example, suppose God created the rose species red in color. He built within it all the many varieties of colors that we now enjoy. But the species of a rose could never develop into any kind of lily.

Genesis 1:12 indicates that the total essence of the plants and trees was in their seeds. There was no more or less in the seeds than in the plant or tree. So maple seed would never produce a tree of a different **kind,** but numerous varieties of maples were in the one seed. Each seed contained both its limits and its possibilities. While **the land** produced **vegetation** (1:12), it took God's creative act to make such production possible. Only God's initiation transformed potential into reality. With this act, God concluded **the third day.**

## ENDNOTES

[1]Derek Kidner, *Genesis,* Tyndale Old Testament Commentaries (Downers Grove, Illinois: InterVarsity Press, 1967), p. 43.

[2]Adam and Eve had to have had the appearance of mature adults at the point of their formation out of "dust" and "rib." Animals created could not have functioned normally if they were not already fully developed. Trees created by God for the Garden of Eden, if cut down, would have had numerous annual tree rings as would be normal from years of growth.

[3]Some claim that Isaiah 14:12-17 gives a more complete account of what transpired in heaven. After Satan was cast down, he is said to be the one "who shook the earth and made kingdoms tremble, the man who made the world a desert, who overthrew its cities. . . ." Church fathers such as Jerome and Tertullian believed these verses did refer to the Devil, causing the name "Lucifer" (Hebrew translated "morning star") to be given to him. But both Luther and Calvin rejected this idea as a gross error.

[4]While the Hebrew words for "wind" and "spirit" are the same, here the meaning is not that God merely caused a movement of air, as the same phrase might indicate in other places (see Psalm 55:8; 1 Corinthians 2:11). Here we do not read *"a* spirit [wind] *from* God," but *the* **Spirit** *of* **God.** Also, if the meaning was "wind," then, since it is just mentioned, it would have existed with God, for there is no mention of "wind" being created.

[5]Lee Haines, *Genesis and Exodus,* The Wesleyan Bible Commentary (Grand Rapids, Michigan: Wm. B. Eerdmans Publishing Co., 1967), p. 27.

# 2

# THE DEVELOPMENT

## Genesis 1:14–2:3

That God is a God of order is emphasized in the way He chose to create. He planned the first three days to set the stage for the second three. The light of the first day is related to the sun, moon, and stars that appear the fourth day. The heavens and waters were created on the second day to provide an environment for the fish and birds that were created the fifth day. The earth was brought into existence on the third day so the creatures intended for it could be created on the sixth day.

## 1. FOURTH DAY (1:14-19)

**The fourth day** of God's creative activity involved the localization of the day/night separation with respect to earth's sky, as compared to the skies of the universe. God created heavenly bodies to **give light on the earth** (Genesis 1:15). The probable source of light on Day One was the sun, as earlier suggested. God brought it into its proper relationship to **the earth** on the fourth day. The God-assigned location of these lights influenced their action in relation to the earth—they separated its day and night.

But God's realignment also established **seasons and days and years** by causing the earth to tilt at the correct angle and to spin at just the right speed. With the world in motion this way, seeds could reproduce after their own kind as God intended.

God designed the heavenly bodies to **serve as signs to mark . . . days and years** (1:14), thus making possible the calendar. And to whom are they to be **signs** for such calculation? Not to the plants, trees, fish, or animals. God built these **signs** instinctively into each of them. The Lord was here preparing for His ultimate creation of the highest form of life, one not guided simply by instinct. This ultimate creation would have the ability to calculate, compare, and intelligently observe, then recall and tabulate. The earthly properties set earth's stage to prepare for God's star performers—Adam and Eve—to make their ordained appearance.

The light-givers God made consisted of one **greater light** and one **lesser light.** The **greater** and **lesser** description of these lights reflect the perspective of the humans who would view them from the earth. The designations greater and lesser do not refer to their relative size, but to the intensity of the light emanated (as in the case of the sun) or light reflected (as in the case of the moon).

God assigned these two lights to **govern** the day and night. **Govern** here does not imply the authority to **rule,** such as a god might have. The Hebrew writers of Scripture strongly opposed any type of worship of heavenly bodies. This view stood in contrast to the concurrent pagan belief that heavenly bodies were gods who ruled the earth.

Here, **govern** means simply when their lights would and would not shine. Their governance was limited to and based on the rotation of the earth, which God set in motion. This pattern of light followed His divine plan, for He pronounced it **good.** God would not have declared His work **good** if the lights were thought to be mini-gods in any way.

## 2. FIFTH DAY (1:20-23)

God began His fifth period of creative activity by speaking into existence all forms of **living creatures** in the **water** which suddenly teemed with life, as well as **winged birds which [flew] above the earth** (Gen. 1:21). Verse 22 seems to say that God spoke directly to the sea creatures and birds, something He did not do to the plants. Rather than a command, these words of the Lord summarized His giving them the ability to **increase on the earth.** He initiated their mission.

## 3. SIXTH DAY (1:24-31)

From our point of view, God was busier on the **sixth day** than on the other five, but more activity on God's part does not involve time as we know it. He began this creative segment by speaking into existence **living creatures . . . that move** on the land. This suggests both the walking animals that people in time would tame and use in one way or another and crawling creatures that creep along the ground. As a separate act, God created **animals** that are instinctively wild. While the word **wild** does not appear in the Hebrew text, the separation of these animals from **livestock** (cattle) in Genesis 1:24-25 seems to suggest it.

Everything God had created to this point helped prepare for His grand finale—the creation of the couple who would begin the human race. They were to be creatures endowed with a will that could turn against their Creator. He could make these creatures robot-like, preprogrammed to do nothing but obey God. And how convenient that would have been, for God could then have made His way the broad way, populating heaven with as many as He wanted, sending few or none on the narrow way to hell.

Why did God reject this possibility? God would rather have the few who would *choose* Him over the many that would have *no other choice* but Him. Before this moment, God acted without prior consultation. This decision required a divine committee of three to decide **Let us make man** (1:26).

And it was not a convocation of gods as pagans might picture, but to many Christian believers, the divine Trinity. Only three are mentioned in Genesis 1:1-3: The **Spirit** of God brooding over the waters (1:2); God's Word, whom John called Jesus, speaking all things into existence (John 1:1); and the Lord—by His name Elohim, its plural encompassing all three. No others existed; no others were present.

Did the author who wrote the divine record use documents handed down to him from earlier authors, such as the patriarchs or Joseph? It could be, for writing has been found predating them by up to two thousand years. But critics who claim the **us** and **our** (1:26) are a reflection of the pagan belief in numerous gods and goddesses have ignored Paul's unequivocal statement: "All Scripture is God-breathed" (2 Timothy 3:16).

Jews claim that the plural forms in Genesis 1:26, as well as one major Hebrew word for God (Elohim), are "plurals of majesty" or a "plural of fullness." The view is that their ancestors who wrote Scripture considered God too holy to describe by a singular noun or pronoun.

Would God have inspired the author to use a plural form when speaking about himself? In our usage today, a person often uses a plural form when he describes himself consulting with himself—for example, the phrase "Let us see." However, this type of usage is not found in the Bible anywhere with respect to God except here and 11:7. Would the **Spirit** in 1:2 and the **Word** (Christ) of John 1:1 have temporarily left the scene so that God was addressing himself? That would be difficult for an omnipresent deity. It seems to support what Christian scholars throughout the centuries have believed: that the Trinity is in view here.

The emphasis in Genesis 1:26, however, is not in the plural forms for God and in the pronouns referring to Him. The text focuses more on God's intent to **make man** in His **image** and **likeness.** These two terms represent the same concept. They fit the pattern of a typical Hebrew parallelism used for emphasis. **Image** in 1:27 merely replaces the idea of **likeness** in 1:26. This does not mean human beings are little gods but that God intended them to have a spiritual endowment. God gave this endowment only to humankind; His gift did not extend to any other animals He created.

Nahum Sarna has observed,

> The idea of man "in the image of God" must inevitably include within the scope of its meaning, all those faculties and gifts of character that distinguish man from the beasts and that are needed for the fulfillment of his task on earth, namely, intellect, free will, self-awareness, consciousness of the existence of others, conscience, responsibility and self-control. Moreover, being created "in the image of God" implies that human life is infinitely precious.[1]

While either image or likeness may adequately cover the meaning of the other, there is some difference between them. We might understand better if we consider a sculptor making a sculpture of a person. He makes the stone reproduction in the model's **image** as he views the stone during the process of his work. When he finishes the work, it can be said to bear the **likeness** of the model. The skill of the artist is evident in both the process and in the end result.

God's Word does not exclude the fact that the Creator and His creature are profoundly different in most ways—necessitated by what might be called the chasm between the divine and human beings. The clear emphasis is on the areas where they are similar by God's carefully planned design.

And it is striking that God made no two people alike. Even "identical" twins have discernible differences. This reveals the multiplicity of God's unity. Every person in his or her uniqueness is a direct reflection of God. If we could isolate the essential God-given differences in each individual, past, present, and future, and somehow put them all together, we would begin to discover what God "looks like." Each one individually, and every one collectively, came from the one **image** God had in mind, and He put all of that potential **likeness** in Adam and Eve.

David recognized the profound significance of humanity's place in the creative collage of God when he asserted, "You have made them [each person] a little lower than God" (Psalm 8:5 NRSV). While sometimes the psalmist's Hebrew word for God is translated "angels" (see the King James Version) or "heavenly beings" (see the New International Version), the writer recognized the high spiritual elevation of humanity's beginning.

Genesis 1:27, unlike 1:26, uses a singular pronoun to describe God. He created **man [and woman] in *his* own image.** The spiritual ingredient in God's formula for creating people came directly from God himself, though in His tri-unity all three were involved in everything that transpired. Why is this aspect of God's endowment emphasized with respect to man? The answer might be that we are being prepared to learn of how spiritually elevated man was in the beginning. We can then understand how far he fell when he yielded to temptation the first time.

Verse 27 further chronicles that what God had contemplated (1:26) was done. Yet we have a new element—**male and female.** These sexual designations, while implied with the animals in 1:22, are specifically delineated concerning human beings. Why is the maleness and femaleness of the human persons more specifically underscored than with all of the rest of God's creation? Perhaps the image-of-God creation requires a greater responsibility in all human relationships, especially in the incomparable physical, emotional, and spiritual merger of a man and a woman in marriage.

God gave the blessing of fruitfulness to humans (1:28) which He had first given to animals, but the difference is that God addressed man and woman directly. This reveals that part of humanity's spiritual uniqueness is to be able to receive and process information spoken by God. Animals are motivated by instinct; people are directed by personal choice.

God could have started with a whole city, countries, or nations of people, making it unnecessary, to a certain extent, to tell them to **be fruitful and increase in number.** But that would have denied humanity the process of learning through the experience of discovery and growth in society, and may have caused them to develop more slowly. If God had begun with whole nations of people, the earth would have run out of space thousands of years ago. God gave the original pair greater responsibility to choose correctly and in the best interest of future generations, according to God's instructions. Sadly, they failed miserably when it came to choosing obedience.

God's instructions did not end with the assignment to **increase** numerically, for He added the phrase **fill the earth** (1:28). We are closer to the fulfillment of this assignment than in any previous generation. In fact, overpopulation in many areas is a growing concern. One could wonder if this has some relevance to the end of the age, and the return of our Lord.

Then the verse continues with an instruction to **subdue** the earth. In God's consultation (1:26), He chose to give humanity authority over the rest of creation. Here, humans are instructed not to let the creation **rule** them. Subsequently, whenever people chose to worship images, they worshiped animals (most often bulls or cows, but also lions, crocodiles, tigers, or some birds) which were created without God's **image** or **likeness.**

In some instances today, people have gone beyond ruling God's creation to "abusing" it, often to the detriment of the greater good for us and our children. Though there is a line between "ruling" and "abusing" which may at times be difficult to clearly define, we must recognize that all that is created beneath us is there for us to rule, not to destroy. Vawter explains, "Dominion [**rule over**] is not a license to caprice and tyrannies, but, in the best sense, a challenge to responsibility and the duty to make right prevail."[2]

Some claim Genesis 1:29 states that God's original intent was for people to be vegetarian, eating only **every seed-bearing plant . . . and every tree that has fruit with seed in it.** Such a view is not tenable. The **every** does not mean that all plants were equally edible for all; some were obviously poisonous. The passage was intended to make a generalization to the effect that, directly or indirectly, life depends on vegetation, and all of it comes from the hand of God. Eating of flesh may have been implicit in the statement. After the flood God told Noah he could eat "every creature that moves along the ground and . . . all the fish of the sea" (Genesis 9:2-3). In the next verse God said, "Just as I gave you the green plants, I now give you everything."

It is at the end of the **sixth day** that God's plan for creation was culminated. God pronounced each of the six days **good.** On the last day, only after man and woman were created, and after He has instructed them as to their diet, God looked over it all and declared it **very good.**

Walter Bowie wrote about Genesis 1:31 as follows:

> This verse is a gladdening thought on which to meditate whenever life seems drab or shadowed. For times come when men are inclined to pessimism. They have reasons for personal depression: They may look out on their world and see it involved in tragic shadows. Nevertheless, this verse exalts the truth that the universe as God made it, and the life which God meant to be lived in it, are beautiful. God looked at everything and saw that it was very good.[3]

# 4. SEVENTH DAY (2:1-3)

The author did not intend the chapter break that occurs after Genesis 1:31. New information does not begin until 2:4, where it is prefaced by a summary statement, "the account of the heavens and earth when they were created." Continuing the story of chapter one, in 2:1 we are told that **the heaven and the earth were completed. . . .** The Lord had assessed His work as **very good.** He affirmed that everything that had been in total dysfunction and disarray earlier had now been set right. Step by step, God organized, added to, gave focus, and assigned specific limits to His creation, making the whole function properly in relation to each part so as to present the entire **vast array.**

Having completed His creative activity, God then **rested from all his work.** Some translations read here "sixth day" instead of **seventh day,** for from 1:31 we know **the sixth day** was the day **God . . . finished the work.** Does that information conflict with what is said in 2:2? No, for the verb tense in 2:2 is past perfect, indicating an earlier action: **God *had* finished** [on the sixth day] **all the work he had been doing.**

Now we come to what is intended by the phrase God **rested from all his work.** God did not need rest, for He had no muscles to use that required rest. Everything He did was by means of His Word. And in Jesus' words, God is at work every day (see John 5:17). This rest was not needed to recover strength on God's part, which most often is why people need rest. Rest can, and here does, mean that the activity God was engaged in during the creative days had ceased. God simply began a different type of "work"—that of a sovereign maintenance and control over His creation.

The emphasis in 2:3 is not on the **rest** God took, but on His blessing and making holy the time immediately following His six creative periods. God had in His mind the man and woman He had created. They would become weary. They would need **rest,** but more importantly they would need worship. This required setting aside a special time for that purpose. Even here, though people tire, **the rest** is really the ending of activity in order to give a fuller focus on worshiping God and to enjoy communion with others. The writer of Hebrews puts it this way: "Let us not give up meeting together, as some are in the habit of doing, but let us encourage one another—and all the more as you see the Day approaching" (Heb. 10:25). While one may appreciate the Sunday afternoon nap, it will not satisfy our basic human need. If this type of rest had been in God's mind for this day, there would have been no need to make it holy. God wanted humanity to elevate their spirits by a special worship every seventh day. And worship of God is enhanced when we consider the length to which He went to make this work special for us.

## ENDNOTES

[1]Nahum M. Sarna, *Understanding Genesis* (New York: McGraw-Hill, 1966), pp. 15–16.

[2]Bruce Vawter, *On Genesis, A New Reading* (Garden City, New York: Doubleday, 1977), p. 59.

[3]Walter Bowie, *The Interpreter's Bible,* vol. 1 (New York: Abingdon Press, 1952), p. 487.

# Part Two

# FOCUS ON HUMANITY

## Genesis 2:4-25

Both Genesis 1:1–2:3 and Genesis 2:4-25 give accounts of the Creation. The climax of Genesis 1 was the creation of humanity. Everything that God did up to that time was to prepare for the creation of Adam and Eve. They needed a garden with trees for beauty, food, and oxygen. They needed animals, birds, and rivers of fresh water. All God's preparations set into motion the complete life cycles of the various forms of life. In Genesis 2:4-25, God turned the focus more directly to His human creation.

One difference between these two accounts is that thirty-five times in the first thirty-four verses of Genesis, God is referred to exclusively by the Hebrew word *Elohim,* while in the account starting with Genesis 2:4 and carrying through Genesis 3, only the title "Lord God" *(Yahweh Elohim)* is used. For some scholars, this change of the divine name signals the work of a different author.[1] (See the introduction to the commentary for a discussion and refutation of the multiauthor theory.)

If one does not accept a multiauthored view, what is the explanation as to why Genesis 2:4 seems to be a second account of the Creation? Believing the Bible to be God's Word given to human authors, we must understand the two accounts to be different ways of looking at Creation. What is presented in the first chapter is God's perspective of what He did. He transcends all He creates. The opening account pictures God standing outside the universe and speaking elements into existence in a chronological, orderly fashion. Adam and Eve were the end focus, but not the primary players.

In the account beginning in 2:4, rather than presenting the writing of a second person, God shows us the Creation from another perspective —

a "this-worldly" one. In it He shows first the desired marriage relation between God and humanity and then the ideal marriage relationship between man and woman.

In this second account, we turn our focus to a more detailed look at the Creation—how God went about His work in relation to a small part of this world. This perspective is that of the Garden—an inside look at Paradise—not of the cosmic universe, as in Genesis 1. There we see Him as the Creation-God, *Elohim,* transcendent and majestic. Here in His relationship with His two stars, Adam and Eve, He is *Yahweh Elohim, a* God of intimacy who desires to be directly involved with them.

## ENDNOTE

¹Though this view has been somewhat tarnished today, many contemporary scholars still consider Genesis 1:1 through 2:3 to have been written by someone other than Moses. In their opinion, Moses likely did not exist. This view holds that Genesis 1:1 through 2:3 was written by an author who lived about 750 B.C. Others think it to have been written as late as the time of Ezra the scribe, or around 450 B.C., and that Genesis 2:4 begins the work of a different author who lived four centuries earlier, or around 850 B.C. These scholars further believe that the work of two other writers, or groups of writers, were blended with these two to make the Pentateuch as we know it a composite collection of four different authors. The scholars believe that these writers do not all agree and that the writers contradict one another in numerous places.

# 3

# ADAM'S COMMENCEMENT

## Genesis 2:4-7

enesis 2:4 begins where Creation began (see 1:1). Then the account jumps to the point paralleled in 1:10. Why speak of the time when **no shrub had yet appeared . . . and no plant . . . had yet sprung up** (2:5)? Because God is setting the stage to tell about the Garden of Eden and all the vegetation and trees found in it. Though it is in the same context, avoid reading that the *cause* for this was that there had been **no rain on the earth** and **no man to work the ground** (2:6). These facts are given parenthetically, but these are not *the reason* for the lack of plant life. In this account the writer details not only Adam's habitat but also his own origin.

There seems to be significance to the double reference in 2:5 as to **shrub** of the field and **plant** of the field. Probably trees are not described because the writer is distinguishing between perennial growth and yearly growth that requires human attention. Perennials appear **on the earth** by themselves, needing minimal or no human attention, while the yearly plants "spring up" from the earth but need cultivation, planting, and nurturing.

Note again that the divine title has a second designation added. God is now called **LORD God** (2:4). If this is not the result of multiauthorship of Genesis, why does the change take place here and not again later? And additionally, why does the divine name change to just "LORD" in Genesis 4?

*Elohim* is a more general name of the Trinity as One in their transcendence, operating from heaven. The title **LORD** means **God** in His close covenant relationship with humanity. *Yahweh* is the way **LORD** would have been spoken and written if the name had not been considered too holy to do either. Since the third commandment stated, "You shall not misuse the name of the LORD" (Exodus 20:7), Jews were fearful that in common conversation or silent thought they might violate this prohibition. So Jewish scribes of the ninth century, who transcribed biblical text from one scroll to another, sought to make it easier not to even think the divine name, lest they do it in vain. Their strategy was to borrow the vowels from another word for "lord" in Hebrew (always translated into English in lower case): *Adonai*. They then added the vowels from this word to the consonants for "LORD." This made the Hebrew word read *Jehovah*. Since God, in the minds of the people, might otherwise lose His transcendence when speaking of people in a covenant relationship, as in this account of Creation, both divine names are used.

There is also another important reason why **LORD** is used when God interacts with His human creation. This name is related to the verb meaning "to be." Its full significance was not grasped during the times of Genesis. God revealed the full meaning of "I am" to Moses. God explained to him that this, God's memorial name, was intended for "all generations" (Exod. 3:14-15 KJV).

Properly understood, God connected His personal, covenant **LORD** to the verb that indicates character: "to be." Common speech more frequently concentrates on verbs of action, such as go, do, send, give, and work. But any action results in empty activity if it does not emanate from a genuine God-given character. Such character cannot be earned by labor. The eternal **LORD** of the universe is the only One who can give godly character to people with an inherently evil nature.

This covenant title also expresses God's timelessness—He is the eternal "I am," meaning that He always was, He is, and He always will be. The emphasis, of course, is mostly on His presentness.

All segments of time are broadly placed in three main classifications: the past, which is enormously vast and growing; the future, which is eternally vast, but shrinking, as far as our earthly future is concerned; and the present, which is squeezed between these two vast parts of time. By contrast to the past and future, the present is minuscule. The present is so brief that before something said reaches the ears of listeners, it is already in the past. But it is in the present moment that God works best.

Sinners often fall into sin because of boredom with what is happening in their lives. Afterward, they have to drag the hopelessly heavy sins of the past, fearful that others may discover how evil their hearts really are if their sins are exposed. To complicate their predicament, they are shackled with anxiety about what the future holds. To escape this fear and anxiety that eats away at any available tranquility, they plunge deeper into sin to obtain some temporary reprieve, then only add more guilt to their troubled consciences.

So, God in His covenant name emphasized that He is the source of genuine peace. His name essentially means "I am there for you wherever you are . . . I really am! If you will allow me, I can eliminate all the cancer-like sin in your life. I can remove the regrets of the past, come into the present moment, and remove the anxieties for the future."

From a glimpse of what God did on the third day of Creation, the picture shifts to the sixth day when God created "man in his own image . . . male and female" (1:27), and we are given a more detailed picture of His process. When God **formed man** (2:7), He did not use new, just-created material. That is, He did not create man out of nothing. He used what was at that moment preexisting material, commonly translated as **dust of the ground.**

The word **dust** in Hebrew does not mean only sand, dirt, or earth, but rather something that was a small part of larger elements. **Dust** often refers to basic elements **of the ground,** as here, but often involves more than dust or clay. The main emphasis though is not on that part of the human's basic elements. Rather it is on what God *did* with them as a whole. He breathed **into [Adam's] nostrils the breath of life.** Until that happened, Adam looked like a corpse. He was no more or less than a lifeless body.

**Breath** here is not just a movement of air. This word includes all the essence of life. God suddenly caused Adam's heart to begin pumping, his arteries to direct clean blood to all parts of the body, and his lungs to exchange oxygen for carbon dioxide. God's breathing into Adam's nostrils is the closest that human language can come to expressing how God gave life in all its necessary activity, and **man became a living being** (2:7).

The Hebrew word often translated "soul" is found several times in Scripture to describe animals as having a "living soul" or the "breath of life" (1:30). If we designated what would seem to be the intended difference, we would say that the animals had a "soul likeness," for God did not **breathe** into them the **breath of life,** or create them in His **image.** Adam, however, had a living, spiritual soul. The Bible expressly states that animals and humans are not, and were never considered to be, on the same level. Killing an animal is never considered murder in the Bible, while taking the life of a human is. That is because human life reflects the **image** and **likeness** of God. Animal life does not.

# 4

# ADAM'S CONTAINMENT

## Genesis 2:8-17

Time came for God to prepare a special place for the test He planned to give the first pair of humans. He needed a **garden.** He decided to make it **in the east,** in **Eden.** The text does not say **garden** *of* **Eden,** but rather **garden** *in* **Eden** (2:8). This information implies that the **garden** was a smaller unit geographically located in a much larger place called **Eden.** From the perspective of the writer, the garden was **in the east,** meaning east of where the writer was at the time of the writing. As for the geographical location of the garden, lower Mesopotamia (*Mesopotamia* is a Greek word for "land between the two rivers") is by far the best candidate.

Genesis 2:9 is not a second account of the Creation, but rather a narrowing down to focus on trees, originally created on the third day. Specifically, the writer focuses on those created for the purpose of setting up the test Adam and Eve would soon face. God made sure the trees Adam and Eve needed would be those **that were pleasing to the eye** (2:9) and would serve as **food** for their appetites. While God provided for physical needs, He also cared about aesthetic beauty.

Note especially that the writer says nothing about "apple trees," though many people think he does. If God placed the garden in Mesopotamia, apple trees could not have grown there since the weather does not get cold enough. Then what kind of trees might have been in the garden? Logically, they were fig trees, date palms, or possibly olive trees. Apparently, God did not think naming the specific type of tree was important enough to include in the biblical account.

Central to the entire garden were two regular trees, for they grew **out of the ground** (2:9). Again, these were regular fruit trees. One was considered **the tree of life,** the other the **tree of the knowledge of good and evil.** The placement of words in any Hebrew sentence intentionally gives words greater or lesser emphasis. Since **the tree of life** is mentioned first, it is the more important tree. Somehow it is connected to maintaining **life.**

The real importance of these trees was that they had been assigned by God to represent abstract ideas of **life** (very probably **life** abundant, for the word **life** appears in plural form in the original Hebrew) and **knowledge** (2:9). Exactly how the fruit of **the tree of life** influenced the subsistence of life is not made clear, but it is in some way unique among all fruit trees. Part of its uniqueness is that it somehow related to "eternal life" (3:22).

> The tree of life, a symbol of eternal life in the ancient East (2:9) must be protected against Adam and all mankind's attempt to reach beyond himself (2:15-17). God has a will beyond the creature, and requires him to live according to the creator's will. Adam is limited; the creature cannot be the creator. The prohibition implies the possibility of the opposite, namely, of the creature acting freely against the Creator.[1]

**The tree of the knowledge of good and evil** was one that related to more than moral information. It included a valued knowledge that would be necessary in order to have the ability to make a clear distinction between what was beautiful or ugly, helpful or harmful, approved or disapproved. Knowledge is obtained from instruction, but what is done with that information can be either **good** or **evil.** Putting knowledge into life requires the ability to discriminate between the two.

In Genesis 2:10, the author refers to geographical details that made the garden luxuriant: **a river watering** it, which **separated into four headwaters.** The names of countries such as **Havilah, Cush,** and **Asshur** were all names of countries that existed much later, during the time the author lived. **Havilah** appears later in Genesis 10:7, 29 and 1 Chronicles 1:9, 23, but in these cases **Havilah** is the name of a son or a people. **Havilah** appears as a place name in Genesis 25:18 and again in 1 Samuel 15:7. These names of places and people may have resulted from the name's original use here in Genesis.

The names of the four streams in the garden were **Pishon, Gihon, Tigris,** and **Euphrates** (2:11-14). The names of the last two are well known today. They flow from Turkey and Syria through modern Iraq into the Persian Gulf. They are easily identifiable on current maps.

Either climatic changes or geographical alterations have made the other two rivers, the **Pishon** and **Gihon,** difficult to locate today. However, recent studies of tree pollen samples taken from boreholes in various places in Israel have verified changes in rainfall throughout the centuries. Studies of soils in Yemen found decayed organic material as much as eight feet deep, indicating there was once a much wetter period than today. And in Saudi Arabia, there is evidence that lakes once existed where today nothing but desert can be found.

Of more interest are the results of remote sensing technology in Saudi Arabia which give evidence that a river once flowed from the low mountains of the far southwest part of the country. This river traveled in a northeasterly direction and finally dumped into the Persian Gulf as the **Tigris** and **Euphrates** do today. It has been named the Kuwait River. It ceased to flow sometime after 3500 B.C. Before that time, grassland covered the present arid Arabia.

Adding to the validity of both research and the biblical record, this ancient "Kuwait River" began near the only place in Arabia where a "Cradle of Gold" once existed and where this precious metal was once mined. It may well be the **Havilah** of the Genesis account. A researcher concluded, "I am therefore inclined to think that the Kuwait River could well be the **Pishon** of the Bible."[2]

The **second river,** the **Gihon,** is not identifiable today, though in ancient times it flowed through **the entire** land of **Cush** (2:13). Often **Cush** indicates an earlier name for Ethiopia, but there are instances in the Bible where the term cannot refer to either this country or to a person from there. It seems in those references to speak of the Kassite land east of the Tigris River. The name **Gihon** in Hebrew means "gushing." Perhaps it was a spring-fed river that no longer flows.

The props of the drama were in place, ready for the star performers. The Lord next put Adam on the stage—**in the Garden of Eden.** But it is clear from Genesis 2:15 that God did not intend for him to have only glorious inactivity with occasional recreation and no responsibility or physical labor. Though some believe differently, work was not intended as a punishment of the Fall. Adam was **to work** his physical muscles and take care of the garden (2:15) to keep it from running wild.

God intentionally did not create the Garden of Eden in perfection. He made it to require such things as planting, hoeing, and pruning. From the beginning, God involved Adam in agriculture. Since God could have created the garden in perfection—to never need work—we know He purposely chose to do otherwise. God gave Adam the command to work before He gave him permission to **eat** (2:16). Could Paul have had this in mind when he said, "If any would not work, neither should he eat" (2 Thessalonians 3:10 KJV)? Rather than being a punishment, God made work a means to accomplishment, success, and fulfillment.

Genesis 2:16 contains the first command of God to Adam. God permitted Adam **to eat from any tree in the garden** (2:16). Then came the restriction: any tree *except* **the tree of the knowledge of good and evil. Any tree** meant even the **tree of life** (2:9) if Adam so desired, for there was no prohibition given concerning it.

Through the ages, people have wondered why the fruit of that one tree was forbidden. God emphatically prohibited it: **You must not eat** (2:17). It is as definite as one of the Ten Commandments. The form of the words in this phrase shows that the prohibition was not based on the possibility that the tree's fruit might poison them. In chapter 3, Eve could tell that the fruit was **good for food** (3:6). Perhaps she based her appraisal on the fact that there were other fruit trees of the same kind, whose fruit she had tasted and which had been delicious.

The significance of the **tree of the knowledge of good and evil** then was not in its fruit, but in the line of disobedience she would have to cross to get to it. Eve had to choose how she would respond: with the sin of disobedience or with spiritual awakening. How would these humans respond? Would their motivation be love for their Creator who deeply cared about them, had provided for their needs and wanted them to choose Him out of love, or would they follow an inner urge for independence?

The **knowledge of good and evil** (2:17) was to be obtained by *not* eating of this tree, rather than the opposite—eating of it. In God's command, eating of the tree was **evil;** not eating of it was **good.** Adam and Eve had known only obedience. If they disobeyed God's command, their consciences would be awakened as had their physical bodies at Creation. God was not trying to keep something good away from Adam and Eve, unless the taking of it would cause them harm in some way. If not physically, then how would it harm them? Harm came in a spiritual way, but they were also affected emotionally and psychologically. Taking the fruit after God had commanded them not to do it would make them insubordinate. Therefore, God was deliberately forcing Adam and Eve to make a reasoned choice between **good** and **evil.** To refuse the temptation, when it came, would provide them with the ability to discriminate between **good** and **evil.** The **evil** was in that to acquire the fruit, they would have to disregard the expressed will of God. God had given them free will for just this specific moment.

## ENDNOTES

[1]*The Anchor Bible,* vol. 2 (New York: Doubleday, 1992), p. 944.
[2]James A. Sauer. "The River Runs Dry." *Biblical Archaeology Review* 22, no. 4 (July/Aug 1996): 64.

# 5

# MAN'S COUNTERPART

## Genesis 2:18-25

Everything that God had done He declared to be **good!** Next God decided that the man He had created must have a companion. Without one, God decided His work was **not good** (2:18). He wanted Adam to discover his need for a companion by himself, so as not to force the decision. God must let Adam determine for himself that everything God created is valuable only for the purposes for which it was created. Adam also needed to discover that he had a dignity that stood markedly above the rest of God's creation, and that consequently he must have companionship. Adam needed love in his life in order to live fully, and so he could only love another one who was on his own level in the truest sense.

God took the time to let Adam name the **livestock, the birds of the air and all the beasts of the field** (2:20), to see if he could find self-completion in them. God knew it would be a fruitless search, but Adam needed the experience of looking among the animals for a **helper suitable for him.** Why did he need the experience? So he would love more completely the mate God would give to him. The literal translation of the Hebrew phrase used here is "a helper as opposite him" or "matching him." This **helper** is to be in every sense a partner who would be a counterpart to him.

After the long process of inspecting and naming all the animals, the author emphatically states, **But for Adam no suitable helper was found** (2:20). Eve's value was to "complete" Adam. God could have created Eve before Adam realized his need for a suitable helper, but He wanted Adam to experience loneliness, and out of it to become aware of his emptiness without a helper. Rabbinic literature describes Adam as looking at the animals in pairs, and after the process making the declaration, "Everything has its partner, but I have no partner."[1]

After his unfulfilled search, Adam was fully aware that he was alone. **God caused . . . a deep sleep** to come to him. Did God do this just to perform surgery? Adam certainly had to have had a most wearying day of activity in reviewing and naming all the animals. Or did God wish to surprise Adam with a new companion?

One writer does not think that the Hebrew word for **rib** is correctly translated here. Instead of being a skeletal bone, as is commonly imagined, he believes the Hebrew word stands for "an aspect of the personality." He states, "Even though the statement 'bone of my bone and flesh of my flesh' might appear to imply such a rendering, a literal bone is not intended to be understood, since the removal of the rib was not accompanied by a corresponding extraction of flesh. Instead, the phrase is simply meant to demonstrate the organic and spiritual unity of the subdivided species."[2]

In most other places when the Hebrew word for **rib** is used, in not one instance does it mean the **rib** of a human body. Its most frequent translation is rather "side," as with the ark of the covenant (see Exodus 25:12), or with the Tabernacle (see 26:20), or the holy altar (see 27:7). In 2 Samuel 16:13, the word is used to describe an elevation above a road, while in 1 Kings 6:5 it represents rooms on the side of Solomon's Temple. Whether God used Adam's actual rib to make Eve, or used Adam's "side," meaning "an aspect" of who Adam was, Eve became Adam's counterpart.

The ideal of a blend of the two personalities in a marriage of harmony and intimacy is certainly the spiritual message. Eve was not another animal creation. She was entirely a part of Adam—his other half. The two were one. God saw them as two equal parts of one whole, not two separate parts of unequal value. Walter Kaiser observes,

> Even though man had a chronological priority in his appearance on the scene, the biblical text takes special pains to raise the woman to an equal level. . . . She was not only to be the one who put an end to his [Adam's] solitude, she was also to be a helpmate especially endowed by God to aid man in fulfilling his calling. . . .[3]

Matthew Henry best captures the proper relationship between Adam and Eve as God intended it: "Not made out of his head to top him, not out of his feet to be trampled upon by him, but out of his side to be equal with him, under his arm to be protected, and near his heart to be beloved."[4]

The early Jewish rabbis noticed that while God **formed** Adam **of the dust of the ground,** the literal rendering of the Hebrew is that God *built* Eve (see 2:22). The original Hebrew here contains a similar noun that means "understanding, intuition." The rabbis then remarked that God had given Eve, and all women, greater intuition than He gave men.

Nothing has yet been said about Eve's ability to reproduce. That comes in Genesis 4.

In making the sexuality of Adam and Eve, God could have made their bodies operate any way He desired. But he built into them their maleness and femaleness to symbolize to them, "Your completeness is not in yourself; it is in somebody else." Perhaps God had in mind that as they would need each other on the horizontal level, so on the vertical level (a cross?) they both would need Him. Their completeness would be found only in Him.

After he awakened, Adam looked at this new gift from God and immediately recognized her as **bone of my bones and flesh of my flesh** (2:23). What he looked for in all the animals but failed to find, he instantly saw in Eve as one on his own level—his equal.

We read next, **for this reason** . . . (2:24). For what reason? That man and woman were a part of each other in marriage. And what existed for Adam and Eve is a principle meant to exist for every marriage! If so, we would expect the text to say, "a woman will leave her father and mother and be united to her husband." But it doesn't! We read, **a man will leave his father and mother and be united to his wife.** Why is it this way? Before marriage, a man's first obligation is to his parents. After marriage, his first responsibility is his wife. She takes priority. And what is true for the wife is true for the husband.

Man is to be **united** (2:24) to his wife. The Hebrew word is stronger. It says he is to "cleave" to her. In more common English, he is to "cling" or "stick" to her. The intended meaning is that his assignment to his wife is to have both passion and permanence in their marriage.

Jesus referred to this passage in Matthew 19:5-6. Pharisees had come to Him to ask if it was lawful for a man to divorce his wife. His replied by quoting this verse in Genesis, making it plain that marriage was a God-given ordinance from the beginning of the human race.

Since sin had yet to enter the world at this point in Genesis, at their meeting Adam and Eve were **naked, and they felt no shame** (2:25).

They had childish innocence. No feeling of guilt existed between them. But it would not last for long.

## ENDNOTES

[1]Bereishit Rabbah 17:5.

[2]Roland K. Harrison, *Introduction to the Old Testament* (Grand Rapids, Michigan: Wm. B. Eerdmans Publishing Co., 1969), pp. 555–56.

[3]Walter C. Kaiser Jr., *Toward Old Testament Ethics* (Grand Rapids, Michigan: Zondervan Publishing House, 1983), p. 154.

[4]Matthew Henry Commentary, vol. 1 (New York: Revell), p. 20.

# Part Three

# FOCUS
# ON THE FALL

## Genesis 3:1–4:26

W hat makes a child early in childhood automatically act badly? Why is it that a father never needs to counsel his son, "Pull your sister's hair once in a while. Don't be afraid to push her around a bit to show who is boss"? Why is it never necessary for a mother to say to her daughter, "Spit on your brother so he won't treat you so roughly. If you need to, bite him on the arm, or even kick him"?

Why is it children never have to be trained how to be bad? Never does a child have to be taught how to get angry. Never does a parent need to say, "Don't be so angelic. Have a temper tantrum if you feel like it." All of this comes naturally. This behavior does not have to be stimulated. Why not? Genesis 3 and 4 answer this question.

In the setting of the Garden in Eden appears **the serpent** (3:1). The text does not say who the serpent is or where it came from. The word **serpent** may possibly relate to a Hebrew verb that is translated "to use divination." **Serpent** may also be related to the Hebrew words for "copper" or "bronze." The word **serpent** may be used to convey the idea of something that shines luminously. Does this picture of **the serpent** relate to Paul's statement, "Satan himself masquerades as an angel of light" (2 Corinthians 11:14)?

Who or what is the **serpent?** A reptile? A symbolism? Satan himself? Whatever the case, the serpent is the instrument of the first temptation. The Apostle John offers insight: "The great dragon was hurled down—that ancient serpent called the devil, or Satan who leads the whole world astray" (Revelation 12:9; 20:2). Paul makes clear that it is "the serpent's cunning" that leads people "astray" (2 Corinthians 11:3).

Since the serpent species would have been created on the sixth day, and since God called everything created that day **good** (1:25), it must have pleased God to make serpents.

It would seem to be a given that God did not create snakes to speak, and yet this **serpent** did. Surprisingly, Eve did not seem surprised by its speaking. Many have offered objections to this vocal ability of the reptile. They believe that including a talking snake in the story makes the whole thing a myth. But if this snake is meant to be symbolic of the most anti-Godlike thing in creation, it qualifies. Is it not a possibility that Satan chose to embody this creature? Luke wrote that Satan "entered Judas" (Luke 22:3). And if Satan "masquerades (literally, fashions himself) as an angel of light," it seems he would not find it difficult to enter a snake.

How then could the snake speak, one might ask? Who would deny that though a cat or a dog does not use words, it often speaks just as effectively without words? And who has not been aware of thoughts that, though silent to the ears, are in reality words spoken by Satan?

In my thirty-five years of experience in archaeological work all over the country of Israel, thousands of figurines have been found of nude women, each with a serpent entwined around her neck. Snakes have been found as decorations on jars, handles on pots, made of brass, curled around cult stands, carved in altars, or dangling from the hands of a female goddess. It appears that people who did not know the true God were fascinated with snakes. Could not all of this date back to the events of the Fall?

# 6

# SIN'S CORONATION

## Genesis 3:1-6

The first verse of Genesis 3 states that the **serpent was more crafty than any of the wild animals** (3:1). **Crafty** suggests being "clever" and "mischievous." The word has its good side, however. It is translated "prudent" in Proverbs 12:23; 14:18. But that same valuable prudence when issued from an evil heart becomes a shrewd and subtle weapon of cunning.

Could not Satan have come in the appearance of an angel to Eve? Indeed he is an "angel of the Abyss" (Revelation 9:11; 12:9). What was his purpose for embodying a snake? Perhaps Satan wanted to appear to Eve as a subordinate, in a way similar to his attack on Jesus through Peter (see Matthew 16:22-23). In such a manner, the Devil could strengthen his appeal to pride without compulsion. He did not want her to feel under duress lest she become more defensive.

The passage emphasizes the words Satan spoke, the topic of the conversation. Satan **said to the woman, "Did God really say, 'You must not eat from any tree in the garden'?"** (3:1).

Note two things about this initial remark.

First, it flattered Eve. It left the impression that what God said was subject to her judgment. Satan's endless attempt in every temptation is to get his target to declare independence from God. Satan would have every person direct attention to self with the idea that God does not have a person's best interests at heart. According to the Deceiver, if a person wants to get ahead in this world, he or she will have to exalt self rather than be humble. It is worthy of note that, throughout the temptation, the pronoun **you** is always plural. Both Adam *and* Eve are being addressed. They were tempted together. "To read the text as the seduction of the man by the woman is to read what is not in the text."[1]

Second, Satan used one of his favorite devices to get Eve to respond with more than a simple "yes" or "no." He intentionally, and with malicious purpose, overstated God's defined limits with the phrase **any tree** (3:1). Satan sought to engage Eve in debate. He worked on Eve's implicit trust. From his viewpoint, he had to have a reply.

Satan couched a carefully planned suggestion within his words. According to plan, Eve should have a suspicion that God had denied her some deserved pleasure of eating of *all* the fruit in the garden. Satan's end desire, of course, was that Eve would come to doubt the precise purpose of God's command. Satan wanted Eve to ask herself, "Is God withholding something vital from me? Is He really being fair in His command?"

Satan was trying to present Eve with a chance to correct God. Much to Satan's delight, Eve did exceed the limits God had given her. God had told Adam that he was not to **eat from the tree of knowledge of good and evil,** for in so doing he would **surely die** (2:17). But Eve added that God's command included an order **not** to **touch it,** lest death be the result (3:3). Had doubt already made an inroad into Eve's heart? Had she begun to move away from God in her attitude, making her an easier prey for Satan's evil explanation? This might be inferred in her reply, which suggested she thought God too harsh and restrictive for not allowing her to touch the tree. Another possible indication was that she left out the word **surely** when she remarked on God's command and its result—that **you will die.** This might have been Eve's way of trying to weaken the penalty.

We also notice that Eve does not call it **the tree of the knowledge of good and evil** as God had named it (2:17). She called it **the tree that is in the middle of the garden** (3:3). The impression given is that, in her mind, she considered the tree to be on the same level as the other trees that were found in the garden. Her only description of it was its location. Had she said to herself, "I don't see why I need to avoid that tree. What is this **knowledge of good and evil** anyway?" Her faith may have already been on shaky ground.

If we could have heard Satan's words, we might have detected an inflection that reflected utter disbelief that God would make such a restriction. Since Eve had moved in the direction of Satan's logic, his approach was calculated to encourage her questions, weaken her trust in God, and feed her seedlings of doubt. The Tempter immediately followed her answer with a flat-out denial: **You will not surely die** (3:4).

Before Eve could fully catch the significance of that blatant contradiction, the Tempter attacked God's truthfulness. Satan wanted Eve to think God was hiding the real reason for His prohibition—His own self-interest. **God knows that when you eat of it your eyes will be opened, and you will be like God, knowing good and evil** (3:5). You will become like God! What a temptation! Not only does Satan make us want to be our own boss, he wants us to try to take God's place. Their temptation was Satan's telling them, "Set your own measure of good and evil. Be autonomous, and live your life without reference to God. He purposely made you weak and limited. You can exert yourself, reach out and beyond, and burst through His restrictions. Show Him you have become **like [Him], knowing good and evil**" (3:5).

It appears that Eve, though beginning to give in to doubt, had not yet allowed herself to even look at the tree. Outwardly, she was obedient. Inwardly, she had been questioning God's logic. Now with Satan's dart, her heart had been pierced. Even more curious about the tree, she turned to see what she was missing. When she looked, she saw that **the fruit of the tree was good for food and pleasing to the eye, and also desirable for gaining wisdom** (3:6).

We might think Eve's response was immediate and thoughtless. This is highly unlikely! She must have been thinking something like this: "I am seeing the *good,* the *beautiful,* and the *true.* That is what the quest of life is all about. Why in the world is God keeping those things from me? Maybe Satan is right. God does not have my best interests at heart. He is looking out for himself. He is trying to keep from me what I need and should have."

God never desires to keep good things away from us, unless they will harm us. While sin is often a misuse of something God intended for a good purpose, at times it is also a taking of something before we are ready for it. With this fruit, it may have been the latter. Had Eve been patient and followed God's instruction, perhaps later God would have come to her and said, "Eve, you can now go eat all of that fruit you want. You have shown that you understand obedience to Me to be more important than any other thing in life. You are now ready for it."

It is striking that the Tempter did not tell Eve to sample the fruit. He instead carefully wove an argument into her in-His-image ability to distinguish between right and wrong. The degree of her ability to discern right from wrong was closely tied to her cooperative obedience to God's specific instructions. Though she could not know the full effect that a disregard for God's command would have on her, whatever caution God may have given her she now discarded by her own choice. Whatever natural inclination she had toward God as a Maker-Father she forfeited. Now her curiosity had her on the road to a catastrophic fall.

Eve's downfall did not come at the moment she took the bite from the fruit. It came when she allowed her trust in God's clear words to erode. Sin crouched at her door (see 4:7). Though at that point she could have chosen to obey, it would have been as difficult as it would be to stop a sled going down an icy hill and make it return to the starting point.

**She took . . . and ate!** (3:6). So simple a sentence; so monumental an act. So quick a choice; so devastating the effect. So easily done; so difficult to be undone. So pure before; so debased after. Thousands of years would pass before "take and eat" (Matthew 26:26) became words of a cure — a cure that required a life's spilled blood to effect.

One might wonder why Satan did not tempt Adam instead of Eve, or both together. One likely reason suggested by Old Testament scholar Victor Hamilton[2] is that Adam had received God's command directly; Eve received it secondhand. Hamilton cites as an example Aaron, who yielded to idolatry in the golden calf incident. Moses got orders directly from God, while Aaron received instructions through Moses.

Could Eve have had the keener intuition and therefore have been more prone to speculation, more observant, more rational? If so, the Tempter saw her as a better prey.

**She also gave some to her husband, who was with her, and he ate it** (3:6). How revealing! In her moment of temptation Adam said nothing. He did nothing to stop his wife. He was a party to what was going on. We might say he abetted the crime. He was just as guilty. When Eve offered the fruit to him, he ate it without resistance. Romans 5:12 tells us "sin entered the world through one man. . . ." It was not Paul's intent in this passage to declare Adam any more responsible than Eve. Adam's responsibility was to help Eve in her moment of weakness. Had he been strong, she might well not have yielded. His silence gave consent. They both felt shame immediately, as is expressed in Genesis 3:7.

> The woman takes some of the fruit and gives it to her husband. As a silent partner "with her" throughout the exchange, the man puts up no resistance, raises no questions, and considers no theological issues; he simply and silently takes his turn. The woman does not act as a temptress in this scene; they both have succumbed to the same source of temptation. They stand together as "one flesh" at this point as well.[3]

Satan duped Adam and Eve into thinking that good lay beyond evil, that wisdom could be obtained by disobedience, that the avenue of greed would lead to greatness. Satan was, and still is, a master at warping the truth. He had told them they would not die, and they did not die at that moment physically, but they were immediately subject to a spiritual and eternal death.

## ENDNOTES

[1]*The Anchor Bible,* vol. 2 (New York: Doubleday, 1992), p. 945.

[2]Victor P. Hamilton, *Handbook of the Pentateuch* (Grand Rapids, Michigan: Baker Book House, 1982), p. 45.

[3]*The New Interpreter's Bible,* vol. 1 (Nashville, Tennessee: Abingdon Press, 1994), p. 361.

# *7*

# SIN'S CURSE

## Genesis 3:7-21

The curse that fell on both Adam and Eve resulted in **the eyes of both of them** being **opened** (Gen. 3:7). Satan's prediction came true, but not in the way they had expected. It was indeed an eye-opening experience! Did they reach to God's level of knowledge of **good and evil?** God said they did (see 3:22), so to His measure they did. In another measure they could not. Think of a physician who knows what a sickness is like. The one who gets the sickness knows, too, but in an entirely different way. The great Physician of heaven wanted to spare Adam and Eve from knowing the **good and evil** through an act that would give them befouled hearts. God had intended that they would know about sin through His loving instruction, but not through actually experiencing it.

Their spiritual death was revealed instantly in two ways: Their clean, clear consciences were tainted with shame—they had to cover parts of their bodies (see 3:7); and their trust was forfeited—they tried to hide from God (see 3:8). They had been clothed in God's glory; it was stripped from them. Their minds had been pure; afterward they were sullied by Satan. They had a moral likeness to God; they gained an immoral likeness of the Devil. God became a stranger and close fellowship was severed.

Adam and Eve endeavored first to cover their nakedness with **fig leaves** (3:7); these leaves were undoubtedly used since they were the largest available and the best suited for what Adam and Eve thought they needed. This indicated their sense of urgency and desperation. How revealing is their act! In innocence, their lack of covering had not been a concern. In guilt afterwards, they felt a need to hide parts of their bodies, possibly from themselves, but certainly from God. They knew they had not obeyed Him. They had mistaken their nudity for a nakedness of ingratitude and disobedience to God's will. They could not hide from themselves or from God.

To announce His approach, and to accommodate His meeting for fellowship with Adam and Eve, God made a **sound** of **walking in the garden** (3:8). It would appear that He had been meeting them regularly **in the cool of the day.** The day cooled in the late afternoon when the evening breeze began to temper the land in the East. Guilt drove the couple into hiding **among the trees of the garden.**

God asked Adam directly, **Where are you?** (3:9). Did He not know? Yes, He knew, but He wanted Adam to see himself as God saw him. And God's words were bathed in grace. God asked the question to *draw* Adam from his hiding, rather than *drive* him out of it. From the moment of the sin, God wanted to heal the rupture. Adam did not seek God. God sought him. How much like God! The Bible as a whole tells not of humans pursuing God but rather of God pursing them. "God created man for the two purposes of fellowship and obedience to him. By disobedience the fellowship was broken, and it is significant that Adam hid himself from God before he was expelled from the garden. Here . . . is found a deep understanding of the character of sin and a clear recognition that man's truest well-being is to be found in doing the will of God."[1]

The response of Adam was immediate. **I heard you in the garden, and I was afraid** (3:10). Here is the first mention of fear in the Bible. It came because of Adam's fallen nature. Inherited by all who have been born since, that human predicament still causes people to shrink from God. Adam's disobedience made him want to isolate himself from God even before he was punished. His sin was against himself as well as against God.

Adam told God that he **hid** because he **was naked** (3:10). His confession was evasive. He hid because he had sinned, but he wanted to sidestep a direct admission. He only admitted to what occurred after his sin. His evasion caused him to stumble into the very proof of his disobedience.

**Who told you that you were naked? Have you eaten from the tree that I commanded you not to eat from?** the Lord queried (3:11). Like a skillful prosecutor probing though the evasive facade in an effort to make the guilty confess, the Lord sought an honest and direct confession. It was the only way to heal the break in fellowship.

Though Adam could no longer hide among the trees, and though his first evasion had been penetrated, Adam tried another tactic to avoid taking personal responsibility for his sin. He impulsively blurted out, **The woman you put here with me—she gave me some fruit from the tree, and I ate it** (3:12). Adam admitted the truth of his disobedience, but only after he tried to divert the blame to Eve and ultimately to God himself. Adam immediately implicated Eve to make sure his part was even more minimized. He tried to justify what was to him a *small* part by pointing to a larger circumstance that had made him sin and for which he was not responsible. Yet God held him responsible for his choice to eat.

Unfortunately, Adam did not know the proverb, "He who conceals his sins does not prosper, but whoever confesses and renounces them finds mercy" (Proverbs 28:13). Adam raised new obstacles to receiving mercy when he retreated from a complete admission of his own sin. He had driven wedges of alienation between himself and his loving Creator, and between himself and his dear human companion. God's silence to his reply must have been deafening.

God then turned to Eve. Satan was addressed later. The order—man, woman, and serpent—showed God's evaluation of the measure of responsibility of each. God expected an account from Eve. Her response was as evasive as Adam's: **The serpent deceived me.** "But Eve," we want to say, "you chose to be deceived!" Both Adam and Eve tried the artful dodge. In effect, both said, "It is not my fault!" But both had to admit, **I ate** (3:13). Adam, Eve, and the serpent each chose their part. All three failed and were guilty for their actions. That guilt was not lessened by trying to shift attention away from themselves.

God did not give Satan a chance to escape responsibility. He immediately informed the serpent that it was **cursed . . . above all the livestock and all the wild animals.** It would **crawl on** [its] **belly and . . . eat dust all the days of** [its] **life** (3:14). Does this mean that until that point the serpent had been walking upright and was reduced to crawling? This view began with a Jewish legend and was held until the eighteenth century. The idea is unbiblical. The true meaning of the Hebrew words is "You shall continue to crawl," meaning "you must live with the deep humiliation typified by your crawling in the dust." God simply gave an existing situation a new significance.

While Satan was being addressed in this curse, the real focus was on what would happen in time to come. **Enmity [will result] between you and the woman, and between your offspring** [literally, "seed"] **and hers** (3:15). This verse gives the first messianic promise of the Bible, the first beam of the gospel. This is the only place in the Bible where a feminine noun has a masculine ending. It is a shrouded reference to a woman's giving birth to the God-man who would be struck on the **heel** (3:15)—a reference to the continuing struggle with evil until the Cross and Satan's presumed victory at Jesus' death. But the Devil would be crushed on the **head**

(3:15)—indicating Christ's ultimate victory in His resurrection. Jesus' resurrection enabled all who will come to Him to be redeemed from the terrible Adamic scourge that infected all of humanity. But the **crushing** on the **head** also prefigures Christ's ultimate annihilation of the evil instigator of sin's curse (see Revelation 20:10). John H. Sailhamer writes that this curse on the serpent was part of God's plan for blessing humankind.

> In Genesis 1, the writer shows that at the center of God's purpose in creating human beings was his desire to bless them. Immediately after creating them, God blessed them and said, "Be fruitful and multiply and fill the land" (1:28). Even after they were cast away from God's protective care in the garden, God let it be known that this act of disobedience would not thwart his plan for humanity's blessing: A future "seed" would one day come and crush the head of the serpent (3:15). Genesis 3:15 shows plainly that God's original intention for the human race was blessing and that his continual concern for humanity remains the same.[2]

Eve's punishment was increased **pains in childbearing** and her husband's **rule over** her (3:16). **Rule** here suggests men's frequent harsh exploitation of women because of sin. "To love and to cherish" is all too often "to rule and to dominate." When God is honored, women are given a higher status. When sin is permitted, a woman's value as a person is demeaned; she becomes more a sex object to be used.

The admonition of Paul for "wives [to] submit to [their] husbands" (Ephesians 5:22) was not in God's original plan; it was part of the Fall. And to insure that a husband keeps a proper relationship between him and his mate, Paul added, "Husbands, love your wives, just as Christ loved the church and gave himself up for her" (Eph. 5:25).

Finally, God addressed Adam. God reminded Adam that he had **listened to [his] wife** (Gen. 3:17). He could have closed his ear to her, but he did not, and he **ate from the tree** (3:17). Adam's punishment was directly related to his act of listening to Eve rather than to God. Five times in 3:17-19, Adam is reminded of his act of eating. From that point on, he would experience **painful toil, . . . thorns and thistles, . . . sweat, . . . and dust.** Before his fall, the **ground** involved labor, but following the fall it would be distressingly more difficult. God told Adam the land would fight back with troublesome growth that would add to the pain, and **sweat** would characterize his work for food until he became again what he once was—**dust** (3:19).

The words of Walter Kaiser help us to see how work was not intended as a curse:

> Work . . . was never meant to be a strain or a curse. True, a curse was *connected* with labor after the fall in Genesis 3:17-19, but it never was put on work itself. The curse was to be found in the pain, frustration, and strain that now accompanied work. God's intention from the very beginning was that people would find joy, fulfillment, and blessing in the fact and consistency of work.[3]

The final two verses of this section contain two items of information. First, Adam gave Eve her name (see 3:20). The meaning of "Eve" in Hebrew is "life," a most fitting name for the **mother of all the living.** Second, God wanted to help the couple obtain more permanent clothing—**garments of skin** (3:21). These would be more durable than fig leaves. Then, too, since Adam and Eve had lost their created high status and marred their divine image, they should not approach God with their private parts exposed. Indeed, this was the requirement God made later (see Exodus 20:26; 28:42).

Though it is not definitely stated, we might conclude that here is the introduction of the need for animal sacrifice to atone for the guilt that sin caused. What seems more certain though is that God intended the clothes not to be an act of grace but to be a reminder of the past sinful acts of Adam and Eve.

## ENDNOTES

[1]*Encyclopedia Britannica,* vol. 10 (Chicago, 1970), p. 94.

[2]John H. Sailhamer, *The Pentateuch As Narrative* (Grand Rapids, Michigan: Zondervan Publishing House, 1992), p. 42.

[3]Walter C. Kaiser Jr., *Toward Old Testament Ethics* (Grand Rapids, Michigan: Zondervan Publishing House, 1983), p. 150.

# 8

# SIN'S CONSEQUENCES

## Genesis 3:22-25

G enesis 3:22-25 reveals that the Trinity in heaven had a convocation concerning what Adam and Eve had done. Because of the knowledge they had gained through disobedience, Adam and Eve had to be punished. Close fellowship with God no longer existed for them. Their relationship with each other reflected strain and alienation. Satan had given them a vision of new knowledge. They had come to know that he used mirrors in his language to warp the truth.

In what sense had Adam and Eve **become like one of us** (the Trinity; 3:22)? They had emancipated themselves from God's requirements and had chosen to live by their own laws rather than His. As a result of their action, they knew **good and evil** on their own terms, and it was a different **good and evil** from that of God's. Additionally, they were no longer fit to eat from the **tree** that represented **life.**

In their sinful condition, there was no way that Adam and Eve deserved immortality. To keep them from **reaching out** and taking **also from the tree of life** (3:22)—trying to obtain eternal life their way, as they had done with the other tree—they must be **banished . . . from the Garden** (3:23). Adam and Eve had tried to become like God, a move toward deifying themselves. God acted so as to prevent a second attempt.

God **banished** them from the **Garden.** He condemned Adam to **work the ground from which he had been taken** (3:23). Adam had cared for the land before the Fall. After the Fall, he labored with pain and sweat as a penalty of sin (see 3:16, 19). The couple faced adverse circumstances, misfortune, and reversals. No longer tending the Garden, they had to make their garden from scratch.

Why did not God just forgive Adam and Eve and let them remain in the Garden, rather than driving them out (see 3:24)? Isn't that what we would expect Him to do? God would not be corrective enough if they could have the blessing of the Garden and their sin as well. Forgiveness frees one from the ultimate punishment by God, but sometimes sin has residual effects, and forgiveness alone cannot stop them from coming.

Knowing that after the sin had had its full recoil and Adam and Eve would yearn to return to what they lost, God caused **cherubim and a flaming sword flashing back and forth** to prevent a return to paradise (3:24). **Cherubim** are heavenly beings that exist in the world of angelic creatures. In gilded form, cherubim guarded the ark of the covenant in the Tabernacle (see Exodus 25:19-22) where "God was enthroned" (1 Samuel 4:4; Psalm 80:1). Olive wood replicas of them were found in the Temple (see 1 Kings 6:23). They even adorned the inside walls (see 1 Kings 6:29).

The original route to life eternal was forever closed. The disobedient acts in the Garden changed everything. In the Garden before Adam and Eve's sin,

> there was no special place for divine-human encounter. There was no sanctuary, no holy place, because the entire Garden was holy. After the fall, however, a sanctuary was needed if human creatures were to meet their holy Creator. God would not meet them just anywhere in the creation; a special place had to be put aside. This arrangement symbolically signaled the gulf in relationship between God and humanity. Sin separated them, and this fact had to be acknowledged.[1]

We will note that the "special place" chosen was an altar. Noah built one after the flood (see Genesis 8:20). Abraham constructed one at Shechem (12:7), another between Bethel and Ai (12:8), and yet another at Hebron (13:18). The most difficult altar for him was the one built on Mt. Moriah (22:9), when he thought he was going to have to sacrifice Isaac. The pattern continued after Abraham's death. Isaac constructed an altar at Beersheba (26:25), as did Jacob at Shechem (33:20) and Bethel (35:1, 3, 7). The patriarchs were aware of God's promises to give land to them, but they were yet to possess it. Their way of laying claim to those promises was to build altars everywhere they went. To them, altars were symbols of a return to the Garden-like relationship that had been restored to them; altars were a way of anticipating what was yet to come.

The ultimate arrival of the "Seed of Eve" would provide the alternative way that would be forever open (John 14:6).

## ENDNOTE

[1]Tremper Longman III, *Making Sense of the Old Testament* (Grand Rapids, Michigan: Baker Book House, 1998), p. 89.

# 9

# SIN'S CONTAMINATION

## Genesis 4:1-26

There is no indication of how much time transpired from the close of Genesis 3 to the beginning of Genesis 4, but chapter 4 recounts the birth of Adam and Eve's first two children. Cain displayed the inbred sin-stained nature as the first offspring of Adam and Eve. The four-word phrase in Hebrew, translated **With the help of the Lord I have brought forth a man** (4:1), is difficult to comprehend fully. Eve was certainly recognizing God's part in the birth of Cain, but **brought forth a man** can also be translated "gotten a husband" (Gen. 29:32). If the phrase points to Adam, Eve might be saying that Cain's birth brought healing to the alienation that existed between her and Adam because of their sin.

The destructive consequences of the Fall extend beyond the relationship of the first couple and God. The vertical rupture with God, described in Genesis 3, resulted in a horizontal rupture in the first family. The family began well. The text does not say how much later Abel was born, but the age span between the sons was likely not long. The boys found their natural God-gifted assignments: Abel, the younger, **kept flocks, and Cain,** the elder, **worked the soil** (4:2) with his father.

During a worship time, when offering sacrifices to the Lord, the brothers brought gifts from their respective occupations. Cain's offering consisted of **fruits of the soil** (4:3), while **Abel brought fat portions . . . from his flock** (4:4).

We cannot assume Cain offered the wrong offering. God did want grain, too; grain later became a required offering (see Leviticus 2:1-16). But Cain's immediate display of anger when God **did not look** on his offering **with favor** is an evidence of his lack of faith (4:5). Cain's anger showed visibly on **his face.** Hebrews 11:4 tells how it was Abel's inner attitude of faith that made the difference in God's acceptance or rejection. God gave most attention to the givers, not the gifts.

God's acceptance or rejection was clearly based on not only the offering itself, but also on the attitude of heart that accompanied it. Several times by the words of the prophets, God told the people He did not want sacrifices offered as substitutes for lives of obedience and inner righteousness (see Isaiah 1:11-20; Malachi 1:6-14). This seems to be the inference given in Genesis 4:7: Cain was not doing **what is right.** Only the best of both the offering and the heart are acceptable to God.

Aware of the attitude of Cain's heart, God queried him, **Why are you angry?** (4:6). Then God offered simple instructions on how to make offerings to the Lord—doing **what is right.** And what is right is to have faith in the God to whom sacrifices are given. Because Cain didn't, God warned that **sin is crouching at your door** (4:6). Is the **pain** reference in 3:16 directed at more than physical suffering in childbirth? The curse may also have referred to the pain that results from sin, which in this case caused a man to kill his brother.

The **crouching at your door** (4:7) metaphor is very vivid. The picture is that of a wild beast, poised at the opening of his lair, ready to leap onto anyone. Beware to whoever slavishly follows the inclinations of the evil heart to enter such a door. If not checked, an evil heart gives birth to more evil, and the evil continues to grow until "when it is full-grown, [it] gives birth to death" (James 1:15).

Cain had come in second best. A sin-directed pride was about to coax him into the most expedient way of taking over first place—blame the winner, then eliminate him!

Cain refused to listen to the Lord's warning that he had the power to turn from his evil intentions—**you must master it** (4:7). The hostility of heart that Cain allowed to fester came to possess him. It robbed him of the power to choose otherwise. Since sin desires secrecy, Cain invited Abel **out to the field** (4:8), away from their parents, who would not hear a cry for help.

The Hebrew arrangement of words, **attacked his brother Abel and killed him,** indicates a particularly ruthless murder. Likely Cain clubbed Abel to death. Cain had become that wild beast that the Lord had told him was crouching at his door.

In 4:9, Scripture says the LORD spoke to Cain. Nothing hints that, like Adam and Eve, Cain was trying to hide from God. He rather tried to hide his sin. Adam had admitted his deed, but tried to shift the blame. Cain denied all responsibility for what happened to Abel and, furthermore, claimed he was not his **brother's keeper** (4:9) anyway.

The content of the oral instructions God must have given the first family to guide them in what was right and wrong conduct is not recorded. But later written rules, which would have codified the "oral law" of earlier times, made it clear that brothers were to have a special relationship that demanded one assist a brother when he needed help (see Leviticus 25:48). And if a man's brother should ever be killed, that man was to become his brother's "avenger," to bring justice to the murderer. Had Cain tried harder to hide his sin, he also would have needed to pretend to find Abel's murderer (see Numbers 35:12-28). So, in effect, Cain's apparent unconcern for wanting in any way to show concern for Abel, or track down his killer indirectly, implicated him as the murderer. Cain's heart was the more crass compared to the heart of Adam, who had told God the truth about his actions (3:10), but Cain did not hesitate to give a bold-faced lie: **I don't know** (4:9).

So foolish is the person who thinks he can hide his acts from God who knows all. God sees all the evidence. In Cain's situation, Abel's **blood** (4:10) was speaking loudly, even though his voice had fallen silent in death. It was crying out to God for judgment.

Throughout the Bible, and especially in the Old Testament sacrificial system, **life** was considered **in the blood** (see Leviticus 17:11). The blood of a sacrificed animal brought to the altar enabled God to give atonement to the guilty party during Old Testament times. But the shed blood of an innocent person polluted the ground (see Numbers 35:33). If God sees to it that each person is born into the world, then when one person murders another, he or she usurps God's role. This person attempts to act as God by deciding when another should leave this earth. There is yet another sense that makes murder an attack on God. Everyone is created in God's image. Killing a person is like attempting to kill God.

In Genesis 3, God cursed both Satan and the ground. God did not curse Adam and Eve. For Cain's vengeful act, Cain was put **under a curse** (4:11); Cain was the first person God so punished. Since Cain had been occupied with tilling the ground and had even presented its "fruits" to the Lord, the curse is especially significant. He was banished from the most fertile ground to less productive soil that would refuse to give him any meaningful production no matter how hard he worked. In the words of Gunkel, "Cain had tilled the land. He had offered the fruit of the land, and given the land his brother's blood to drink; but from the land the blood cries against him, for which the land refuses him its fruit, so he is banned from the land."[1] He became a restless vagabond, **a wanderer on the earth** (4:12). If he ever tried farming again, he would come up empty-handed and be required to move on restlessly and endlessly.

Such a punishment was especially heavy to a farmer who likely had learned to love his occupation, to work hard, and to see quickly the fertile results of his labor. Cain complained, **My punishment is more than I can bear** (4:13). Cain had finally admitted his guilt, but he complained about the severity of the sentence. He was not truly penitent. He considered himself a better judge than God.

However, Cain did recognize that he would be **hidden from your** [God's] **presence** (4:14). He might not have missed fellowship with God, but probably feared exposure to vengeful relatives. He had to have spoken the phrase, **whoever finds me,** with other brothers and sisters in mind. How many children Adam and Eve had at this point is not mentioned. Scripture later says Adam **had other sons and daughters** (5:4). It is even possible that Abel could have had children of his own before he was killed. If so, they might have sought to make Cain pay for their loss. Even at the moment of Cain's punishment, he was more concerned about what would happen to him than what had happened to his defenseless brother. His self-centered appraisal of all of life still plagued him.

Yet God affirmed, **If anyone kills Cain, he will suffer vengeance seven times over** (4:15). God had mercy on Cain and desired that blood revenge not take root in society. Even so, it did later and necessitated the establishment of cities of refuge where one could be tried without the threat of an avenger taking his life (see 35:9-15).

In both Adam's ejection from the Garden in Eden and Cain's assignment to a life of wandering, one truth stands out. Sin causes not only a loss of status but also a loss of fullness of life that can be found only in the presence of God.

In Hebrew usage, **seven times over** means being punished completely or in full measure. It is used this way in describing the heating of the Persian furnace for Daniel's three Hebrew friends (see Daniel 3:19), meaning to heat to the maximum temperature.

Even though Cain's fear came from a skewed sense of justice, God did not overlook it, so He put **a mark on Cain** (4:15). This was not likely a mark that Cain had to wear visibly, for that would only have increased his chances of being targeted by an enemy. It may indicate that God's promise was a sign of His protection to give Cain peace of mind, in that God was his assurance of safe conduct. What an expression of love for the unrepentant sinner! As ever, God wanted to forgive and redeem Cain, but Cain was more concerned with the level of his punishment than forgiveness for his sin. In later biblical law, he would have received the death penalty. That he did not is evidence of God's abundant grace. No indication of the nature of the sign is recorded, but its purpose is very clear: **so that no one who found him would kill him** (4:15). As to the location of Cain's new home, it was **east of Eden.** Perhaps the **land of Nod** was not so much a place as it was a lifestyle, one of nomadic wandering.

Genesis 4:17 gives the impression that Cain was already married, most likely to a sister, for there is no record of a special wife being created for him as for Adam. Circumstances required the marriage of relatives at this time, but God prohibited that practice when the necessity no longer existed (see Leviticus 18:6-18).

Cain's son, **Enoch** (4:17), came while Cain was **building a city** that he chose to name after his newborn son. The name **Enoch** is related to the verb meaning "to initiate." Was this an attempt by Cain to express his own independence? Since God had sentenced him to the life of a vagabond, this verse might indicate that Cain tried to reverse the penalty by attempting to settle down in one place. If so, Cain failed, for there is no record anywhere of the completion of the city of **Enoch.** Notice, though, that the Hebrew word for **city** stands for a human settlement of any size, from a few dwellings to a metropolis.

The author of Genesis now gives a quick lineage that traces the family tree of **Cain** through many generations to **Lamech** (4:18), who was the first polygamist (4:19). To this point in the odyssey of the human family, emphasis is given to the continued decline in human life caused by sin. God's people experienced a loss of status, a changed destiny, and a dilution of His intended plan for marriage. Sin always leaves its mark.

But not all the descendants of Cain were bad. God never punished people by taking from them bestowed gifts. These gifts eventually gave birth to tending and selectively breeding livestock (4:20), to creating music (4:21), and to mastering the techniques of metallurgy (4:22). Sin would misdirect them but would not immediately destroy them. And the rapid decline sin caused is evident. Cain had bowed to it, and Lamech reveled in it. Cain wanted protection from its ill effects, but Lamech gloated in blood lust. If sin is not eradicated from the life, it will ultimately destroy its host.

Likely by this time God had given the principle orally that a punishment must fit the crime and not be overly retaliatory. This would later be put in writing (see Exodus 21:23-25). What a contrast to Lamech's **seventy-seven times** (4:24)! His chip-on-the-shoulder existence led him to an unbridled reaction to any affront to his supposed honor. For an infraction he would strike back hard; for a misdemeanor he would devastate; for a wound he would kill. Humankind was on a collision course with destruction. The flood was coming!

Genesis 4:25-26 moves from Cain's family to the genealogy of Seth, who in a sense was Abel's replacement. Eve considered this so, for she considered her new son **another child in the place of Abel** (4:25). Within this one verse, Eve showed that she could not forget any son, for she named the newborn, the murdered, and the murderer. She had given birth to all.

Mothers had named all of the children up to this point, but Seth named **Enosh.** More importantly, though, **At that time men began to call on the name of the Lord** (4:26). The Hebrew word for **call** is stronger than the English word reveals. It has the force of the beginning of organized public worship. It is used in this sense elsewhere (see Psalm 116:17; Zephaniah 3:9). Jerome translated this passage in the Latin Bible in such a way as to indicate that Enosh was responsible for the general turn to the Lord. We are not explicitly told what precipitated the change, but it is revealed that the change came from the line of Seth. His line was the one that kept alive the faith that would guide Noah and later the patriarchs in their worship of God.

## ENDNOTE

[1]Herman Gunkel, *Genesis ubersetz und erklart,* 9th ed. (Gottinger, Germany: Vanderhoeck and Ruprecht, 1977), p. 45.

# Part Four

# FOCUS ON JUDGMENT

## Genesis 5:1–11:9

A
s Judge of all the earth (see Genesis 18:25), God is always reluctant to bring judgment on His creation. He much prefers to act in mercy, but for Him to do so depends on such things as His grand design and on cooperation from humankind. He has always expected a right order in society, one that had a moral fabric. Though not everyone in it follows Him, nor even recognizes Him, righteousness has at least been given a chance to breathe and grow. When, however, wickedness became so great on the earth that **every inclination of the [human heart] was only evil all the time** (6:5), when evil began to smother righteousness, the wheels of God's cataclysmic judgment began to turn.

From the first bite of the forbidden fruit (3:6), to the first murder (4:8), to a vengeful, remorseless killing (4:23-24), and through long generations following sin, evil grew unabated. There were some bright spots, like Enoch, who had special intimacy with God (5:22). But as the genealogy of Genesis 5 makes clear, as it traces the faithful line of Seth all the way to Noah, evil came ever closer to choking righteousness to death. Had it not been for Noah, the only righteous person left, God might have destroyed everything and begun again with another Adam and Eve. But Noah "found favor in the eyes of the Lord" (6:8).

# 10

# FROM ADAM TO NOAH

## Genesis 5:1-32

Genesis 5 gives the genealogy of Adam through Seth, the son introduced at the conclusion of Genesis 4. There is no question but that the author wrote under the inspiration of the Holy Spirit. Yet the opening phrase of 5:1, "This is the book," might indicate that the author possessed genealogical records that had been passed down to him. The phrase "This is the book" was used when other books were referenced, such as "The Book of the Wars of the Lord" (see Numbers 21:14) and "The Book of Jashar" (see Joshua 10:13; 2 Samuel 1:18).

At the time of the author of Genesis, books as we know them had not yet been made. Writing was done on either small clay tablets, or on vellum sewed together into lengthy scrolls. The term **book** referred to any written document, small or large.

While the information in Genesis 5 may not be interesting reading today, the genealogy served the Hebrews' need for connection in lineage. Cain is not mentioned in this chapter. His violent and godless line is the antithesis of Seth's line. Seth's lineage lets the reader know the connection between Adam and Noah. And that connection involved more than simple reproduction. As Adam had been created in the **image** and **likeness** of God (1:26), so Adam passed on that **likeness** and **image** to Seth (5:3). Note that the description of **likeness** and **image** are reversed from Genesis 1:26. Since Hebrew writers considered word order in a sentence indicative of their importance, reversing the order here probably showed that the words essentially have the same force of meaning.

The lineage of Genesis 5 seems rather monotonous in form until the birth of Enoch where the format is broken with the fact that he **walked**

**with God** (5:24). And the author says this twice, giving added emphasis to Enoch's righteousness. This phrase, used later of Noah (see 6:9) and of the patriarchs (see 17:1; 24:40; 48:15), indicated a life of intimate and pious fellowship with God. Such a walk was, according to Micah, the divine plan for all God's creatures (see 6:8). But Enoch's walk with God exceeded that of all the others of his family.

While the phrase **and he was not; for God took him** (5:24 KJV) was a poetical expression used for death, it was more specifically substituted for the repeated phrase "and he died." Clearly though, Enoch did not die in the normal way, as Hebrews 11:5 confirms. No physical organ ceased working, causing a physical death. Somehow, he simply left his body and entered the presence of God. Later, God would take Elijah from earth in an unusual way (see 2 Kings 2:11).

**Lamech,** a different person from the man with the same name in the Cain lineage (see Genesis 4:19), was introduced as the father of Noah. Lamech expressed a prayerful yearning that Noah would be the one to **comfort us in the labor and painful toil of our hands** (5:29). What he hoped for could not become a reality, for the world was headed for a devastating destruction; evil was winning the race to control more of the hearts of humankind. Yet, because of Noah's piety and righteousness, Noah would be chosen to preserve God's plan for the "seed" of woman to make possible the ultimate birth of the God-man "Seed."

Genesis lists ten men between Adam and Noah, and later ten names represent the generations between Noah and Abraham. When Bishop Ussher, a renowned Bible scholar who lived in the seventeenth century, added up all the years indicated in the lives of men in these and other biblical genealogies, he arrived at a date of 4004 B.C. for the creation of Adam. He assumed that each generation followed immediately on the heels of the previous one. Yet other genealogical lists skip generations; for example, Matthew 1:8 names Uzziah as the son of Joram. Uzziah is indeed the descendant of Joram, but that lineage completely omits Ahaziah, Joash, and Amaziah. It is clear from this, as well as other lineage lists, that "son of" can mean "grandson of" or "great grandson of" or, in its longest reach, "descendant of." Consider the phrase "Jesus, son of David" (Matthew 1:1). In reality, there is nearly a thousand-year period between their lifetimes.[1]

Archaeological records from the city of Jericho indicate that the city had occupants dating back numerous millennia without evidence of any flood deposits. So, the ten men in Genesis 5 appear to be reference points rather than unbroken links in the lineage from Adam to Noah. The total number of years that existed between the two is not indicated.

With respect to the very lengthy life spans of the pre-Flood population, the Bible is not alone in chronicling such a phenomenon. The ancient literature of the Egyptians, Sumerians, Phoenicians, and Chinese all speak of ancient ancestors living for extended periods of time before a world flood. It would appear that aging factors—preventing people today from living much beyond one hundred years of age—did not exist before the Flood.

The Bible records two separate lines that developed from the first two parents: the descendants of Cain and the descendants of Seth. The former grew in evil and ungodliness, moving farther and farther away from God; the latter, while most of them lost their moral direction, did maintain a line of godliness that ended in Noah and his immediate family. God saw no other option than to bring judgment on the entire human race and begin all over again with Noah.

### ENDNOTE

[1]Gleason L. Archer Jr., *A Survey of the Old Testament Introduction,* 2nd rev. ed. (Chicago: Moody Press, 1973), pp. 185–89. For additional reading concerning the gaps in biblical lineages, see *The Five Books of Moses* by Oswald T. Allis (Philadelphia: Presbyterian and Reformed, 1943), pp. 261–64.

# 11

# JUDGMENT NEARS

## Genesis 6:1-22

The history in the first eleven chapters of Genesis appears in skeletal form. One cannot know how much time transpired between chapters or, in some instances, between sets of verses. There are times when the events of one chapter may have actually begun in time before the events occurred at the end of the previous chapter. One gets the impression that God and the human author wanted quickly to get through the preliminary information to reach the story of Abraham. The early accounts give just the high points before God slows the pace of storytelling. The opening phrase of this section of Genesis 6, **When men began to increase in number** (6:1), gives the feeling that some time had elapsed since chapter 5 or, just as likely, that the author was reaching back to an earlier time.

### 1. CORRUPTION GROWING (6:1-12)

The understanding of Genesis 6:1-12 has been debated for many years. The big problem is the identity of the **sons of God** (6:2). Some have insisted that, as in the book of Job (see 1:6; 2:1), the sons of God were angels who had fallen and then married into the human line. But how could it be possible for an unbodied spirit to marry and have physical relations with a human woman? Why did not God punish them? And how would such a union be possible when Jesus said categorically that angels neither marry or are given in marriage (Mark 12:25)? Some think the **sons of God** may refer to the offspring of a ruling class, what we would call the nobility, marrying the offspring of commoners. But how could that be so wrong as to add to the growing evil and necessitate the Flood?

The more probable understanding is that **sons of God** indicated followers of God, as is found in the New Testament. The **sons of God** would then have been the descendants of Seth, who intermarried with the descendants of Cain (**daughters of men**). While it is true that the phrase **sons of God** does refer to angels in the Old Testament, such as in Job 1:6, it also refers to followers of God, as in Psalm 82:6. If the author meant to portray **sons of God** as angels intermarrying with earthly women, then we must recognize that Satan appeared as one of the **sons** in Job 1. If these sons were angelic beings, we would have to wonder why God did not judge the angels who participated in carnal intercourse.

The expression seems rather to be a typical Hebrew parallelism. To illustrate what this means, Hebrews liked to use two lines to emphasize a thought. In the first line the statement was made; then, for emphasis, the second line gave the same idea with synonyms so as not to sound monotonous. Another type of parallelism, as would be the case here, is when a statement is made in the first line; then follows a contrasting idea in the second line.

If this literary device is what the author is using, then Genesis 6:1-12 tells of the time when believers decided to marry unbelievers (both **sons** and **daughters** has the broader meaning indicating both sexes). It speaks of a time when faith found common cause with doubt, and people thought that they could go separate ways together in marriage.

Sin multiplies more quickly it seems when someone of faith enters an intimate relationship with one of unfaith. The sacred more easily becomes diluted and eventually desecrated. Today's believers need to remember not to violate Paul's principle of being unequally yoked to unbelievers (see 2 Corinthians 6:14).

The mixed marriages caused God to give a warning: **My Spirit will not contend with man forever** (6:3). The meaning of **spirit** here seems best understood as the life-giving power of God given at the Creation (see 2:7) which is translated there as "breath" of life. But it is more than just "breath," for if it were only breath, then humans would die when it was withdrawn. Concerning the bones getting new life in Ezekiel's vision, recorded in Ezekiel 37, God explained to him that the bones were the people of Israel in the graves of the Exile. God was going to put His spirit (breath) within them so they could "come to life" (Ezek. 37:5). This life force that makes the flesh and soul live, which cannot exist without God's Spirit, would be withdrawn if evil continued to add to man's depravity, says Genesis. People would continue to breathe, but God's Spirit would no longer be a part of their lives. God's mercy always has its limits. Judgment is inevitable at some point.

God set a limit for people to mend their ways of **a hundred and twenty years** (Gen. 6:3). Does this mean that He would reduce the human life span to this number of years? That is a possible interpretation. But since people continued to live past this age throughout the patriarchal period, the more probable explanation is that God would extend His mercy for up to three more generations, or a total of 120 years.

Who are **the Nephilim** (6:4)? Were these "giants" the result of the mixed union of the **sons** and **daughters** (6:2)? Though some have maintained this view, the author mentioned them only to establish a point in time. They were in the land when this unholy union occurred; they were not the result of it. The author mentioned them with the definite article **the** (6:4), indicating a specific group that presumably his readers would recognize. These "giants" had created a name for themselves through their great physical strength, which they may have expressed through violence.

In the context, perhaps we are made aware of the growth of evil in people and that rather than physical "giants" they were "giants" at committing evil. Admittedly, there were men later who, like Goliath, were of large physical proportions, but they were considered exceptions rather than the norm for an entire tribe or clan of people.

However difficult the exact understanding of the various possibilities of these verses, the overarching purpose of the passage is that God was fully aware of the moral climate, of its rapid decline, and was reaching the limits of His patience to endure it. Genesis 6:5 suggests that humankind was now near the end of the grace period. **Wickedness on the earth** had significantly worsened since evil was not an occasional interlude in moral living. It was so ingrained in the very nature of all thought and activity that **every inclination of the thoughts of [man's] heart was only evil all the time.** God's plan had run aground, mired in evil so deeply that it seemed nothing of His creation was worth redeeming.

Because of the limits of human understanding, God sometimes stoops to human levels to communicate His truth. Since God wanted His people to know about Him and His "feelings" to the limit of their comprehension, He chose to describe everything about himself in human terms. We call these descriptions "anthropomorphisms." God used this method when He said that **the Lord was grieved** at having made man, and **his heart was filled with pain** (6:6). In reality, God cannot be grieved at anything He has done; that would give the idea that He had made a mistake. But God wanted His people to know the sorrow and hurt He felt. The free will He gave people took a route that moved them far away from their Creator. They became captives of evil, unable to choose otherwise.

The writer of Genesis gives the distinct impression that there was no possible way to lift humanity out of its cesspool of existence and so change the course of history. The depravity was so deep, so pervasive, so all-encompassing that destructive judgment was God's only option.

God chose a dramatic intervention that nearly wiped all humankind **from the face of the earth** (6:7). As one would wipe a dish clean of its soil, so God decided to **wipe . . . the earth** clean of the evil contamination embodied in human hearts and minds. Preferably, one uses water to clean a dish. Perhaps the word **wipe** showed God's preferred way to bring judgment. Unfortunately for the animals who had not sinned—since they had no free will to choose to be disobedient—they too would be subjected to the "wiping." There was no way to separate them from the destruction that came. They had to share in the doom the people deserved.

God was ready to make His judgment complete, and yet **Noah found favor in [His] eyes**—another anthropomorphism that indicated God's approval of Noah's character (6:8). Why did God approve Noah? God saw in Noah what He wants most in every person in every generation—a righteousness that brings a blamelessness among people (see 6:9). The Hebrew word for **blameless** carried with it also the idea of a level of completeness, of perfection on the moral level. This word described one whose every inclination was only good all the time. And how was this made possible? Noah **walked with God** (6:9). We read earlier that Enoch also **walked with God** (5:22, 24). The phrase indicates that someone is in close communion with God.

To this point, the author has described the history of heaven and earth, which began in 1:1 and is specifically indicated in 2:4, giving us lineage from Adam through to Noah. But there came a second beginning of sorts, with only eight people (see 1 Peter 3:20) who, while escaping judgment, really were indebted to this singularly holy man, Noah (see Hebrews 11:7).

To be the only one in step with God must have been incredibly difficult, but Noah proved it was possible. On a day-to-day basis, everyone with whom Noah had dealings wanted to take advantage of him, but if tempted to return in kind, he did not yield. Noah was an example to all, though it was much harder to be honest when everyone else was dishonest. Outside the circle of his own family, his example was scorned.

Before being given more information of the pending judgment, the writer of Genesis introduced the three sons born to Noah before the

Flood: **Shem, Ham, and Japheth** (6:10). How long before the Flood they were born is not recorded, but they all had wives who made up three of the eight who entered the ark.

Genesis 6:11 reveals that only minutes remained before the hour of judgment tolled, for all **the earth was corrupt.** God had intended that people full of character would fill the earth (see 1:28), but there were only people **full of violence** (6:11). The Hebrew word for **violence** stands for what we might term today a cold-blooded, dog-eat-dog society, motivated mostly by hate and greed which expressed itself in brute force. Humankind had become little more than beastly animals ever ready to fall on weaker prey or spring on the unsuspecting. Society as a whole (**all the people on earth** [6:12]) was in the midst of fully developed anarchy.

## 2. COMPENSATION IN SIGHT (6:13-22)

The hour of reckoning had arrived. The ruling Judge of all the earth, before whom all facts and all evidence comes, was now ready to inform Noah of His sentence, since Noah would have to make preparations to avoid the inevitable destruction of both **them** [the people] **and the earth** (6:13). The earth's inhabitants would be wiped out completely, but the earth would only be stripped to a state of barrenness. It would revive, but humankind would not except through Noah and his family.

To endure the coming cataclysm required planning. God gave Noah careful instructions as to what to do. Likely, contemporary knowledge of boat construction was elementary at best. God told **Noah** to build **an ark** and to use **cypress wood** (6:14). The Hebrew language here used the word for "gopher" to describe that type of wood, and that word is found only here in the Bible. The true type of wood is uncertain, but it was most likely, as it is translated in the New International Version, **cypress**—a wood rather durable in water. Other scholars have thought God instructed the use of "reeds," which might have helped seal the lumber of the boat. The only other place in the Bible where **ark** appears is the boat that Jochabed, Moses' mother (see Exodus 6:20), made of reeds to set her infant son afloat in the Nile (see Exodus 2:3).

Noah's vessel was to have **rooms.** The root word used here is more exactly translated "nests," undoubtedly pointing to their intended occupants. These were necessary for an orderly division of the animals and also to give the boat balance. If there were too much movement to one side, the ark would be made to tip terribly and possibly sink. To insure the ark's seaworthiness, God instructed Noah **to coat it with pitch**

**inside and out** (6:14). It is noteworthy that the word for **pitch** is closely related to the word meaning "atone" in Hebrew, which the author may have intended. Since the boat needed a covering to keep it from sinking, the occupants also needed a covering (atonement) of God's grace to keep them from sin's destruction.

The size of the vessel (consisting of about one and a half million cubic feet) would seem to have been the largest boat structure known up to that time. It roughly was the size of a modern ocean liner. Its walls were to be topped with a space of eighteen inches between them and the **roof** (6:16), undoubtedly for proper ventilation and possibly to protect Noah and his family from viewing the full fury of what was occurring outside. Noah provided only one **door** to enter and exit the **lower, middle and upper decks** (6:16).

Noah learned of the full intent for all the instructions: God was **going to bring floodwaters on the earth to destroy all life . . . , every creature that has the breath of life in it** (6:17). The word for **flood** means literally "devastation," which indicates that the people who had come to live **with violence** (6:13) were about to be destroyed by violence, when **everything on earth would perish** (6:17).

In the midst of all this devastation, God told Noah that He would **establish** His **covenant with** him (6:18). **Covenant,** the word that signals a relationship in the context of an agreement, appears here for the first time in the Bible. Admittedly, the covenant is not an agreement of equals. In this case, both members did not have responsibilities toward each other, for Noah had none specified toward God. Noah simply acted in obedience to what God directed. But the Lord showed intimacy and affection for Noah by revealing to him the plans necessary for him and his family to escape the coming deluge.

The first glimmer of salvation had been given in Genesis 3:15. It was God's announcement of grace for all people that was to come through the "Seed." To make a covenant possible, Noah and his family, because of their righteousness and by means of the ark, preserved the "Seed" when the rest of humankind was eliminated.

God could have made provision for subsequent animal life by simply repeating the process of creation that had brought them into being the first time. Perhaps He chose not to act in that way because part of human responsibility was to "rule over . . . every living creature that moves on the ground" (1:28). And being righteous (see 6:9) did not qualify Noah to escape that assignment. The Hebrew word for "rule over" has the intended inclusion of the concept of "care for" or "tend." It does not suggest a rule expressed by dominating. God's instructions necessitated months, perhaps even years, of work. Noah had to fell the trees, then prepare the lumber for the construction of the ark, both inside and out. He constructed all things necessary to house **two of all living creatures, male and female, to keep them alive** (6:19) with him and his family.

Then Noah undoubtedly gave attention, perhaps through several harvests, to obtaining the food he, his family, and all the animals would need to survive (see 6:21). Whatever occupation Noah may have had before receiving his orders from the Lord, he and his family turned their full attention to the many responsibilities that lay before them at that point. And regardless of the amount of work involved, **Noah did everything just as God commanded him** (6:22), in spite of likely constant daily ridicule. His faith held him steady in his obedient walk with God.

# 12

# JUDGMENT NOW

## Genesis 7:1–8:14

How much time elapsed between the end of Genesis 6 and the beginning of Genesis 7? Some contend that Noah and his sons spent the entire "one hundred and twenty years" (6:3) building the ark. Since the number of years which had passed before God spoke to Noah with instructions to build the ark is not known, no one can calculate how long it took to complete the project. However, consider how much time it would take to build such a huge ship without the use of modern cranes, sawmills, trucks, and automated equipment. No matter how long it took, the day came when the last tree had been felled, the last plank had been hewn, the last peg had been driven, and all the waterproof covering had been applied. The ark was ready for its voyage. Judgment time had arrived for the whole world.

## 1. COMMAND: ENTER THE ARK (7:1-10)

Noah obeyed God and completed the ark despite no visible evidence that a flood would come. God told him to enter the vessel with **your whole family, because I have found you righteous** (7:1). Noah had obeyed God's directions even to the smallest detail. He was righteous before beginning the construction of the ark; he was the same after building the ark and readying it for its voyage.

Earlier God had told Noah that he was to preserve two of every kind of animal so as to enable the continuation of their kind after the flood (see 6:19-20). At that point, God gave additional instructions. Noah was to bring into the ark **seven of every kind of clean animal** (7:2). Why so many of the clean animals? It seems most likely God was making provisions for sacrifices that could be made while the ark was afloat. That Abel presented an animal sacrifice proves God's people had been offering such sacrifices for generations.

How could Noah possibly have known what was meant by "clean" and "unclean"? That distinction would not be put in writing as we have it in Hebrew manuscripts until Moses received the written Law on Mt. Sinai many years later (see Leviticus 11). Likely an oral law had been passed down from father to son and ultimately to Noah. Its writing in Leviticus was simply a more permanent written statement of what their ancestors had been told.

Had some time passed between the events of Genesis 7:3 and 7:4? It could be. Or if not, a time span may have elapsed after the events at the end of Genesis 6, during which time all the preparations were being made. Noah next learned that he had just seven days to get the clean animals aboard before the rain started to fall. On this occasion, too, God told Noah of the duration of the Flood. It would last **forty days and forty nights** (7:4).

Note Noah's age. When **the floodwaters came on the earth,** he had passed his six hundredth birthday. Noah's sons had passed their one hundredth birthdays (5:32).

## 2. THE FLOOD BEGINS (7:11-16)

Skeptics have noted at least two arguments against the validity of the Flood account.

First, they state that there is no way enough rain to flood the earth could have come down in a mere forty days. This is true. But the Bible states that not only **the floodgates of the heavens were opened, [but] all the springs of the great deep burst forth** (7:11). Somehow God caused pressure to force water up from underground sources, while rain was falling from the sky.

Second, some argue theoretically that if all the water in the air was liquefied and the world's ice was melted, the world's water line would not be raised more than nine or ten inches. Since no water is ever lost, and no more is being generated, where then is all the water that flooded the world?

The answer must be that the world today has a very different configuration than it had before the Flood. A sonar probe of the bottom of the Atlantic Ocean has revealed a seam in the middle of it. It somewhat matches the continents of North America and Europe with South America and Africa. The impression is that at one time the Atlantic Ocean did not exist, perhaps before the Flood. But through a cataclysmic fissure, the ground opened to make the water recede quickly. This indicates that it is really too difficult to determine what might have happened during the

Flood. One is much safer simply to take the Word of God as a factual report of a totally unique and one-time event on the earth.

The information about the beginning of the Flood—**the seventeenth day of the second month** (7:11)—is dated from the **six hundredth year** of Noah's life. This would be more helpful information for us if the month of Noah's birthday could be known, but that remains a mystery since there is no hint of it in the text.

Some critics claim that 7:13-16 indicates that not only Noah's family entered the ark on this date but all the animals as well, and that a normal day is too short a time for all this to happen. Reading these verses as a report of a grand procession gives that impression. But an alternate reading helps simplify the matter. Rather than **They had with them [as they entered the ark] every . . . animal,** one could translate the Hebrew text to read, **They had with them [in the ark] every . . . animal** (7:14). This alternate reading leaves the impression that the animals had boarded before the human family, and **on that very day** refers to time after the humans entered (7:13).

After the entrance of Noah and his family, **the Lord shut him in** (7:16). What could this phrase mean? Surely it indicates that any other person wanting to enter the ark later would have found that impossible, for Noah did not control the door. Perhaps the door was below the water line and was sealed in such a way that the force of the water kept it closed during the Flood. That made it impossible for anyone on the inside to open it until the waters of the Flood receded.

## 3. THE FLOOD COVERS ALL (7:17-24)

Water rising from subterranean sources and rains falling steadily during the forty days caused **the flood** to keep **coming on the earth** (7:17). Altogether it took forty days for the water to reach its maximum height when **all the high mountains . . . were covered** (7:19). If one could have viewed the earth from some point in space, all that would have been visible was water over the entire ball, for even the highest peaks were twenty-two and a half feet below the water's surface (7:20). The highest peaks would not have been, it would seem, as high as current mountain ranges. Possibly the mountain ranges of today arose after the Flood from a thrust caused by activity within the earth. Genesis 7:21-23 tells how not only **all mankind** perished, but everything **that had the breath of life in its nostrils.** So the animals that died were limited to those that lived on dry land—that is, water animals survived.

After the waters reached their maximum height, the ground was so saturated that the waters could not recede. The waters stayed **for a hundred and fifty days** (7:24).

# 4. THE FLOOD CONCLUDES (8:1-14)

Genesis 8 begins with the fact that **God remembered Noah** and those in the ark (8:1). This in no way implies that for a time God had forgotten them. It simply indicates a turning point in the story. The waters of the Flood had served their appointed purposes—the complete end of air-breathing life on the earth. God was ready to prepare the earth for the reintroduction of life. The significant change in the **wind** that God caused to pass **over the earth** (8:1) helped the water level to drop.

The water probably was beginning to recede during the one hundred and fifty days even before the wind had started to blow, for at the very end of the period—on the seventeenth day of the seventh month—**the ark came to rest on the mountains of Ararat** (8:4). If these mountains were the tallest mountains in the area, then the water had dropped twenty-two and a half feet (see 7:20) from its maximum height. Noah's salvation was about to be completed.

Though a quick reading of the text has made many believe that the ark landed on the mountain (singular) called **Ararat,** the Hebrew word used is in plural form: **mountains** (8:4). The precise location where the ark came to rest is not identified.

The water level continued to drop for another two and a half months, making it possible for **the tops of the mountains** to be seen (8:5). For some unrecorded reason, Noah waited another forty days before he sent **out a raven** (8:7). This he did in order to obtain some clue as to when would be the most appropriate time to leave the ark. Since mountains surrounded them, Noah's perspective on the condition of the earth was too limited to make a good judgment without additional information. And there was a probability that the window he used to free the raven was placed too high for him to view the land conditions for himself. Until the recent use of electronic instrumentation to determine the proximity of land, sailors depended on released birds to do that for them.

The raven apparently flew until it found sufficient ground to make survival possible. It did not return to provide Noah with the information he needed. He then released a **dove** (8:8), a much more sensitive bird. He believed it would be more reliable in helping him determine the appropriate time to release the animals, which he certainly was most anxious to do. The dove returned because it did not find suitable nesting conditions.

Aware that each day brought an improvement in conditions, the patient Noah allowed another week to pass before sending the dove out again. On this occasion, the dove found more to occupy its time. It stayed out the entire day and returned with a freshly plucked olive leaf in its beak. There was every reason to believe that during the Flood Noah had tamed the dove. He expected it to return. Since olive leaves can sprout even under water, Noah knew the tree this leaf had come from had survived the Flood. That it was growing in the ground convinced Noah the waters had nearly all subsided.

After another week, the dove was sent out a third time. When it did not return, Noah knew it had returned to its normal pattern of existence. Yet, as the text states, he waited another two months before removing **the covering from the ark** to confirm **that the surface of the ground was dry** (8:13).

The removable covering apparently was made of animal skin that had somehow been secured and made watertight. Its removal signaled the soon-to-be-given order to leave the vessel. It is likely that, given the confinement time for all the animals, Noah was anxious to air out the ark. Just as God had concern for the animals, so did Noah.

# 13

# JUDGMENT PAST

## Genesis 8:15–11:9

The Flood had passed. Noah and his crew gladly anticipated leaving the confinement of the ark. But they did not get the order to leave until the earth was sufficiently dry to allow the group to descend the mountains. Noah did not know when the instructions would arrive, so he did his best to determine the condition of the ground by the use of a raven and a dove.

Noah's understandable desire to exit the ark and return to a normal existence was tempered by his patience to be in step with God. The dove did not return after its third flight, but that was not sufficient cause to uncover the vessel or even open the door. Noah waited another two months.

There is no record that God told Noah to remove **the covering of the ark** (8:13). It would appear that He let Noah decide for himself when to do it. God always wants people to use their own endowed wisdom to assist Him in fulfilling His plan.

Throughout the Flood story, God dealt with Noah alone. The entire plan of salvation focused on Noah exclusively. His family, which would become more active, had been consistently in the background. They benefited from Noah's righteous walk with God. Though Scripture does not explicitly mention it, Noah was God's second physical Adam. True, Noah had lived in a society deeply contaminated by sin, but he was ready to enter a world where judgment by water had cleansed it of all contamination.

## 1. THE COMMAND TO LEAVE THE ARK (8:15-22)

Noah had obediently followed God's commands. And although he knew he could leave the ark, he waited for the Lord's orders. They came. God told Noah to **come out** (8:16) with all the members of his family and to **bring out** (8:17) all the animals. All inhabitants of the ark returned to their natural habitat.

The deliverance from the Flood can best be described in one word— spectacular![1] Though God told Noah to leave the ark, He did not tell him what to do next. Noah did not need such instruction. His righteous heart made him want to commune with God, so his first act was to build **an altar to the Lord** (8:20), and on it he **sacrificed burnt offerings.** His first thoughts were of the deliverance from the Flood and of God's part in it. But his mind also must have been humbled at the responsibility that lay before him in starting a renewed world.

We read that Cain and Abel sacrificed to the Lord, yet Scripture does not mention the use of an altar. This is the first mention of one (see 8:20). Also, the writer uses a different word for sacrifice here than what he used with Cain and Abel (see 4:3-5). The word in the Law (see Leviticus 2:1) given at Sinai stood for "gift" of a "grain offering." The word used in Genesis 8:20 had its origin in the idea of "ascending." It pictures perfectly the rise of the fire and smoke of the sacrifice going up to God.

The **aroma** of that fire and smoke was **pleasing** to the Lord. God **smelled** it (8:21), an obvious human expression to show God's acceptance of both Noah and his offering. On Noah's part, the sacrifice first expressed gratitude for what God had done for him, but it was also a prayer for God's continued protection.

The Lord answered that prayer immediately **in his heart** (8:21), meaning "to himself." The public announcement followed, recorded in the next chapter of Genesis. God pledged **never again . . . [to] curse the ground because of man** in spite of the fact that **every inclination of his heart is evil from childhood** (8:21). Why just from his **childhood?** The concept given is "from the age of accountability." Though one's heart is contaminated at birth, a person is not guilty for what it tempts him to do until the dawn of his discernment of good and evil.

God assessed the sinful corruption that passed through Adam and Eve to the whole human race. Without grace and mercy, all people are hopelessly corrupt. Adam's stain still contaminates all.

Genesis 8:21 indicates that while the Flood was intended by God as punishment for the human family for allowing sin to dominate society so completely, it was also intended to give newly born people a second chance to contain their evil inclinations by a greater reliance on the Lord. They failed again and continue to fail. But when evil's needle rises to God's allowed limit, destruction will come again, this time not by water but more likely by war.

In order to get the correct sense of the verse (8:21), a better translation is "Even though I brought destruction on the world because of the *results* of the evil inclinations of men's hearts, I will not do it again." Putting it in human terms, God's "change of mind" was not because of humanity's inherited evil nature. It was because He accepted the sacrifice and prayer given by Noah; this was paving the way for the more perfect sacrifice of His Son. There is the sense too that God was saying, "From this point on I will not punish the human family as a whole; I will now punish individual sinners."

In poetic form, God said that after the Flood, life would follow in normal patterns of **seedtime and harvest, cold and heat, summer and winter, day and night** (8:22). The last phrase, **will never cease,** is qualified by the first phrase, **as long as the earth endures.** He was not saying the earth would continue forever. Rather, He was saying that there would not be another universal interruption in these things until the final judgment and the end of this earth.

# 2. THE CHARGE GIVEN (9:1-7)

God spoke to Noah but also addressed his sons for the first time (see Genesis 9:1). God did not yet tell them what He had decided to do with the earth and all humanity. He was first concerned with restating to them what He had previously told Adam (see 1:28). They were heads of a new race of people who would have to start over and, in some respects, at a lower place. The world they faced was in a ruined condition and must be rebuilt. They could not do it alone. They needed to **be fruitful and increase in number and fill the earth** (9:1).

In His words to Noah, God did not mention "ruling over" all living creatures as He had commissioned Adam. Why the change? Humanity's relationship to the world had changed, so their ability to rule the animals had diminished. It would be less peaceful; there would be **fear and dread** (9:2). Animals would be more dangerous than before, so the Lord put a measure of fear into them. Otherwise, they might have brought an end to the human family.

Next, Noah and his sons received an entirely new permission on God's part. Animal flesh could be consumed. Adam, Eve, and their first descendants might have lived on "a vegetarian diet" (1:29), though this does not mean that there was no consumption of animal meat before the Flood, as some have interpreted. Had it been prohibited, there would have been a stated prohibition against it. People had been permitted to kill animals for sacrifices and for clothing, but as of this time they are told they can consume (or continue to consume) meat for food.

While God approved the consumption of animals for food (see 9:3), He did not permit the eating of **everything that lives and moves** (9:3). For example, he subsequently forbade the eating of animals that had died of natural causes (see Deuteronomy 14:21). The very important reason for this provision, aside from the danger to one's health, was the danger of consuming blood (see 9:4). God wanted a holy respect for blood, both human and animal. It was later spelled out in Deuteronomy 12:23: "Be sure you do not eat the blood, because the blood is the life, and you must not eat the life with the meat."

Modern thought is that life is in the brain waves, for when these cease, one is declared dead, though the heart may still be pumping. But God was speaking to the ancient people at their level of understanding: When blood is drained from the body, one's vitality is drained with it until the heart stops.

Two reasons for this prohibition seem prominent. This command prevented cruelty to animals. Primitive races thought nothing of barbarously cutting a leg from a live animal, causing terrible suffering. God did not want such disrespect for animal life. If people exercised some humane way of taking the life of animals, they would be more likely to respect the blood of humans. More importantly though, God knew that Christ's blood would have to be shed, and true life without His blood in sacrifice for sin is impossible (see Acts 4:12). God let Noah know (see Genesis 9:5) that relationships between people and animals (as well as relationships among people) were among His main concerns. God **demands an accounting** of responsibility even **from every animal** (9:5). A natural question arises: "How can a carnivorous animal be held responsible for doing what his nature demands? Exodus 21:28-29 gives some clarification. There the Law says, "If a bull gores a man or a woman to death, the bull must be stoned to death. . . ." It would appear that this law was established to some degree to help "breed out" domestic animals' propensity to kill.

Yet relationships between people are of greater concern to God. The animal is not a brother to humans; rather other people are. While humans are broadly classified as animals, it is with other humans that man is most closely related, and his **blood** (life) must be considered sacred. Human life is supremely sacred, **for in the image of God has God made man** (9:6). Those who oppose capital punishment see verses 5 and 6 as a convincing argument.

## 3. THE COVENANT ESTABLISHED (9:8-17)

At that point, God publicly expressed what He had decided at the time of Noah's sacrifice (8:21), to **establish** His **covenant** with Noah, his sons, their **descendants after** them, and **with every living creature . . . on earth** (9:9-10). **Never again will . . . a flood . . . destroy the whole earth** (9:11). As a symbol of the sign for this covenant, God said, **I have set my rainbow in the clouds** (9:13). God considered this covenant important, for it is mentioned six times in 9:11-17. The covenant is mentioned in five different ways:

- **between me and you and every living creature with you** (9:12)
- **between me and the earth** (9:13)
- **between me and you and all living creatures** (9:15)
- **between God and all living creatures of every kind on the earth** (9:16)
- **between me and all life on earth** (9:17)

The importance of the covenant is underscored like a signaling drumbeat—repeatedly—for Noah's day and for the future.

Was this the first appearance of the rainbow? Many have claimed this, but the Hebrew words do not intimate that it had just been created. Rainbows come from sunlight shining through moisture in the air between earth and the sun. The sun was shining from the time of Creation on, and 2:6 states that there was a "mist" (better than "streams," as the New International Version has it) "that watered the whole surface of the ground." Could the sun have made a rainbow every day as it shined through this moisture? If so, then God subsequently chose it to be the sign of the covenant, for it appears only when there is sufficient moisture in the air. There are those who point to God, saying it is His **rainbow** (9:13) and suggesting that this confirms it had already existed. The timing of this sentence points to the past, not the present, in that the Lord said, **I have set,** indicating something that He had already done. But regardless of when the rainbow first appeared, God intended that when people saw it they would think of His promise.

## 4. CANAAN CURSED (9:18-29)

Noah's three sons have already been introduced, but only by their names. As would be expected, they became the forebears of all subsequent people. But parenthetically included is the fact that Ham had a son named Canaan. Focus shifts to this son of Noah.

Noah had been a farmer, **a man of the soil** (9:20), before God charged him to build the ark; literally, he was called "Noah the husbandman." Somehow he had discovered the art of grape growing and actually had planted a vineyard. Botanists say that the grapevine originated in Armenia, exactly where the ark landed. While the text says that Noah **proceeded to plant a vineyard** (9:20), the Hebrew word gives the sense that he "began" to plant, lending credence to the idea that this was a new experience for him. Nothing written here reflects disapproval for what Noah did. Did he fall into sin by his act, and was he still considered righteous? Nothing was said to the contrary. Would he fall into sin by simply growing grapes? No, but his innocent experimentation led him into it. He had discovered a way to press out the juice of the grape, and after letting it age for a time, he noticed that it had a different taste. He was totally unaware of its intoxicating effect. His drunkenness resulted from an accidental discovery rather than a calculated, premeditated act. His act did not merit condemnation. Noah was still blameless.

But Ham was not. A recovering Noah lay in his tent. Did Ham, while passing by, simply take an accidental glance at his father's uncovered body, then go to tell his brothers? Where was the great sin in that? And why would Canaan be the one cursed for what Ham did? If Noah's righteousness was not affected by what he had unintentionally done, can we blame Ham for a similar infraction? These are questions that some find difficult to answer.

The tenor of the Bible is, "The body is holy, cover it" (see Exodus 20:26; 28:42; Leviticus 18:1-30; 20:17-18; Habakkuk 2:15-16; 1 Corinthians 6:13b, 20; Revelation 3:18; 16:15). The pagan idea current at the same time was, "The body is evil, uncover it." Nakedness after the Fall could no longer be countenanced, for the evil heart always seeks an unbridled expression of sex rather than containing it within marriage as God intended (see Genesis 2:24-25). Still, this does not answer the questions raised.

One explanation is that Ham somehow enjoyed the nakedness of his father, maybe even committing a homosexual act, then relating with delight to his brothers what he saw or did. This still does not answer the question as to why Canaan was cursed by Noah (see 9:25) for what Ham had done.

References in Leviticus 18 (see verses 11, 18-19) frequently have statements like, "You shall not uncover the nakedness of. . . ." Then a person of the opposite sex is identified. These are all possible cases of incest and have nothing to do with homosexuality. It has been suggested that what Ham actually did while Noah was drunk and uncovered in his tent was to have relations with his mother,² whose nakedness belonged to Noah alone. By this interpretation, Canaan then was cursed because he was the offspring of an incestuous relationship.

While this theory leaves a few unanswered questions, such as how Noah would learn so quickly of what Ham had done, this explanation more readily explains why Canaan was cursed. Noah knew others would blame Canaan for his illegitimate birth, though he had nothing to do with it. Noah's words then were prophetic. This would explain why Shem and Japheth **took a garment and laid it across their shoulders;** then, with their faces turned away, **they walked in backward and covered their father's nakedness** (9:23), meaning they were covering their mother. Noah's wife may not have been a willing partner to Ham's act. Perhaps she too was semiconscious from having tasted the same fermented juice that Noah drank, though admittedly this is not stated.

Whatever happened here, the Ten Commandments later codified expected behavior of children toward their parents. It was above all to "honor" (Exodus 20:12), a most sacred duty. The first four commandments point to God (see Exodus 20:1-11); the fifth, honoring parents, heads the ones pointing to people, even preceding murder and adultery (see Exodus 20:13-14).

Canaan's destiny through his race, as predicted by Noah, would be one of virtual enslavement to the descendants of both Shem and Japheth. It was widely believed that a father's blessing would cause his son to succeed; conversely, a father's curse would cause a son to fail. Three times in three verses Noah cursed Canaan, an emphasis to the extreme. The curse came true. The Canaanites were among the most morally depraved peoples of their time. They were virtual slaves to sex in every form.

Some have viewed the color of black peoples as evidence of the curse, and then find legitimacy for bigoted feelings. Such a view is a misunderstanding of the text. While Ham's descendants did populate parts of Africa, he was not cursed; rather Canaan was. One cannot consider Canaanites to have been a black race, so skin color had nothing to do with this incident.

After the curse on Canaan, Noah blessed both Shem and Japheth— Shem with a doxology to God for being **the God of Shem** (Gen. 9:26), and Japheth with an enlargement of land. Genesis 9 ends on a note that Noah **lived 350 years** after the Flood, **950 years** altogether (9:29).

## 5. THE FAMILY SPREAD (10:1-32)

Genesis 10 may be heavy reading for a student of the Word today, but it offers a link. From the new start for humankind by means of one family, it takes us to the life of Abraham, the man chosen to give rise to the race of people through whom the Redeemer was to come. Some of the names are meaningless today because of limited information of that period of history. Other names of nations are not found at all.

There is no obvious reason as to why God inspired this entire chapter. It names the peoples who sprang from Noah's family. Admittedly though, people of earliest times were more concerned about ancestry and lineage than are people today. Perhaps it was intended more for them. It is a limited analysis of the descendants of the nations and tribes of the Near Eastern World to the time of Abraham. There seems to be a focus on the East. God (see 2:8) had placed the Garden of Eden there. The entrance to it was on the east, for the cherubim blocked it on that side (see 3:24). Cain lived on that side of Eden (see 4:16). Some of Shem's descendants "lived . . . in the eastern hill country" (10:30). The plain of Shinar was in that direction, and it was where many people wanted to live (see 11:2).

## 6. THE FUTILE TOWER (11:1-9)

As the record of Genesis 11 begins, **the whole world had one language and a common speech** (11:1). This is commonly thought to mean that before the Tower of Babel attempt, there was only one language spoken. The broader context seems to say quite the contrary is true. Three verses of Genesis 10 (verses 5, 20, 31) mention **languages** being spoken by the descendants of the three sons of Noah, and that to some extent these linguistic differences were part of the reason they were living in their **clans . . . territories and nations** (10:31).

Philologists, scholars in linguistics, affirm that all languages that can be studied—even extinct ones that appear only in written form—show undeniable affinities with one another. These affinities, so numerous, indicate intensive borrowing. This may point back to a time when there was only one language. Spoken languages appear to have existed long before writing came into being. Therefore this first language cannot be isolated. The invention of writing only goes back to the fourth millennium. The first language cannot have been Hebrew, for it came quite late in the history of writing.

It would seem that groups of nations spoke differing dialects, called **languages,** which in many cases may not have been known or understood by other groups. Yet all people apparently also had one language by which they could communicate with one another. This would have been what we call a *lingua franca*—a common language they all used in cooperating with each other. It tended to bring the peoples too much together and reverse the design God had for them "to multiply, and fill the earth" (1:28 RSV). This common tongue of communication would have been the language that God confused. Each group continued speaking its own vernacular, but suddenly people could no longer give and receive information by means of their universal language.

It would seem that all early building projects in that area of the world used a more moist mud for mortar, but these people decided to use **tar** (11:3). Perhaps they had an oversupply of it, since in that area a by-product of underground oil deposits oozes to the surface as a dark brown substance.

These people seem to have had absurd reasoning. They hardly had the ability to build **a tower that reaches to the heavens** (11:4). Admittedly, the phrase in Hebrew expresses an exaggeration for "as high as we can." If God had allowed it, their harebrained idea would have involved great danger of harming themselves physically—there would have been an overcrowding in the plain of Shinar. Spiritually also, with their away-from-God direction, they were headed for collective apostasy rather than righteousness. Without a concern about God in their lives, they wanted **to make a name** for themselves (11:4). One of the first marks of the rebellious spirit is to disobey God and at the same time to elevate self and try to act like a god.

On an archeological note, some two dozen mud-brick towers, built in pyramidal form, have been discovered in present-day Iraq. One found at Ur, dating from around 2000 B.C., measured three hundred feet on each side. They were likely their builders' efforts to make elevated temples to worship the supposed heavenly deity they venerated. They are called "Ziggurats," a word meaning "mountain peak" or "to be high." For centuries, local inhabitants have plundered the structures to obtain the mud bricks for other building projects. These structures might well have been copied from the original one described here in Genesis.[3]

In 11:5, the scene switches to heaven. Perhaps worded to help people understand the scope of this project from God's perspective, we read that God viewed it from heaven. From that vantage point, it was so insignificant that God came **down to see** (11:5). God was already at the site on earth, but this was a graphic way of expressing that this great human achievement was but a puny effort to build as high as God.

Are people capable of doing anything they put their minds to do? Is nothing impossible for them? In a relative sense, perhaps, if they will commit time and money to the project. Much of what has been developed by human ingenuity and experience today was thought impossible by previous generations. If time lasts, much will be invented that we now think impossible. But no matter how ingenious the plan, how ambitious the effort, or how skillful the execution, God limits what He will allow people with free choice to do. And it is in our best interest. One who elevates himself or herself to a presumed divine eminence becomes dictatorial, turning brutal if necessary, to get his or her way.

Knowing these people were in no way capable of listening to God's instructions, God simply chose to **confuse their language so they will not understand each other** (11:7). This caused them to separate into groups with their various dialects and spread **over the face of the whole earth** (11:9).

## Endnotes

[1]The Apostle Peter much later saw deliverance from the floodwater as a symbol for baptism. And the water of baptism symbolizes the from-death-into-life experience made possible "by the resurrection of Jesus Christ" (1 Peter 3:21).

[2]F.W. Basset, "Noah's Nakedness and the Curse of Canaan. A Case of Incest?" *Vetus Testamentum* 21, 1971, pp. 232–37.

[3]Andre Parrot, *The Tower of Babel* (New York: Philosophical Library, 1955), p. 9.

# Part Five

# THE CHOSEN RACE: ABRAM, BUT NO SON

## Genesis 11:10–14:24

This block of Genesis opens with a furthering of lineage. Chapter 5 records lineage from Adam to Shem. Genesis 11:10-26 begins that lineage where it stopped and takes it to Abram, later called Abraham. The universal history, necessary to set the stage, has been completed. The record moves on to the purpose of Genesis. The writer of Genesis first chronicled the descendants of the human family as a whole. The focus then moved to the lives of the patriarchs of the chosen race. From Shem came the descendants leading to Terah, the father of the man originally called **Abram,** and his two brothers, **Nahor and Haran** (11:26). It is likely there were other children, but they are not named.

We will note that for some unexplained reason Terah decided to leave Ur with the purpose of going **to Canaan** (11:31). Why he took Abram, Sarai (later called Sarah), his wife, and Lot, but not his other children is not mentioned. Terah may have been some type of merchant who had traveled that way before.

What changed Terah's mind so that he chose to stay in Haran instead of continuing on to his original destination of Canaan is not revealed, but he remained there until he died. Abram had a more compelling reason to leave. "For He was looking forward to the city with foundations, whose architect and builder is God" (Hebrews 11:10). Before his call, his family gods of wood and stone never heard or acted on a request he had made. They were always silent—never a reply.

While the Lord appeared to have been silent about the Promised Land until Abram arrived at Shechem, there He removed the mystery by informing Abram that it was the chosen place for him and his descendants (see Genesis 12:6).

Why Abram chose to venture farther to the south (see 12:9) is not mentioned. But while he was there, a famine made him decide to go on farther still to Egypt where, because of the ever-flowing Nile, food was usually abundant.

We will learn that Abram left Egypt with less credibility than he had when he went there, for he resorted to what we can term a third-grade truth, causing him to be ordered to leave. He was even escorted to the border. Abram later experienced the departure of Lot after Lot decided to settle in a place that would lead to temporary captivity, great sorrow, and eventually the loss of all he owned.

# 14

# ABRAM IN MOVEMENT

## Genesis 11:10-13:4

ollowing the account of Shem (11:10-26), we are given **the account of Terah** (11:27). He was the clan leader. At the time, such leaders were highly respected. To whatever they decided to do, the extended family agreed. Of the three sons, **Abram** (God later changed his name to Abraham; see 17:5) was likely the oldest, for his name precedes the others. Little information is given about **Nahor,** the second oldest. He seems to have been named after his grandfather (see 11:24).

Lot was born to the youngest son, **Haran** (11:27). At some point after Lot's birth, Haran died. The impression given is that he died prematurely, for his death happened even before Terah, Haran's father, died (see 11:28). Abram married **Sarai;** Nahor married Milcah, who happened to be his niece, one of the daughters of Haran (presumably a sister to Lot). Later the text states that Abram and Sarai had the same father, but different mothers (see 20:12). The Law given later at Sinai forbade unions such as these. But the cultural customs of Abram's period seem to have encouraged such unions.

## 1. THE UNCOMMON HERITAGE (11:27-32)

From what Joshua later said in his farewell speech (see Joshua 24:2), Terah and his extended family had been taught and early practiced idolatry. It would be interesting to know under what circumstances Abram became convinced that his native gods were powerless, even lifeless.

Geographers have been puzzled by the information that the homeland of the patriarchs was in **Ur of the Chaldeans** (11:28), in lower Mesopotamia near the Persian Gulf in the present country of Iraq. The

117

homeland for the wives of both Isaac and Jacob was in Paddan Aram (see Genesis 25, 28, 31), which is farther to the north in present-day Syria. There is no record that the families of the patriarchs lived so far south. Some have concluded that there had to have been another city of Ur to the northwest of the Ur mentioned in 11:28, in what was later called Paddan Aram. The other possibility is that the original home of the families of Terah was indeed in the north, but that Terah, for some unexplained reason, migrated for a time to the south. He lived there until he decided to go to Canaan, but en route stopped at Haran (in the same general vicinity of Paddan Aram) where he later died, never having reached his intended destination. It must be admitted, though, that the names of Abram, Sarai, and Nahor are found in Babylonian inscriptions where **Ur** was known to have been located.

The text states that **Sarai was barren** (11:30), a fact that was considered unbearable, especially to women. A woman's whole purpose in life was to grow up, get married, and have children. A life of barrenness was almost totally unacceptable, again a pagan-influenced cultural custom.

Some years ago at a city northeast of Babylon called Nuzu, thousands of clay tablets were found which chronicle the societal practices of the biblical Horites (see Genesis 14:6; 36:20; Deuteronomy 2:22), a group of tribes who had amazingly similar customs to those of Abram, Sarai, and their descendants. Based on this list of ancient customs, it would be correct to surmise that at Haran's death Abram adopted Lot, since Abram had no son of his own. He would not have done it so much for Lot's benefit as for his own. Abram wanted someone to care for him in his old age. And when Abram died, Lot, as an adopted son, would inherit Abram's property.

The Bible indicates that when Terah left Ur with his extended family, his intent was **to go to Canaan** (11:31). What caused him to change his mind and settle at **Haran** instead? Perhaps it was religious, for both Ur and Haran were centers of moon-god worship. Another possibility could be that Babylon was destroyed by the Elamites soon after the beginning of the second millennium. Terah might have fled to safety away from these warring people. Perhaps the presumed protection of the gods of Haran might have caused him to decide to change his original travel plans. Whatever the reason, Terah **settled there** in Haran, where he lived until age 205, when **he died** (11:32).

One gets the impression that Abram did not leave for Canaan until after Terah passed away, but based on information about their ages,

Abram left sixty years before his father's death. The purpose of its being recorded at this point is to end the story of Terah. The text shifts its concentration to Abram.

## 2. THE UNIQUE CALL (12:1-3)

Genesis 12 begins with God's calling Abram to leave his country, his relatives, and his close family members and **go to the land I will show you** (12:1). From what Stephen later said in Acts 7:2, there must have been an original call to "Abraham while he was still in Mesopotamia [Ur], before he lived in Haran." Could it be that, so fresh from idolatry when he received his initial call, Abram lacked enough clarity about it that God knew Abram needed a confirmation? If so, that call came again while Abram was at Ur.

Why did God think it necessary to keep secret from Abram the place where He wanted him to go? Indeed, the location of Canaan was where Abram could maximally influence society without being overly influenced by it. It was a land bridge that connected the three continents of Africa, Europe, and Asia. Travelers often had to traverse this land en route to their intended destination. An international highway partly passed through the land near the Mediterranean Sea, then turned to the center of the land in its northern part.

God still could have told Abram where he was to go. But perhaps God thought the best way for Abram's faith to grow was in the dark. Often, the more we know, the less we trust. It is never easy to surrender the known in order to embrace the unknown. Abram needed most to learn to trust God. In the words of Hamilton, Abram "does not have, in terms of personal realization, all the promises of God. But he does have the God of all the promises."[1] That was all he needed.

Not knowing exactly where he was supposed to go, Abram wisely decided to stay on the course—toward Canaan—that had been decided before his family group left Ur of the Chaldeans. Why Terah decided to remain behind is not stated. Perhaps his idolatry, as well as the growing faith of Abram, made him feel increasingly ill at ease with his son—who was turning from his childhood religion to an invisible God—and thus Terah felt more secure in Haran. Abram may not have wanted Terah to go, because God had told him to leave **your father's household** (12:1).

What a promise accompanied the call! Abram had to have been excited at the possibilities: He was to be the father of a **great nation;** he was to be blessed by being given a **great name;** and he was to be the means of blessing **all peoples on earth** (12:2-3). Yet how could all this happen? He must have immediately thought of Sarai's barrenness, of the days—perhaps even years—she had yearned to have children, of her increasing age. Then, too, he realized he would not live to see the **great nation** (12:2) which was to be part of his reward, nor could he assess the full **blessing** (12:3) of which he was to be the means. And how could he measure what others would think of his **name?** He had every reason to believe that these words were all part of an illusionary dream. Likely with questions, but without argument, Abram **left** Haran, **as the Lord had told him** (12:4). What faith! What amazing faith!

## 3. THE UNUSUAL PROMISE (12:4-9)

While people in Abram's day generally lived longer than people do today, even at **seventy-five** years of age this had to be a most traumatic move for Abram. He might not have had all the **possessions** most contemporary people do, but he likely **had accumulated** a fair amount, including large herds of animals. With him, too, were additional **people [he] had acquired in Haran** (12:5). These required much planning for a long and arduous trip, one that would take weeks, if not months, and perhaps even longer. Abram had no way of knowing how far he was to go or even when he would arrive. But he went.

This very large group had traveled some four hundred miles south from Haran when they arrived at **the site of the great tree of Moreh** near the town of Shechem (12:6). In Hebrew, this tree is called a "terebinth" tree. Oaks of several kinds used to grow abundantly in the Holy Land. This particular one likely was taller than the others. Some authorities think it was a "turpentine tree," which could grow from twenty to forty feet tall. It may have served as a landmark among numerous smaller trees. That it was called the **tree of Moreh** might indicate a tree in a grove worshiped by the Canaanites. They had their worship sites at such places, for **Moreh** is the Hebrew word for "teacher." The text says that **the Canaanites were in the land** (12:6).

It is reasonable to think that Abram simply stopped at this well-known spot to rest and to obtain supplies from nearby Shechem. **The Lord appeared** to Abram there and told him that he had arrived at the place where God wanted him to be. If Abram was near this tree of idol worshipers, it was of little concern to him. He was not ashamed of his faith. He let everyone know he worshiped a different God—one who had made the very special tree which these inhabitants likely venerated—so right there **he built an altar . . . to the Lord** (12:7).

The Lord used a vision to speak to Abram in a later setting (see 15:1). But in 12:7, God **appeared** to him directly. What visible form did God use? Only Abram knows, but the word suggests that God used not a vision but an objective reality that could be seen and recognized as God. The term "theophany" expresses this appearance as "God in visible form."

Having left the altar as a visible witness of his God to the Canaanites, Abram moved farther south to a point between **Bethel** and **Ai**, a journey of another day or two from Shechem. While traveling, Abram and Sarai likely mused on the words God had spoken to Abram until finally, so moved, **he built [a second] altar . . . and called on the name of the LORD** (12:8). This suggests public worship, however simple and elementary it may have been. By the time Abram built this second altar, his entourage numbered in the hundreds. It is not hard to picture him calling them together and leading them in public prayers to God.

It would have been an informed addition if the author had given some window into the thinking of Sarai through all these wanderings. Her barrenness had to have been especially burdensome, and her having to leave all her familiar surroundings unsettling. But there is no indication that she objected to Abram's migration. Abram may well have sought her advice about the move from Haran; he may have confided in her numerous times along the way.

## 4. THE UNFORTUNATE DEVIATION (12:10-20)

Abram had not been in his new country long before something unexpected happened. In Ur, and even in Egypt, river civilizations benefited from abundant fresh water, even when it seldom rained. Canaan was almost totally dependent on seasonal rains that fell from about October through April, the wet season, before the dry months of summer came. If the rains did not come, drought and famine were always a threat. Soon after Abram's arrival, a lack of moisture over an extended time caused **severe** drought (Gen. 12:10).

God had told Abram that the land of Canaan would be his, but Abram did not have a deed to a square inch of it when a need for food forced him and all his people to leave there in search of sustenance. Historically, Egypt welcomed the masses, for the Nile's waters made it possible for them to grow an abundance of produce. Numerous records have been found showing that many outsiders found food in Egypt, as Abram did. In another recorded case, groups of Semites (an ethnic group of which Abram was a part) arrived with goods to trade for food.

Abram could not afford to have his large herds and employees with their families go hungry. Assessing the Canaan famine to be unusually severe, he decided **to live there** [in Egypt] **for a while** (12:10). Sometime during his long trek over the Sinai Desert, Abram began to worry that the Pharaoh might become interested in his wife enough to want her for his harem. In Old Testament times, the acquisition of multiple wives was a statement of influence and affluence. Many leaders coveted large harems to stress their power and wealth.

In a moment of weakness, Abram chose a strategy that, while risking Sarai's future, might save his own. To make his twisted logic more palatable to her, he opened his suggestion with, **I know what a beautiful woman you are** (12:11). One wants to say, "Yes, but Abram, what an ugly plan! You need to protect your wife, not use her to save your own hide."

Abram employed a partial truth, one that gave misleading conclusions. Knowing that Sarai was his half-sister (see 20:12), Abram told her to pretend to be his **sister** (not his wife) so his life would be **spared** (12:12-13). He also knew that if the Egyptians believed this story, he would be favored with many gifts. Did Abram not realize he would lose Sarai to Pharaoh's harem? It seems unlikely that Abram thought through to the end result of his scheme. Those who make decisions based on selfish self-interest seldom do. At that moment Abram took himself out of God's hands and tried to run his own life at the expense of his wife.

From the clay tablets found at the city of Nuzu, it was often the custom that once a man got married he would adopt his wife as a full sister, so that the title "sister" would then have been a term of endearment, such as "honey" or "darling." Additionally, this "sistership contract," along with a marriage contract, was intended to give a wife additional protection.[2] It worked the opposite for Sarai in this instance. But Abram knew Pharaoh would not know of his home custom, and more to the point, that Sarai was his wife.

The plan worked! Abram was **treated well for her sake** (12:16), while poor Sarai had to enter Pharaoh's palace as part of his harem. Abram realized he had really messed up his life. If he stayed in Egypt in order to be near his "chosen" wife, he could not return to the "chosen" land. And if he returned to Canaan without her, she could not bear the many nations God had promised to send through Abram. Abram faced trouble either way.

But God intervened with a mysterious sickness that raised suspicion in Pharaoh's household. Perhaps everyone there became sick except

Sarai. After an investigation, it was determined that Sarai was a married woman. Pharaoh called Abram and sternly interrogated him.

Abram acted out of fear that he might be killed (see 12:12). How much more likely was he to get killed for having made Pharaoh look like a fool and endangering the physical health of the whole house? As a result, he was kicked out of Egypt. Was God being unnecessarily severe in allowing that to happen? No, God knew that was the way to get His grand design back on track. Abram did leave Egypt much richer but, more importantly, much wiser. Though he fell into a similar trap later with the Philistine king, as we will soon see, his new wisdom had a lasting impact on his life.

## 5. SPIRITUAL REPAIR (13:1-4)

Lot had been with Abram on his trek to Egypt and now returned to Canaan with him (see Genesis 13:1). Could this whole experience also have influenced Lot, making him yearn for "the good life" which he later sought in Sodom? Though Abram returned **very wealthy in livestock and in silver and gold** (13:2), his spirit was surely troubled. He had to have realized how close he had come to ruining the future fulfillment of all God's promises.

Abram returned to the southern area of Canaan, called the **Negev** desert (13:3). It is an area of "dry land," which is the meaning of its name—fertile but lacking enough water for very successful farming. Still restless, Abram went from place to place. Something was going on deep inside him. The original Hebrew text gives the sense that Abram traveled in stages, as if he was still trying to make sense of what had happened. When the next test comes, Abram would react differently.

Abram finally realized he needed again to call **on the name of the LORD.** As if on a pilgrimage, he returned to **Bethel, to the place . . . where he had first built an altar** (13:3-4). He had built his very first altar at Shechem (see 12:6), but maybe he did not consider going to that altar because it had been built near a pagan shrine. Perhaps he wanted more seclusion than the Shechem altar afforded. He had built this altar at Bethel between two pagan cities, where he could be freer in his expression of gratitude and adoration. He needed to recapture his earlier experience with the Lord.

There is no substitute for prayer to God when events have not transpired as expected. It is not uncommon to think God will lead one way, and then He goes another. Since our insight is limited and our view of the future somewhat shrouded, we must always trust the greater knowledge and wisdom of God. He knows what He is doing, even when we do not. We must always learn to see things from the highest point of view, which is always God's point of view.

The stories of the Fall and the Flood have this to say—because of man's guilt, man and the world did not remain as God had desired them and created them. But even so, the world and man are not forsaken by God. God seeks out a man who, bound by him in inviolable religious communion, is to become the father of a people who are blessed and who are destined to be a blessing for mankind. Even if obstacles appear again and again in his way and that of the bearers of the promise who follow him, obstacles which threaten the fulfillment of the promise, God can overcome them all and bring the story to the conclusion he intended and wants to have. . . . The view of the world and of history which is expressed here stands at the very pinnacle of Christianity.[3]

## ENDNOTES

[1]Victor P. Hamilton, *Handbook of the Pentateuch* (Grand Rapids, Michigan: Baker Book House, 1982), p. 95.

[2]See "The Wife-Sister Motif in the Patriarchal Narratives" by Ephraim A. Speiser, *Biblical and Other Studies,* A. Altmann ed. (Garden City, New York: Doubleday, 1963), pp. 91–94.

[3]*The Interpreter's Dictionary of the Bible,* vol. 2, p. 380.

# 15

# ABRAM IN CONFLICT

## Genesis 13:5–14:24

The life of a shepherd was not easy in biblical times. Often shepherds needed to roam to find adequate pastures. One area could be lush with grass, yet another lacking grass for sufficient grazing. Rains in the Holy Land were seasonal, making it necessary to go where they had fallen, farther north in the summer and south in the winter.

Prosperity sometimes created additional problems. Disagreements often necessitated separation. So it happened with Abram and Lot and with their herdsmen (see Genesis 13:7). Each had been singularly successful in animal husbandry. For their increased number of animals, pasturage was in short supply.

One commentator's observation is worthy of note here:

> Abram and Lot feared God; they were related, and fellow-travelers. Poverty, hunger, toilsome journeys to and from, could not bring about any strife, but the abundance of temporal possessions had nearly accomplished it, when Abram saw and marked the cunning of the devil. If this could happen to holy men like these, we may easily see how far Satan may carry those whose hearts cling to the world's goods.[1]

## 1. STRIFE ARISES (13:5-13)

Abram already had been rich in livestock and had gained even more in Egypt. Lot, too, had many **flocks and herds and tents** (13:5). The land simply **could not support** the animals of both men (13:6). Perhaps the problem first presented itself in a field with some animals competing for the same pasturage, causing the herdsman of both men to quarrel. **The Canaanites and Perizzites were also living in the land** (13:7). This suggests that the solution was recognizably not simply a matter of moving a few acres away. These other peoples would have had flocks, too. A time had arrived when Abram and Lot had to separate their flocks by some distance.

Wanting no quarrel to develop between Lot and himself, as it had with their herdsmen, Abram humbly approached his nephew on even terms— **we are brothers** (13:8). It was a normal custom for an elder clan leader to have the first choice before allowing a younger member to choose. The address of Lot as a brother is striking. Abram gave Lot the opportunity to choose first, leaving himself the other option. Lot looked over the **well-watered** and fertile **plain of the Jordan** (13:10) and quickly responded, "That's my choice."

A pre-Egypt Abram might have shot back, "Nephew, what is the matter with you? I gave you a chance to let you show respect for your elders. You were supposed to say, 'Uncle, you first.' Will you never learn?" But there is no indication in the text of these thoughts in the mind of Abram at all. Had he learned that when he tried to look out for himself first, he messed up? It seems that having returned to the altar near Bethel was the right thing to do.

When one goes to the plain of the country of Jordan today, the area around the Dead Sea is barren and bleak. It may well have been that way when Genesis 13 was written, because there is a parenthetical statement: **This was before the LORD destroyed Sodom and Gomorrah** (13:10). Archaeological activity on the eastern side of the Dead Sea appears to have located some cities in that region, two of which were destroyed rather suddenly. The entire area is now without significant population. Perhaps before the destruction of Sodom and Gomorrah this area was a very fertile plain, which was ruined in the upheaval at that time.

The concluding statement of this paragraph in Genesis (see 13:13) describes Sodom's terrible wickedness. Yet Lot decided to pitch **his tents near Sodom.** Why? There was plenty of pasture available away from Sodom. Was he curious? Curiosity is sometimes the scourge of the soul. It can be the Devil's best weapon to tempt. Later Lot moved inside the city of Sodom. While he was subsequently considered righteous enough to spare before its destruction, if he had stayed away he might have avoided being taken as a hostage (see 14:12). Had he not been in the city, he would not have lost everything he owned when Sodom was destroyed, and he also might not have lost his wife.

## 2. SUFFICIENCY PROMISED (13:14-18)

The turn of events drove a knife into the heart of Abram. As mentioned earlier, the probability of Abram's having adopted Lot gives reason to believe that he considered Lot his son and perhaps even believed him to be the only son he would ever have. In Abram's mind, they each would move to either the **right** or the **left** (13:9), depending on where Lot chose to go. To Lot, the whole plain (see 13:10) looked too inviting, but that was where the wicked cities were located. Compare a contemporary saint who might move into a drug-infested area, but only if God called him or her to do so. Otherwise, that person would be putting himself or herself in unnecessary danger. So, as the two men looked south, to the left were the plains Lot chose, and to the right was the Negev where Abram would go. Lot moved to an area about forty miles due east of where Abram settled.

In the midst of Abram's bitter disappointment, God spoke to him. God knew his thoughts, "I may have lost all hope of any posterity." God gave him a promise that in every direction he looked, **north and south, east and west,** the land would belong not only to him but also to his **offspring forever.** And his descendents would be as numerous as **the dust of the earth** (13:16).

The first promise God had given Abram came at the time when God called Abram to leave his home in Haran, a most unsettling and traumatic time. God then had promised Abram a name, a reputation. In 13:14, God has appeared to Abram again, immediately after another traumatic incident: when Abram thought perhaps he had lost the only "son" he would ever have—Lot. But God had promised not only a son but descendants too numerous to count. God came to Abram at the times of need and promised to give Abram exactly what he most wanted—a reputation and children.

Assured that God had not forgotten him, Abram moved back to the Negev to the great oaks of Mamre, near the town of Hebron. And what did Abram do immediately? **He built an altar to the Lord** (13:18). By now we can begin to call him "an altar builder." Likely, when he worshiped the Lord at the altar in Mamre, he prayed a prayer for Lot, knowing that Lot was where he should not have gone.

# 3. KINGS INVADE (14:1-12)

Lot may not have considered the rocky hills as productive as the fertile valley areas, but when kings come raiding, they do not consider the barren hill country; they look toward the rich cities with much for the taking. Lot's choice soon proved to be a bad one, while Abram's choice was the wiser one.

For a total of **twelve years,** four eastern kings of Mesopotamia had subjugated the people of the plains, but **in the thirteenth year they** [the people] **rebelled** (Gen. 14:4). This apparently caused the four kings to fight the peoples of surrounding areas, who perhaps had sided with the rebellion. Likely hoping that the four kings might be somewhat weakened by their battles, the five kings of the cities of the plains marched **out and drew up their battle lines in the Valley of Siddim** (14:8) in hopes of defeating the invaders.

The fiercely fought battle went against the five kings. The kings of Sodom and Gomorrah fled. Unfortunately for them, **some of the men** stumbled into some of the area's numerous tar pits, while the remainder of the army fled to the hills (14:10). Interested now in grabbing all the booty, the foreign kings raided Sodom and Gomorrah of **the goods . . . and all their food** (14:11). And before starting their return journey to their homelands, they decided also to take with them many people from that region, including Lot, **since he was living in Sodom** (14:12). There is little doubt that at that moment Lot regretted the choice he had made regarding what land to take.

# 4. ABRAM INTERDICTED (14:13-16)

Fortunately for Lot, a man in the fray had escaped and apparently ran the forty miles to inform Abram of what had happened (see Genesis 14:13). The text here mentions Abram as **the Hebrew** for the first time in the Bible. Israelites never named themselves by this title. Non-Israelite people used it only when they referred to the Israelites. Some have thought that a group of brigands, nonsocial outcasts, whom the local people called "Habiru," was the reason for the designation here. Pagan peoples living in Canaan might have seen Abram as an outsider, an outcast. If so, the term originated more as a social category than as an ethnic term. But it may have stated that Abram was just one of the many descendants of Eber, a forefather (see 11:16-27).

Upon hearing the news of the battlefield, Abram quickly decided what to do. He immediately **called out the 318 trained men** (14:14). These servants of his, **born in his household,** evidently had received some military training, perhaps to prevent thieves from stealing Abram's herds. Genesis 14:24 states that Abram received help from allied tribal leaders **who went with** him.

The kings had a long head start, so Abram and his men did not catch them until they were nearly beyond the northern limits of the land, at **Dan** (14:14). Nightfall helped Abram gain the advantage on the more numerous army of the kings, so Abram **divided his men to attack them** (14:15). The text does not say what battle plan—besides the element of surprise at night—he used. Like Gideon many years later, though outnumbered, he chased the panicked enemy for about forty miles to make sure they would not return.

The brevity of the account of Abram's successful attack might give greater credibility to the success of his speedy attack and victory. Had he had more difficulty, it might well have been included in the account. Abram used a strategy that may have made the enemy kings think they were being attacked from all sides. This frightened them to the point of retreating in complete disarray, leaving their booty, as well as Lot, **the women and the other people** (14:16).

## 5. MELCHIZEDEK INSPIRED (14:17-24)

Successful in his venture, Abram returned down the Jordan Valley. When he arrived at **the King's Valley,** the king of Sodom met him (14:17). This king apparently had heard the news of Abram's successful foray, freeing the captives and recovering the stolen booty. But an extraordinary figure named **Melchizedek** also appeared at the same time (14:18). He is called a **priest,** the first person so designated in the Bible. He brought with him **bread and wine** (14:19) and blessed Abram, giving special honor to **God Most High,** who was really responsible for delivering Abram's **enemies into [his] hand** (14:20). In appreciation for his blessing, Abram **gave him a tenth of everything** (14:20). According to Hebrews 7:4, it was "a tenth of the plunder," probably an offering of thanks for his success in battle.

Who was Melchizedek? He is called **king of Salem** (14:18), but the location of this town **Salem** is unclear. If Jerusalem is intended, it is a strange abbreviation of the name, for from the time of Abram, Jerusalem was already named by its full name in nonbiblical texts. The meaning of

**Melchizedek** is "my king is righteous." The meaning of **Salem** is "peace." In Joshua's time, the king of Jerusalem was named Adoni-Zedek. The meaning of his name was "king of righteousness." Yet he was a pagan king whom Joshua defeated. Melchizedek seems to have been serving the same God as Abram; otherwise the patriarch would not have paid tithes to him.

One of the messianic psalms states, "You are a priest forever, in the order of Melchizedek" (110:4). The description of "priest" gives one a picture of Melchizedek's occupation, but the word "forever" adds another dimension. The appearance of this king-priest so suddenly, and with little explanation, gives him an aura of timelessness. The New Testament writer to the Hebrews states that Melchizedek "was without father or mother" and was "without genealogy, without beginning of days or end of life" (Heb. 7:3).

It is very difficult to separate Melchizedek from Jesus. He is at least somehow related to Him. Some have conjectured that he might have been a Christophany, Christ appearing in visible form. Though not widely accepted, it has enough credibility that some consider it the true explanation of this priest-king.

**Melchizedek . . . brought out bread and wine** (14:18). For friends to dine together on bread and water was normal. It was simply a token of good will. But bread and wine was royal fare. According to Numbers 15:2-10, bread and wine normally accompanied animal sacrifice.

After Abram met with Melchizedek, the king of Sodom addressed Abram, telling him he could **keep the goods** (plunder) for himself, but the king wanted his **people** back (14:21). Abram had not forgotten his unfortunate deviation in Egypt and how God had helped him to escape a more serious situation. Perhaps, too, Abram's having so recently been **blessed** by Melchizedek made him more aware that the **God Most High [had] delivered [his] enemies into his hands** (14:20). Abram told the king that he could have the goods. Abram would not be made rich by the king with **even a thread or the thong of a sandal** (14:23). Thomas Whitelaw notes, "If Abraham had taken all the spoil, it would only have been in accordance with the general practice of that age; but a principle and not a custom, is his guide."[2]

Would the pre-Egypt Abram have been so selfless? He normally would have thought, as most victors did, "The spoils are mine. I earned them." It would seem Abram had come to realize that "what I take for myself, I lose; what I let God give me, I keep." Though Abram later would have a situation with another king similar to what he had experienced in Egypt, it is clear that Abram was a changed man. Abram reinforced his commitment to **the LORD, God Most High** (14:22). He came through as a shining example of selflessness.

## ENDNOTES

[1]John Lange, *Commentary on the Holy Scriptures: Genesis,* vol. 1 (Grand Rapids, Michigan: Zondervan), p. 400.

[2]*The Pulpit Commentary,* vol. 1 (Grand Rapids, Michigan: Wm. B. Eerdmans Publishing Co., 1978), p. 215.

# Part Six

# THE CHOSEN RACE: ABRAM, A SON PROMISED

## Genesis 15:1–20:18

As Abram did when Lot decided to leave him to move to the cities of the plains (see Genesis 13:11), this aging man must again have felt great disappointment that his nephew—whom he had wanted to be his link to the future—decided to return to wicked Sodom. Lot did not see the folly of his choice. After all that Abram had done for Lot, saving him from a life of slavery, Lot seemed at best ungrateful. The patriarch must have had another low point. One can almost read his thoughts: "What am I going to do now?"

Adding to the fact that societal norms of the day caused a woman to carry an unbearable stigma if she was married and yet unable to have children, it is easy to imagine how Sarai's growing sense of desperation would cause Abram also to feel additional uncertainty.

Abram had to have felt like a lonely man on an island since he was virtually the only believer in the true God. All about him were idol-worshiping pagans who would give him no encouragement in faith. They were everywhere around Abram: at the wells where he would water his flocks, in the cities where he would buy and sell, along the roads as he traveled from place to place. Thankfully for Abram, the Lord was not unmindful of these crucial times. God came to Abram once again with the promise that both he and Sarai longed to see come to pass.

# 16

# GOD'S WILL: A SON TO COME

## Genesis 15:1–17:27

### 1. A NEW CONCEPT (15:1-6)

magine in the midst of the turmoil of Abram's heart, **the LORD came to Abram in a vision** with a new revelation (Gen. 15:1). This time Abram saw God without using his normal senses. The assurance is, **Do not be afraid, Abram. I am your shield . . .** (15:1).

Perhaps Abram had experienced a narrow escape in his victory over the four kings. Maybe in discouragement he even speculated that the next battle could be his last. God told him, **"I am your shield** (15:1). I will protect you, so don't worry about your next battle."  But with the departure of Lot, Abram feared that his last hope for posterity had just left him for good, so God added, **I am your . . . very great reward.**

God works through things, events, and circumstances, but faith must not be anchored in these.  If it is, then when these do not materialize or turn out the way expected, faith weakens.  If our hope is in a cause, and the cause fails, our hope falters.  Our trust must always be rooted and fixed in the person of God.

Abram divulged the thoughts of his mind to God.  Help in understanding the reason Abram was so troubled can be found from the clay tablets discovered at Nuzu in present-day Iraq.  If a person failed to produce heirs through an adopted relative, the social custom of the day gave another option.  It allowed a man to adopt a servant as a son, who would then take care of his master until the master died, after which the servant would inherit his master's property.[1]  With this in mind, Abram spoke with a wrenched heart:  **O Sovereign LORD, what can you give me since I remain childless and the one who will inherit my estate is Eliezer of Damascus?** (15:2).  Earlier, God had promised Abram a reputation, a name (see 12:2). Abram had become famous even as far away as Mesopotamia. Certainly four of their kings would have been reluctant to meet him again in battle (see 14:1, 15). Abram had acquired land (see 13:14-15), but he still had no children as heirs. So Abram prayed, **You have given me no children; so a servant in my household will be my heir** (15:3).

God was ready with His reply, for He knew the heartache of His faithful servant. He quickly and emphatically replied, **This man will not be your heir** (15:4). Instead God told Abram he would have an heir who would come **from your own body** (15:4). God had waited until now to assure Abram that he would in fact father a son. Why had not God been more specific earlier? He waited until Abram came to a level of faith where he would trust God for what seemed impossible to him.

Abram sensed his advancing age, but he was even more aware of Sarai's barrenness. So God made the step as easy as possible with an illustration that would help his faith. He took him outside and told him to look up **and count the stars** (15:5). Abram may have started to do so, but would have eventually stopped, saying, "I can't do that, Lord!" With solid reassurance, God said, **So shall your offspring be.** Abram believed **and he credited it to him as righteousness** (15:6). What a powerful statement! What a glorious concept! The divinely chosen means for salvation has not changed (see Romans 4:3; Galatians 3:6).

John Sailhamer underscored the basis of Abram's faith when he wrote,

> The appeal to the number of stars of "the heavens" looks back to Abraham's own words in 14:22, where his hope for reward was based solely on the "creator of heaven and earth." If Yahweh was the creator of the great multitude of stars in heaven, it follows that he was able to give Abraham an equal number of descendants ("seed"). Thus God's faithfulness in the past was made the basis for Abraham's trust in the future.[2]

There was nothing Abram could do to bring about God's promise. As Paul said, Abram had contemplated "that his body was as good as dead . . . and that Sarah's womb was also dead" (Romans 4:19). Yet, with *all* evidence to the contrary, "he did not waver through unbelief regarding the promise of God, but was strengthened in his faith and gave glory to God" (Rom. 4:20). For Abram knew that if God had promised it, He would make it happen. Abram was "fully persuaded that God had power to do what he had promised" (Rom. 4:21). But his faith had to hold him for another twenty-five years before God gave him the son he longed for.

## 2. A NEW COVENANT (15:7-21)

A time span of perhaps a day or two must have existed between Genesis 15:6 and 15:7. Verse 7 mentions no vision, and the subject of conversation changes to Abram's inheritance of land. God told Abram that the Lord who spoke to him was the same **LORD** who **brought** him **out of Ur of the Chaldeans** in order **to give** him **this land** so he could **take possession of it** (15:7). This is one of only four times where Scripture quotes God calling himself "Jehovah," His personal name.[3]

While Abram was aware of the name the **LORD** (15:2), he did not at the time understand its full significance or its greater meaning. God told Moses this fact in Exodus 6:3 when He said, "I appeared to Abraham, to Isaac, and to Jacob as God Almighty, but by my name LORD I did not make myself [fully] known to them." While the patriarchs did know and often used the name, the people lacked the miraculous demonstrations connected with it during the time of the Exodus. Its full grasp was unrevealed to them.

Abram needed some sign that would give him assurance. He responded with an honest question: **How can I know that I will gain possession of it?** (15:8). This may have been so different an idea to Abram, as a Bedouin roamer, that he needed some sign. Seeing the need, God elaborately gave it. God was not impatient with Abram. He did not reprimand him for his request for some indication of how God would make the land his. Instead God condescended to Abram's level, an excellent Old Testament example of divine grace. God could not overlook Abram's humble query, for "God opposes the proud but gives grace to the humble" (James 4:6).

God instructed Abram to obtain **a heifer, a goat and a ram, each three years old,** and two birds, **a dove and a young pigeon** (Gen. 15:9). After securing them, Abram cut each animal in two and laid each half a distance apart. He left the birds intact, probably one on one side, the other opposite. Why he placed the dissected animals in two rows is not explained, but the words God gave Jeremiah (see Jeremiah 34:18) give some insight. "The men who have violated my covenant . . . I will treat like the calf they cut in two and then walked between its pieces." All were being readied for establishing a special covenant between Abram and the Lord. A true sacrifice was different from the covenant. It involved placing the animal on an altar. A covenant was an agreement made between two parties who would walk between the halved animals and say, "May we become like these dissected animals if either of us breaks this agreement."[4]

After making all the preparations, Abram had to wait. **Birds of prey** descended on the meat for a meal, and Abram **drove them away** (15:11). As the sun was setting, he became weary and fell **into a deep sleep** (15:12). Since God had told him to look at the stars (see 15:5), perhaps this whole procedure began the night before and concluded the following night. While asleep, **a thick and dreadful darkness came over** Abram. This was all calculated to impress Abraham with the awe-inspiring activity of the Lord as He readied the atmosphere for the covenant to be made.

Probably while Abram was still asleep, God told him that a period of Egyptian bondage would last **four hundred years** (15:13), to **the fourth generation** (15:16). The impression one gets is that the two periods are the same—in this case, a generation equaled a century. Further information from the Lord was that after the time of bondage, His people would **come out with great possessions** (15:14) and would return to the spot where Abram slept. God told Abram that he would die peacefully **at a good old age** (15:15). Did God read Abram's yet-to-be-expressed thought, "I am too close to death to appreciate what you are saying"? If so, Abram was informed that he had many years left before he would die.

The covenant was ready to be **made** (literally, "cut") between Abram and the Lord. Abram saw a vision **of a smoking firepot with a blazing torch** pass **between the pieces** of the animals (15:17). Then the Lord said, **To your descendants I give this land . . .** (15:18). God defined the limits of the gift as from the river of **Egypt,** generally identified as "the wadi of Egypt," which flows in the north of the Sinai to the **Euphrates** in the far north. The inhabitants of the land then were identified. It was not until the kingdoms of David and Solomon that the full scope of this prophecy was realized.

God patiently worked with Abram to bring him from his pagan beginnings to become a giant of faith. What God had promised required much trust for many years. It had taken over ten years for Abram to gain the reputation he had been promised (see 12:4; 16:16). In some respects, the ownership of the land Abram was promised would be realized only after he had died. And he was getting to an age when childbearing was less and less a possibility. It takes some faith to believe the possible, a greater faith to believe the improbable, but the biggest faith of all to affirm what seems impossible.

## 3. GOD'S WILL, MAN'S WAY (16:1-16)

Ten years before the time of the events of Genesis 16, God came to Abram with a promise of offspring. God gave the promise soon after Abram had entered the land (see 12:7), and restated the promise several times. But a decade is a long time to wait for fulfillment. Likely Abram and Sarai had talked about the possibilities numerous times. For a while, they probably made plans for a new baby. By this point, days had stretched into months and on into years. Their faith had been tested severely. They surely reminded themselves, "God said this and this and this, but He hasn't come through. We know what He wants us to have. Maybe He wants us to work it out *our* way." And they fell into the desperate trap of doing God's will *their* way, ignoring the fact that God always wants His will done *His* way.

As Genesis 16 opens, the writer describes Sarai as desperate to have a child in any way possible. We first learned of her barrenness in 11:30, a situation that had been aggravated by God's promise to Abram that his servant "will not be your heir, but a son coming from your own body will be your heir" (15:4). At the time of chapter 16, a sense of hopelessness had faded Sarai's faith. The most common cultural custom of the time was for the barren wife to provide a surrogate wife to bear a child in her place. In such cases, the wife was required to make the arrangements.

Hagar was the servant companion of Sarai. This speaks of Sarai's wealth, for rich women usually received a maid as part of their dowry. Such maids did not merely serve their mistresses, but were owned by them (see Psalm 123:2). The text reveals that with respect to Hagar, Sarai had control over her, and she could make an order and her instructions were followed.

Sarai approached Abram one day and instructed him to **sleep with my maidservant; perhaps I can build a family through her** (16:2). Why didn't the Lord interdict to prevent Sarai's plan? He certainly was not pleased with the suggested deviation. But people in that culture at that time thought there was nothing wrong with this option. God allowed it because the practice was so ingrained as to make it impossible for a change in the practice at this time.[5] Later in Genesis, Jacob would take his wives' maidservants and father children by them. Although the Lord tolerated the practice, He inspired the writer to describe the major problems of jealousy, alienation, and separation that resulted from such customs.[6]

When the people of God's covenant had advanced further in faith, having more adequately assimilated God's truth, the practice became taboo. This situation helps us to realize that God does not create cultural practices; people do, and His preferred way of handling such situations is to change people so they will then change cultural practices. Sometimes that may be the best way to permanent learning. Cultural practices that are now known to be counter to God's laws always have their devastating results.

Abram's faith had apparently weakened to the point that he was deceived into thinking, "Maybe this is God's way of doing His will, His way of giving us a child." Instead it was *their* human way of trying to bring about God's will. There was no indication of protest on Abram's part. He carried through with Sarai's plan. Abram's relationship with Hagar was more than a sexual convenience. In reality, when Abram had married Sarai years before, Hagar had become his secondary wife.

Almost immediately, when aware of her pregnancy, Hagar began to look with disdain on Sarai (see 16:4). If not in words, her actions said, "Old woman! You tried and tried, and you failed. Look at me! Look what I've done." It had been many years since Sarai had acquired Hagar in Egypt (see 16:1). Likely their relationship was good before this episode, but it soured. Hagar must have felt secure, but her attitude was a dangerous one to take since she was subject to Sarai, not just as her maid. In reality, Sarai owned Hagar.

Yet Sarai could not reprimand Hagar without the approval of Abram. To sharpen her desire to rid herself of this daily reminder of her own failure, Sarai charged Abram with the responsibility of everything that had happened, even though she had originally taken the initiative, as she was supposed to have done. And what had happened was exactly what she had planned. However, she did not expect Hagar to heap haughty mockery and a sneering attitude upon her.

The results of this human attempt to fulfill God's will are evident in a false pride on the part of Hagar, a false blame on the part of Sarai and a false neutrality on the part of Abram.

Hagar likely did not know that Abram had told Sarai, **Do with her whatever you think best** (16:6). She likely felt sure Abram would continue to protect her from Sarai's reprimand, as he likely had been doing. But now with Abram's approval, Sarai **mistreated Hagar** (16:6) so oppressively that Hagar set out, apparently intending to head for her homeland of Egypt. Not having made adequate preparation for such a journey, she would have died of exposure and thirst.

She had traveled only a few miles to **the spring . . . beside the road to Shur** (16:7). This certainty of location is suggested by the definite article **the** identifying the source of water. It was likely a spring all travelers knew existed and used on the road connecting Egypt with Canaan. She may have delayed her departure, knowing that her life might be threatened over the more difficult part of the desert ahead. At the spring, an **angel of the Lord found her** (16:7), and told her to **go back to your mistress and submit to her** (16:9).

Was this the proper advice? Yes, for three reasons. First, it was for her protection; she could not have survived the trip to Egypt. But even if by some unusual circumstance she would have made it, a newly born babe would not. Second, God is always more concerned with attitudes than with what has caused them (see Genesis 4:6, Matthew 5:21-22; James 4:3). He always wants reunion and forgiveness, which in Hagar's case would not be possible unless she returned. Third, as events had turned out, everyone had lost. Sarai had lost her maid, Hagar had lost her home, and Abram had lost the child he was hoping would give him the heir he had been promised.

The angel told Hagar of the benefits that would result from her obedience. First, she too would have **descendants . . . too numerous to count** (16:10). Next she was told that the baby she was carrying was a boy, and that she **shall name him Ishmael,** which means "God hears" (16:11). Her son's name was intended to remind her of how in her misery God had heard her and had told her how to relieve it. (She is the first person in Scripture to receive an angelic message.)

At the beginning of the conversation with the angel, Hagar did not know to whom she was talking. The angel apparently looked like a common man who had stopped for a drink. But she took special notice when the visitor addressed her as **servant of Sarai** (16:8). She had to have thought, "How does he know who I am?" By the end of the conversation, Hagar recognized the presence of God and affirmed, **You are the God who sees me** (16:13). Her reply showed she was aware that God is the all-seeing God. And she recognized that God saw her in the moment of deepest distress and gave her hope when all her hope had vanished. She then named the well **Beer Lahai Roi** (16:14), which means "The well of the living One who sees me." And when the account was written (as much as several hundred years later), the spring was still flowing and called by the same name.

Genesis 16:15 indicates that Hagar gave birth to Ishmael. (Thus several months had passed since the angel had appeared to her at the well.) It is striking that nothing is said about Ishmael's being Sarai's son. That had been the plan all along. He was the offspring of Abram and

Hagar. For all the cruel treatment she had received and the suffering that followed, Hagar was rewarded by her son's birth. In spite of all Sarai's scheming to have a son by this unapproved-by-God plan, it did not work out as she had hoped. Ishmael was not hers.

Genesis 17 gives the information that Abram had already adjusted his thinking; he saw Ishmael as the fulfillment of God's promise (see 17:18).

Another lesson is evident. God is concerned about oppression no matter who suffers it. A downtrodden foreigner has God's attention as much as a parent of the chosen Israelites.

## 4. GOD'S WILL, GOD'S WAY (17:1-27)

The opening words of Genesis 17 inform readers that thirteen years had passed since the close of chapter 16. These thirteen years have been filled with wondering on the part of Sarai and Abram. "Did we get ahead of God?" "Is Ishmael the son of the promise, or have we messed up God's plan?"

Why did God choose to delay the fulfillment of His promise of a son to Abram? Did God want him and Sarai to live with the misery of doing God's will their own way, of taking events into their own hands, of messing up His plan? Was God saying, "I want you to live out the full consequences of your act until you get your just desserts"?

While some may think these factors caused God's silence, more likely something else was involved. Could it not be that God simply waited these thirteen years until Abraham was ninety-nine and Sarai was ninety, when both were even further past childbearing age? If so, God knew that when a child was born to parents that old, there would be no doubt in anyone's mind that their son was a God-given miracle. Finally, God was ready to get things back on track. How singularly amazing is a God who can make a ninety-nine-year-old man a father!

God came again and spoke to Abram: **I am God Almighty** (17:1). God was introduced as "God Most High" with Melchizedek and as "God who sees me" with Hagar. Here for the first time in Scripture God refers to himself as "God Almighty." Scripture mentions God by this name "El Shaddai" only two other times (see Exodus 6:3; Ezekiel 10:5). It is especially significant here. To Abram, it was meant to convey that God can make nature bend to His will; He can make the barren fertile; He can cause age to loosen its grip. He is **Almighty** indeed!

God's instruction was **walk before me and be blameless** (17:1). The word **blameless** means "whole-hearted." God is saying, "This time

Abraham, there must be implicit and unfaltering trust in Me alone. I want you to abandon all other options." This was necessary for Abram if he really wanted God to ratify His covenant. When God inaugurated the covenant (see Genesis 15), it was His initiative. For Him to confirm it, He must have a concordant human response, a blameless walk before God.

Abram needed no words to express his thoughts. As soon as God spoke, he **fell facedown** in humble worship (17:3). By his prostration, Abram showed himself ready to listen to anything God had to say.

God told Abraham that he would be **the father of many nations** (17:4). This promise expanded the previous promises when Abraham was told he would be the father of "a great nation" (12:2) and when Hagar was told that the son Abraham sired would have "descendants . . . too numerous to count" (16:10). To adequately impress the patriarch with the promise, the same phrase was used again (see 17:5-6). And then God added, **kings will come from you** (17:6).

Meanings of names were much more important to people in biblical times than they are today. When Abram's mother gave him his name, she was expressing her hope that he would be a "great father." In this encounter, God changed Abram's name to **Abraham,** indicating that he would be the "father of a multitude." Never again would Abraham forget the covenant God made with him at this point. His very name would remind him of this moment.

"The covenant I am making with you, Abraham," God continued, "is also being made with **your descendants after you** (17:7, 8, 9). Abraham was hearing this news for the first time. In 13:15, he had been promised that all the land he could see would be given to his descendants. In the next verse, he was told his descendants would be numbered "like the dust of the earth." In 17:7, God included all these descendants in the covenant. And this began a unique relationship: **I will . . . be your God** (17:7), and **I will be their God** (17:8). This was the best gift of all—not just forgiveness, not just acceptance, not just grace. God was giving *himself!* And the full realization of that gift came to all people when Jesus gave *himself* to the whole world.

But Abraham could not possibly grasp the full scope of this promise, for it included not only his physical heirs but the spiritual heirs of which Peter spoke: "The promise is for . . . all whom the Lord our God will call" (Acts 2:39). Through the centuries, many Hebrew people thought they were the exclusive benefactors of the promise. Never did God have such a restriction in mind. It was hard for Jonah to think God would stoop so low as to accept the hated, cruel Assyrians. But he and all

Hebrews had to learn that the most undeserving can choose to become a part of God's **everlasting covenant** (17:7) and that even the Hebrew people would suffer if they broke off their relationship with Him.

This covenant had strings attached. Both Abraham and his descendants **must keep my covenant . . . for the generations to come** (17:9). Involved in the covenant Abraham and his descendants were to keep was its **sign** (17:11), the sign of circumcision. It would be administered as a rite to yet unborn descendants at the age of **eight days** (17:12).

Records have come to light showing that many peoples in Abraham's day practiced circumcision. The surgery was not something entirely new. But God was designating the practice as a special sign of the covenant He was making with Abraham and his descendants. Intentionally, it would seem, God chose a sign that could not be reversed. This sign's permanence would reflect the eternal aspect of the covenant and would be a reminder of the spiritual bond that existed between the chosen and the Chooser.

This sign perhaps had a special significance to Abraham that did not exist with others. During the thirteen-year period since Ishmael's birth, Abraham had become impotent. By then, he knew there was no way he could father a child (see Hebrews 11:11-12). If he had one by Sarai, it would have to be all God's doing. So Abraham was directed to put this special mark on the reproductive member of his body so as to remind him, "God, where I failed in my human attempts at fulfilling Your will, You succeeded."

In my opinion, circumcision was intended to be a special sign to all humanity, that the member of the body that so often leads away from God really should be dedicated to Him. One might then wonder why a special mark was not required of Sarai. God's plan was that husband and wife are considered one by God (2:24), so a mark on the woman was not necessary. And if the reproductive members of the "one flesh" belong to God, they were not to be used outside God's designated limits. The process of bringing a new baby into life is the most creative physical act, given by God alone, which brings us closest to His ability to create. And when the sexual act is cheapened by making it merely a joking matter or throwing it about as if it is loose change, the holy thing God intended it to be is lost.

In our day, more and more doctors are trying to direct parents into not circumcising their babies. This is not new. In the time between the Old and New Testaments, Jews often suffered because they held to the practice with an unbounded and loyal devotion. When Greek kings were trying to force their customs on the Jews, mothers were put to death for circumcising their babies. To make these mothers a public example, "they hanged their babies about their necks" (1 Maccabees 1:61).

Why did God make circumcision a sign of the covenant? In his "Special Laws," Philo—a Jewish philosopher who lived at the time of Christ—listed four reasons Jews gave for following the practice: (1) to prevent infection and disease; (2) for purification; (3) to tie together procreation and the thought process; and (4) to increase fertility. He follows this by two reasons of his own: (1) in a symbolical way, it helps a man remove lust from his mind; and (2) perfection can only be achieved by removing all evil from the heart.

Circumcision was important to God at the time of the Old Testament. The Lord made it clear that **every male among you shall be circumcised** (17:10). Then He added, **Any uncircumcised male, who has not been circumcised in the flesh, will be cut off from his people; he has broken my covenant** (17:14). The inference left was that there could likely be either excommunication from the community or premature death of that individual. Walter Kaiser has observed,

> Circumcision became a sign of the covenant in which those who obeyed participated, but circumcision never became the grounds or the meritorious basis on which faith or personal relationship with God was bestowed. Faith was or was not already present—circumcision did not change that fact.[7]

Could circumcision have had another significance—that God wanted no class distinction? Those who were in servitude should rank as high with God as those who were free.

We must recognize that Paul affirmed in New Testament times that circumcision of the heart was far more important than one that is physical and outward (see Romans 2:29). And to the Galatians he concluded his letter with these words: "Neither circumcision nor uncircumcision means anything; what counts is a new creation" (Gal. 6:15).

God next turned Abraham's thoughts to Sarai. As God had changed Abraham's name, so now Abraham was told his wife's new name was Sarah. Her former name was of archaic Babylonian origin; her new name spoke its meaning more forcibly: "princess." What a surprise hit Abraham when God told him, **I will bless her and will surely give you a son by her** (17:16). It was likely Abraham received the news in sudden disbelief, his lower jaw dropping nearly out of its socket. Then he again **fell facedown** (17:17), this time laughing to himself. He was not thinking about God's ability, only his own.  He could not grasp the possibility that he, approaching one hundred years in age, with a wife that had passed her ninetieth birthday, could have a baby.  He knew Sarah was barren, and he knew he had lost his ability to have children.  The only solution that came to his mind he expressed to God, **If only Ishmael might live under your blessing** (17:18).

While God did not reprimand Abraham for his disbelief, He did confirm to him what He had just told him, and then He added that Abraham was to name his son **Isaac** (17:19).  Should this name be considered punishment for Abraham's temporary disbelief?  The root meaning of the name is "to laugh."  While the name reflected Abraham's and later Sarah's laughter (see 18:12) at the idea of having a son together, it may well be that God was, so to speak, laughing with them, for He knew that what was about to happen was a herald of what was to come.  In time, when His own Son would be born by miraculous birth, people then would not believe it possible.  Perhaps God was happy because He wanted to use this occasion to give a picture prophecy of what was to come in the future to all people.

As God wanted Abraham to know, He would have us realize that though His promises are sometimes delayed longer than reasoning would think necessary, they are reliable.  And even though to experience them the miraculous must be called upon, His promises are trustworthy.

While Ishmael and his descendants would not be a part of the eternal covenant, God heard Abraham's prayer for him and informed Abraham that Ishmael would be blessed with many, many descendants.  Ishmael would **be the father of twelve rulers** (17:20), the same number of the tribes that would issue from Abraham's grandson, Jacob.  Both Ishmael and the yet unborn Isaac were to have special blessings, but only one could be chosen to be the recipient of the revelation, and one from whom the ultimate descendant, Jesus Christ, was to come.  Just before ending His revelation and leaving Abraham, God concluded with the announcement that in a year Isaac, Sarah's first and only son, would be born (see 17:21).

Though Abraham's thoughts are not recorded, his actions speak eloquently enough.  Without delay, **on that very day** (17:23) he brought all the male members of his household, beginning with himself and including Ishmael, for circumcision.  He included every servant, born in his house or purchased, to comply with God's human obligation for the covenant to be ratified.

## ENDNOTES

[1]William F. Albright, *The Archaeology of Palestine and the Bible* (Cambridge, Massachusetts: American Schools of Oriental Research, 1974), p. 138.

[2]John H. Sailhamer, *The Pentateuch As Narrative* (Grand Rapids, Michigan: Zondervan Publishing House, 1992), p. 151.

[3]In Hebrew, "Lord" was written with only four consonants. Rabbis from the ninth century A.D., who invented a Hebrew vowel system, spelled it as "Jehovah." It is certain it was not pronounced that way. These scholars did so intentionally to keep one from even thinking God's personal name, lest it be done "in vain." It is believed that if they had verbalized it, it would have been "Yahweh."

[4]Frank S. Frick, *A Journey Through the Hebrew Scriptures* (New York: Harcourt Brace College Publishers, 1995), p. 168.

[5]Eds. M. Avi-Yonah and Abraham Malamat, *The World of the Bible* (New York: Educational Heritage, 1964), p. 80.

[6]See, for example, Genesis 21.

[7]Walter C. Kaiser Jr., *Toward Old Testament Ethics* (Grand Rapids, Michigan: Zondervan Publishing House, 1983), p. 78.

# 17

# GOD'S WILL: CLARIFIED

## Genesis 18:1–20:18

n *The Screwtape Letters* of C. S. Lewis, there is a passage where the senior devil Screwtape is speaking to one of his junior devils. Screwtape tells him,

> "There is nothing like suspense and anxiety for barricading a human's mind against the Enemy [God]. He wants men to be concerned with what they do; our business is to keep them thinking about what will happen to them.
>
> "Your patient will, of course, have picked up the notion that he must submit with patience to the Enemy's will. What the Enemy means by this is primarily that he should accept with patience the tribulation which has actually been dealt out to him—the present anxiety and suspense. It is about *this* that he is to say, 'Thy will be done,' and for the daily task of bearing *this* that the daily bread will be provided."[1]

Abraham was about to learn of the imminent destruction of the cities of the plains, including the city of Sodom where Lot lived. God knew the news would fall most heavily on Abraham. God planned not only to send His angels to help Abraham cope, but God himself would appear. Before, God had come to Abraham rather quickly after Abraham had endured very crucial turns of events that were most unsettling.[2]

The Lord knew this news He had for Abraham would be much more devastating, so before the message was delivered, Abraham learned that a year later Sarah would give birth to a son. Abraham's reaction was not recorded; the news caused Sarah to laugh in disbelief. At that moment, Abraham and Sarah's faith was too weak to grasp the full significance of God's will in giving not only *a* son to them but *the* son God had promised.

## 1. SARAH'S TIME IS AT HAND (18:1-15)

Genesis 18 opens with Abraham's resting after his noon meal. In that area during patriarchal times, as in Israel still today, one avoided much physical activity during the hottest part of the day, from about 1:00 to 4:00 P.M. It was and is most advisable to stay out of the direct light of the sun. Most people therefore have learned to spend an afternoon more at ease.

Abraham's tent had been set up in the shade of the great oak trees of Mamre, and he was sitting at the tent's entrance. Perhaps he had begun to nod in his weariness. He came to full consciousness and saw three men **standing nearby** (18:2). He must have thought, "I did not see those men approaching. Where did they come from?" He had no idea they were heavenly visitors.

Though unaware of who these men were, Abraham did what is still practiced today among Bedouin peoples. He took them to be simply travelers—perhaps hungry, thirsty, and weary—who had come to his tent in hope of finding hospitality. He **bowed low to the ground** (18:2) and set about hurriedly to prepare a sumptuous meal for them.

Perhaps the Lord stood out in some way from the two angels, for in 18:3 Abraham was addressing one of them individually, while in 18:4-5 Abraham was addressing all three, for he then used plural pronouns. In 18:5, Abraham tried to persuade his visitors to stay—literally, "while I fetch a morsel of bread"—all the time hoping to prepare a feast. Perhaps he did not let his guests know of his desire for fear that if they knew of his plan to be a gracious and generous host, they would feel they were imposing on his generosity and pass on.

The visitors did not reveal their true identity; they allowed Abraham to continue to think they were just men passing by. Abraham's offer of a meal was accepted, and the guests patiently waited for the meat to be killed, prepared, cooked, and served. Like an attentive waiter, Abraham **stood near them under a tree** while they ate (18:8).

While Abraham did not know the true identity of the men, did he somehow sense they were special? His order for **a choice tender** [bull] **calf** (18:7), far more than enough for three men, might indicate this. Why not a lamb or goat? He also told Sarah to prepare **three seahs of fine flour** (18:6), an amount of bread that would normally serve far more people. While this sumptuous fare could represent Abraham's high social status, he seemed to be aware that there was something very different about these "men."

Almost nonchalantly, after the meal the men asked Abraham, **Where is your wife Sarah?** (18:9). While Sarah was not in sight when the question was asked, the men certainly could have surmised where she was, for she had been baking the bread. Probably this question was calculated to give Abraham a clue that they were not ordinary men. For although he answered immediately—**there, in the tent** (18:9)—Abraham had to have thought, "How did they know her name?"

Now the Lord informed Abraham that **about this time next year, . . . Sarah your wife will have a son** (18:10). There is no record of Abraham's reaction. The writer rather gave a glimpse inside the tent where Sarah overheard the remark. She discreetly stayed in her tent, for since she was a married woman, custom said she should not display herself. The author noted that she had already reached menopause: **She was past the age of child-bearing** (18:11). She knew there was no way, humanly speaking, that she could bear a child. She **laughed to herself** (18:12). While she did not believe the event possible, she was much more reserved than Abraham had been, for when he first had heard the news "he fell on his face, and laughed" (17:17 RSV).

Sarah's laughter did not come from a sneering arrogance, for it was based on her physical condition. She knew in her mind that, with her **worn out** body and Abraham's advanced age, **this pleasure** was out of her reach (18:12).

Was this the first time Sarah had received the news? If so, Abraham had kept from her the announcement he had earlier received (see 17:16, 19). Had he felt it would be too much for her faith to grasp? It was, even if she had been informed of the promise made earlier.

At this point, the writer says directly that this one "angel" was the Lord himself (see 18:13). No longer was there any uncertainty, even on the part of Abraham. Had Sarah muttered her words audibly after laughing to herself? Perhaps, for the Lord asked Abraham, **Why did Sarah laugh?** (18:13). Tent material had little sound resistance.

While the laugh of disbelief might be considered normal for a woman of Sarah's age, it prompted one of the premier promises found in Scripture: **Is anything too hard for the Lord?** (18:14). The thinking of both Abraham and Sarah had been too earthly, too human. Their thoughts were not lifted to the heavenly, the divine. With emphasis, Abraham was told that **at the appointed time next year and Sarah will have a son** (18:14).

Perhaps with a bit of shame, but with far more fear, Sarah stepped forward. Trapped in her disbelief, she directly denied that she had laughed. She apparently was not totally aware of who the visitor was. As a parting statement, the Lord rebuked her with **Yes, you did laugh** (18:15). He made sure Sarah would not forget this incident of laughter, for her child was to be named Isaac, meaning "laughter."

## 2. SODOM'S TIME IS AT HAND (18:16-33)

Seeing that the visitors were intent on leaving and were heading **toward Sodom,** Abraham, the gracious host, accompanied them **on their way** for an undetermined distance. Perhaps he walked as far as three miles to a spot where one can see the Dead Sea through breaks in the hills. This was probably where Sodom and Gomorrah were located, on the eastern side of the Dead Sea.

Since Abraham had such a special relationship with God, God could not allow himself to act without consulting Abraham, for **all nations on earth will be blessed though him** (18:18) and God had made a special covenant with him. Yet God knew that the iniquity of these two cities deserved immediate punishment. God would not, however, take the step of judgment without bringing Abraham in on the decision.

Genesis 18:17-21 gives, from a human perspective, God's mind as He contemplated whether He should inform Abraham of His "going down" to see if Sodom and Gomorrah really deserved punishment as the **outcry** (18:21) concerning these cities seemed to have indicated. At this point, because God had made Abraham His friend, God chose to communicate His plans and give Abraham a chance to ask Him to change His mind.

God is never indecisive because of a lack of knowledge. Being omnipresent, He does not need to "go down" to see what is going on; He is already there. And being omniscient, He knows inerringly everything He needs to know. This way of stating what happened was to let us know that God never acts unjustly, without full information of every situation.

Genesis 18:22 states that while the two angels (in human form) turned to go to Sodom, the Lord lingered a bit to allow Abraham to ask Him to spare the city of Sodom. Remember that Abraham's nephew, Lot, and his family lived there. Did they possess enough righteousness to be spared from its destruction?

Lot was obviously on Abraham's mind as the patriarch asked God, **Will you sweep away the righteous with the wicked?** (18:23). Abraham was confident that Lot was not the only one to be found there who was righteous enough to be spared, and he wanted to pray for their deliverance. With his question, Abraham inferred that God was too righteous to ignore those of good character who live among the wicked. Abraham was counting on God being more concerned with a small number of righteous people than with the many wicked ones. Yet Abraham did not know exactly how many people fit into which category. Not wanting to presume on God's mercy, he first wanted to know that if the Lord found **fifty righteous** there, would He spare the city (18:24). God confirmed to Abraham that He would **spare the whole place** if He found only that many (18:26).

In his continuing intercessory prayer, Abraham felt confirmed enough to lower the number by five, once (see 18:28), then again (see 18:29), and God agreed to each reduction. Abraham was likely fearful that the total number of righteous people would not even reach this number, but at the same time he felt confident of God's mercy, so he lowered the number by ten three times (see 18:30, 31, 32) arriving finally at the number of **ten** (18:32). With God's agreement at this lowest number requested, **Abraham returned home** (18:33).

This passage indicates that righteous people do make a difference in God's decision to bring punishment on a place. And we learn, too, that the number may vary with the amount of wickedness or the number of righteous people. On another occasion, speaking of Jerusalem, Jeremiah was told by God that if he could "find *but one* person [in Jerusalem] who deals honestly and seeks the truth, I will forgive this city" (Jer. 5:1). The situation had worsened in the holy city not many years later. God told Ezekiel, who was prophesying to those who had already gone into captivity in Babylonia, that "even if these three men—Noah, Daniel and Job—were in it, they could save only themselves by their righteousness" (Ezek. 14:14).

Two things are noteworthy about the passage in Genesis. First, it was God in this passage who wanted the intercession to be made, and He wanted Abraham to "stand before [Him] in the gap on behalf of the [city], so [He] would not have to destroy it" (Ezek. 22:30). Second, Abraham had become aware that Lot was not in God's plan for his direct descendants, since Abraham had been told that a son "from your own body" (at that point he believed it was Ishmael). Still Abraham felt a concern as a "parent" for Lot's welfare and interceded for him.

Abraham likely stopped praying because he was rather convinced that the Lord would indeed find ten righteous people in Sodom. Would God have considered an interceding saint so influential that He would have considered a smaller number if Abraham had requested it? Maybe, but the wickedness of Sodom was too great for only four (Lot and his immediate family) to make a difference.

# 3. SODOM'S TIME HAS COME (19:1-29)

The scene shifts to the evening arrival of the two angels at Sodom's main gate. The events of Genesis 18 took place earlier that same day (see 19:1). If the city was, as many believe, on the southeastern side of the Dead Sea, the angels would have traveled forty miles, an unlikely distance for anyone but angels in so short a time. But there was intended haste on the part of the heavenly visitors to emphasize that judgment was imminent.

What a contrast to the rest of the city was the righteous Lot! He was **sitting in the gateway** (19:1). He was totally unaware of the little time he had left in the city. He was likely not the only person there, for the gate area was often the most active part of any city. That was where court was held, where tradesmen presented their wares, where the latest gossip could be heard, and where the official business of the day was conducted. It seems probable that Lot was a member of some standing in the city, though it must have been difficult for him to stand alone for what was right.

When Lot saw the visitors, **he got up to meet them and bowed down with his face to the ground** (19:1). This was what Abraham had done, but Lot seems to have added to Abraham's respect. He wanted the "men" to come to his house. Although Lot was not fully aware of their identity, he may have sensed that they were special visitors. In any case, he appeared to have little concern for the city of Sodom. He seemed quite happy living there and implored these "men" to spend the night at his house where they could **wash [their] feet . . . and then go on your way early in the morning** (19:2). They declined Lot's offer, saying they would stay in the square all night.

But Lot, with a strong persistence, would not take "no" for an answer. It seems that part of Lot's urgency was because he knew just what kind of city he lived in and what could possibly happen. Perhaps the willingness of the angels to stay was in Lot's best interest, to make him more fully aware of the great depth of the wickedness that existed in the city. As a result of Lot's insistence, the angels relented and followed Lot to his house. Like Abraham, Lot **prepared a meal for them** (19:3), although it did lack the grandeur of his uncle's banquet. Bread without yeast could be prepared more hurriedly. By about bedtime, the news of the arrival of the visitors spread all over town. All the men from every part of the city converged on Lot's house (see 19:4). Scripture (see 19:5) makes clear that all the inhabitants of the city were addicted to an unnatural, homosexual depravity.

The intent of Sodom's citizens was to *know* these men not on any social terms but entirely on a sexual level. It is not difficult to understand the origin of the term "sodomy." We learn here how unbridled sexual focus on same-sex relationships may lead to relationships for no other reason than sex. It often has a self-gratifying end. Some who are addicted to this sexual practice approach life on the basis of "what I can get from it to please me" rather than "what I can give to make another happy." Homosexuality tends to lower relationships to the level of what Paul called a "shameful lust" and "indecent acts" (Romans 1:26-27).

For these reasons, it would seem that the Bible comes down hard on the sinfulness of homosexual practices. The Law made it a capital offense, along with incest and bestiality (see Leviticus 20:13). Paul affirmed to the Corinthians that people who engage in such acts will not inherit the kingdom of God (see 1 Corinthians 6:9-10).

Lot had apparently developed some ability in mediation. He bravely tried to prevent his fellow citizens from persisting in their evil intentions. His desire was to strike some kind of compromise. With great courage, he went outside his house to face the mob alone; he even **shut the door behind him** (19:6). Lot had become extremely desperate after assessing the full intent of these citizens. Knowing the seriousness of the situation, he made an offer of his two daughters. He hoped that as a substitute, they would be more desired since they were virgins. The culture at that time held it as a sacred duty to protect guests who had **come under the protection of [one's] roof** (19:8), at the expense of anything and anybody.

Although one might want to excuse Lot because of the cultural practices of his day, in truth Lot had a serious moral vacuum, no doubt brought about by the influence of his environment. What he tried to do was to propose what seemed to him a lesser evil to avoid a greater one. He saw the situation as so completely hopeless that he thought there was no other option than for him to offer his daughters to the lust-crazed mob. The offer "evidenced a serious moral weakness on Lot's part. Even so, it must be seen as the product of sheer desperation. . . . His reasoning seems to have been that it would be better that they satisfy their uncontrollable sexual cravings through natural acts than by grossly unnatural excess."[3]

The passions of the men peaked, and one of them yelled out, **This fellow came here as an alien, and now he wants to play the judge!**

(19:9). Then another yelled, **We'll treat you worse than them.** By then it seemed that Lot was about to be pushed out of the way so they could **break down the door** (19:9).

Seeing the seriousness of the situation, the angels quickly reached out to bring Lot back inside and then shut the door. But that was not enough to redeem the situation. **They struck the men who were at the door . . . with blindness** (19:11). This word for **blindness** is found only here and in 2 Kings 6:18. The Hebrew word does not indicate "lack of vision" but rather something like a "dazzled state of mind." They could still see, but their minds were so totally confused as to make it impossible for them to **find the door.**

The hour of judgment had arrived. Little time was left. The Lord had decided not to destroy Sodom until He had let Abraham know and intercede. The angels delayed carrying out their assignment until they informed Lot and gave him time to escape. If the angels had unlimited knowledge, they did not exercise it. They advised Lot that anyone who belongs with him must leave **because we are going to destroy this place** (19:13). Lot's patriarchal authority covered his sons (if he had any) and daughters. Lot seemed not to worry about others, or else he assumed none but the two daughters would heed any plea; he was immediately concerned, however, with the welfare of his **sons-in-law** (19:14).

His daughters had **never slept with a man** (19:8). One might wonder, then, how Lot could have sons-in-law. In Bible times, as with Joseph and Mary, engagement was a pledge to marry that involved a relationship "as if" the marriage had already taken place, but with no sex involved. The New International Version translates the relationship as **pledged to marry.** If this was not the case here, then perhaps these men were husbands of other daughters of Lot who would not be saved.

When Lot informed his sons-in-law of the imminent destruction, they **thought he was joking** (19:14). Perhaps they thought that Lot was trying to call off their marriages. Maybe they thought Lot's earlier offering of their future wives to sexual violation made Lot unworthy of being heeded. Another possibility is that perhaps the men thought Lot was overreacting to what had happened to him at the hands of the town's men and was in his own way threatening judgment on the town.

The events of Genesis 18 had taken all night. The angels had arrived **in the evening** (19:1), and now the time for **the coming of dawn** had arrived (19:15). Those who had come to Lot's house, the place of refuge, directed Lot, his wife, and two daughters to leave the city. They were urged to **hurry . . . or you will be swept away when the city is punished**

(19:15). Lot had urged his sons-in-law to flee, but then he hesitated. Was he discouraged that so few of his family had come? Could there have been other family members for whom he felt concern? Did he suddenly become aware that he was going to lose everything that he had worked so long to obtain? Whatever the cause for his hesitancy, there was no time for reconsideration. The angels **grasped** the hands of all four and **led them safely out of the city** (19:16).

After they all had been saved, in spite of Lot's momentary indecision, they were going to lose their divine escort—a test to their resolve now that the destruction was certain. Instructions were very deliberate, very strong, and very insistent. **Flee for your lives! Don't look back, and don't stop. . . . Flee to the mountains or you will be swept away** (19:17)! At this point, each person needed to exert some individual effort on his or her own to avoid the imminent disaster. Almost immediately, Lot verbalized his inner struggle. The emotional and physical roller coaster had exhausted him. After thanking the angels for their great kindness to him, he protested that he could not **flee to the mountains** because **this disaster [would] overtake** him and he would die (19:19). There had to be some doubt in his mind that God could save him from the disaster, even though the destruction was under divine control.

Lot looked for an alternative and, seeing a **small** (and he emphasized **small**) **town** that he thought was **near enough to run to** (19:20), he requested permission to go there, thinking that at this place his life would be spared. Terribly sinful people might be found in this town also. At the moment, he felt no concern for the condition that was causing Sodom to be destroyed. He was thinking mostly of his own survival. At this critical moment he was fearful and self-centered and had weak faith. Not because of but in spite of Lot's slumping spirit, the Lord—who seemed to have arrived—consented to Lot's alternative, agreeing not to destroy the small town. But Lot was instructed to flee there quickly, **because I cannot do anything until you reach it** (19:22). Divine leniency is not always dependent on a person's faith; God's grace is always the basic reason for His mercy. The town to which Lot chose to flee had been named Bela (see 14:8), and afterwards, because of its insignificance, it was named **Zoar.** (The Hebrew root behind this name means "small.")

Lot had hardly set foot in the town when **burning sulfur** rained down on **Sodom and Gomorrah** (19:24). All of the cities of the plain except Zoar were destroyed so quickly that no one escaped. Even the vegetation was destroyed. The Hebrew words for this mode of destruction were "fire and brimstone," indicating burning bituminous material. While explanations have been suggested for the catastrophe, such as an earthquake's putting pressure on underground oil deposits, causing them to spew up through the fault lines on both sides of the Dead Sea, the author makes clear that it all was **from the LORD out of the heavens** (19:24).

How unfortunate that **Lot's wife looked back, and . . . became a pillar of salt** (19:26). While Lot's wife had left Sodom's city gates, she still had the love of the city within her. Was she curious about exactly what was happening to the city? Were there friends she did not want to leave? Did she momentarily regret the loss of her possessions? Whatever the cause of her lingering, even momentarily, it was in disobedience to the clear, emphatic instruction given by the angel (see 19:17). Though she was not physically in Sodom, her glance back identified her with the evil populace of the cities. Her sympathies at that moment were not completely with her husband, and it caused her to find her end in death with the people of Sodom.

The description of what happened has all the ingredients of a natural disaster. The Dead Sea area "was full of tar pits" and, lacking vigilance, one could fall into them (14:10). That area is prone to earthquakes. It has many flammable deposits such as sulfur, asphalt, naphtha, and numerous compressed gasses. "The Dead Sea region was rich in minerals, and the sea was known in Roman times as *Asphaltites,* from the lumps of bitumen often found floating on its surface, especially in the southern area. These can be quite massive objects."[4] But it is impossible to rule out its divine origin. Its intensity, its limited location, and its timing all speak to God's control of the catastrophe. **It was from the Lord out of the heavens** (19:24).[5]

It is no wonder that the curiosity of Abraham made him wonder if his prayer had been effective enough to save Sodom, or if God had not found even ten righteous people. As soon as Abraham arose, he hurried to the spot where he had pleaded before the Lord and where the Dead Sea plain could be seen. There he realized that his worst fears had happened, for **he saw dense smoke rising from the land, like smoke from a furnace** (19:28).

Imagine Abraham's first thought: "God did not find ten righteous!" But might he not also have wondered, "Has Lot escaped?" He knew that Lot had had a choice to settle elsewhere but had decided to return to Sodom after he had been freed from captivity. Abraham also would have known of the evil influences to which Lot had daily exposed himself.

As a summary, the writer states that Lot was not spared from the disaster because of his own deeds but because of his praying uncle. How many of us as children were saved from calamity because of a praying mother or father? And for how many others was disaster averted because they were remembered in prayer by some faithful saint? Indeed, "more things are wrought by prayer than this world dreams of."

## 4. GOD'S WILL, MAN'S WAY, AGAIN (19:30-38)

Lot had lost his wife. Just he and his two daughters were left of the citizenry of Sodom. With the ashes of the cities all about him, Lot saw the wisdom of the angel's original instructions to "flee to the mountains" (see Genesis 19:17). He did so and settled down to live in a cave. What a change! Lot had considered his uncle's tent too mundane, too common, so he had chosen the high life of the cities. He ended up in the confines of a dark cave with nothing but his honor, which those who should have loved and protected him literally stole from him. Lot could not have been more pitiable.

It is difficult to understand the rationale of the **older daughter** (19:31) when she voiced to her sister her plan to trick their father into drinking an intoxicating drink so they could each have children by him. Perhaps they thought the destruction was more widespread than being restricted to the plain only, and that they would never have the chance to get married and have children. They made their plans out of desperation, as if their only option was to **preserve our family line through our father** (19:32). To them, the fate of dying childless would have been worse than never having been born. But their plan not only sacrificed their own virginity; it also dishonored their father.

Though the Law had not yet been given against incest, they knew it was wrong. The fact that the daughters knew their plan would succeed only if their father did not know what they were doing indicates that fact. As with other social customs of the time that could not have pleased God, the writer provides a simple report of what happened, in no way showing any approval of it.

The whole situation might have been averted if only Lot's wife had not disobeyed and had survived the holocaust. It is less likely they would have carried out their plan with their mother present, and, soon too, they would have learned that the destruction was not universal. One sin committed often leads to others being done. We are left to wonder if Lot's sense of caution was not working any better than when he decided to take up residence in Sodom, for he might otherwise have suspected his daughters were planning something.

The two sons born from this unvirtuous strategy were named by the act. The name **Moab** (19:37) means "from a father," and **Ben-Ammi . . . the father of the Ammonites** means "son of my kin." Conflicts persisted with Abraham's descendants and the descendants of these two sons. Numbers 25 portrays the most carnal seduction in the entire history of Israel at the hands of the Moabites at Baal-Peor. Israel's history reflects the influence of the pagan Ammonite god Molech to whom the Israelites sacrificed many of their children in flames (see Leviticus 20:2-5). Even Solomon succumbed to the gods of both of the peoples descending from these daughters (see 1 Kings 11:7).

No other twenty-four-hour period in Abraham's life is related more fully than that described in Genesis 18–19: a midday lunch with three angels that ended with the destruction of Sodom and Gomorrah early next morning. This gives a hint of the importance of this story for the writer of Genesis—a hint that is certainly noted in the rest of Scripture, for the fate of Sodom and Gomorrah became a by-word in the prophets and the NT, and still lingers in popular religious consciousness.[6]

## 5. GOD'S WILL, MAN'S WAY, YET AGAIN (20:1-18)

The events of Genesis 20 have been the point of attack by critics. If Sarah was, in her own words, "worn out" (see 18:12), how could she possibly have been desired by King Abimelech? The story is generally considered to have come from a much later writer and in reality is a rewriting of Abraham's experience in Egypt. Such dissecting is not necessary. The story stands in its own right if we must assume that by this time Sarah was pregnant, although her condition was probably not apparent. Perhaps she evidenced that "glow" some women show when in this condition, and it could have caused her to regain some of her attractiveness. Yet, what makes women attractive to men today likely was not the same as what appealed to men of that time. From what can be surmised, kings especially wanted a harem filled with as many women from as many different backgrounds as possible to give them more influence and power. Women generally were used in marriage for political influence, to seal treaties, and to assist in peaceful relations between tribes. For example, a son was less likely to attack his father-in-law, and vice versa.

How much time transpired between the events of Genesis 19 and 20 is not directly stated in the text. We are told that Abraham **moved on**

**from there** (20:1). If his move was almost immediate, then the place from which he saw the destruction was intended by the word **there.** If the reference was his home, then Mamre is intended (see 18:1). But he went to the border of his country to live as an alien in Gerar. Some reasons for the move can be suggested. While Abraham had stayed where he was for some twenty years (see Genesis 12:4; 21:5), it may be that he wanted a change of scenery. Then, too, it could be that the tragedy of Lot and Sodom may have precipitated his move. Additionally, we know from references to the Hittites in Genesis 23 that these people, from what is now central Turkey, had moved into the area of Hebron, so it could be Abraham was seeking a more secure place to live. As it turned out, for whatever reason, his move was unfortunate, for it brought about another deviation from God's will.

By the time Abraham arrived in Gerar, he seemed to have forgotten the lesson he had learned in Egypt. This new deviation from God's will occurred twenty-five years after the Egypt incident, but even so Abraham should have remembered. God never likes His children to have to learn the same lesson twice. One might be more inclined to excuse Abraham while in Egypt when he was still developing his faith, but why did he make the same mistake at this point in his life? He was years older. He had demonstrated a growth in faith by his reactions to Lot's choice (see 13:9) and with the King of Sodom's offer to give him the captured booty (see 14:22-24). God had delivered Abraham from danger. Why would he fear for his life at this time? From his high point of intercessory prayer for Sodom, Abraham had fallen to a level where he was scared that there was **no fear of God in this place** (20:11).

But how wrong he was! Abimelech did fear God (see 20:4, 8). Had Abraham's experience in having misjudged how many righteous people lived in Sodom caused him to assume that all foreigners held no awe for his God? For whatever reason, Abraham fell into the desperate trap of pawning off Sarah for fear of his own safety by his announcing, **She is my sister** (20:2). When King Abimelech got the news, he sent for Sarah to become a member of his harem. Fortunately for Sarah, the Lord intervened before the foreign king approached her intimately. God gave the king a dream in which he was told, **You are as good as dead because of the woman you have taken; she is a married woman** (20:3).

We are not told how Abimelech was able to recognize God as the one who was speaking to him, but he did. (Another example of this type of recognition is found in 2 Chronicles 35:21-22. The author there makes it clear that, in the battle in which King Josiah was killed, God had commanded Pharaoh Neco to pass through Judah and assist the Assyrians in their battle with the Babylonians. Neco heard about Josiah's attempt to stop him, so he sent messengers to warn him about the divine instruction, but Josiah refused to listen.)

Throughout the ancient world, it was held that adultery was considered a capital offense punishable by death. The literal Hebrew phrase for **married woman** is "owned by the owner." Since a wife was considered the property of the husband on the basis that the two were "one flesh" in God's eyes, for another man to take her was thought to be theft in the worst sense.

Apparently still in his dream, Abimelech defended himself before the Lord, stressing that he had taken the word of both Abraham and Sarah as truth, and what he had done was **with a clear conscience and clean hands** (20:5). God informed him that he was correct in his assessment, and partly for that reason God had kept him from committing the sin of immorality with Sarah. Strikingly, in the Lord's own assessment, if Abimelech had committed a sin, it would have been first and foremost a sin against God.

Abimelech's dream occurred at night, and when he awakened he wasted no time, for **early the next morning** he informed his officials of everything that had happened, including the revelation God gave him in his dream. It caused great fear among them (see 20:8). His next course of action was to summon Abraham. Abimelech blasted Abraham with many questions to determine the cause of Abraham's subterfuge. Abimelech ended with **What was your reason for doing this?** (20:10). It was rather unusual for a king like Abimelech to publicly admit he had been deceived. He would more readily punish the culprit or drive him from his presence.

What a contrast! Abraham, the man who should have been open and honest, was deceptive. Abimelech, a pagan who would have been expected to be devious and crafty, was seriously honest. Additionally, the man who selflessly had given first consideration to Lot's choice of land (see 13:8-9), who had stood in the gap in intercessory prayer for the righteous in Sodom, had once again put himself above his wife and a friendly king. His actions jeopardized Abimelech's entire kingdom. When Abraham decided he could not trust God with his life in that situation, when he thought he could do a better job of taking care of himself, his actions were actually more inglorious than those of a sinner.

Furthermore, the promised son, Isaac, was on the way. Sarah was actually carrying the one through whom the divine "seed" God had promised was to come (Genesis 3:15). Abraham's actions put this part of God's plan in jeopardy. Indeed, God could have chosen another to bear the "seed," but His credibility based on His promises to Abraham would have been damaged. And for all of his caution and concern, Abraham was wrong in his assumptions. There *was* a fear of God among the people and their king. No one was going to kill Abraham, and their hospitality was so gracious that he was invited to stay wherever he chose among the people (see 20:15). One of the first evidences of weakening faith is a loss of discernment.

Abraham and Sarah should have shared their family history (see 20:12-13) when they first had met Abimelech rather than at this point. The patriarch then would have been spared shame, his wife would have avoided extreme embarrassment, and Abimelech would not have had to suffer guilt and fear. Usually the sin of one causes many to suffer.

Abimelech was so shaken by what had transpired that he gathered **sheep and cattle and . . . slaves and gave them to Abraham** along with Sarah (20:14). Then he offered them permission **to live wherever you like** (20:15). But Abimelech thought this was still not enough. He informed Sarah that he was **giving your brother a thousand shekels of silver** (20:16). By ancient standards, this was an enormous sum of money. From ancient texts, one gets the impression that six to eight shekels a year would have been a common laborer's salary (see Judges 17:10). At this time a shekel was a weight, not a coin. Each shekel weighed about .4 ounces. Abraham was given 25 lbs. of silver.

In spite of his generosity, Abimelech resented what had happened to him. To Sarah, he pointedly referred to Abraham as **your brother.** But likely still ill from the experience (see 20:17), he was leaving no stone unturned so that Abraham would pray for him. Abimelech further absolved Sarah of any complicity in what had happened. He told her, **You are completely vindicated** (20:16).

God did in this instance more than He had done in the Egypt situation (see 12:17). Pharaoh had had to determine for himself the cause of the plague that had struck his house. Here God used a special dream to warn Abimelech. In Egypt, it appears that Sarah had been accepted in the harem for a time. Here God permitted no sexual contact at all. It would appear that Abimelech's illness was somehow related to impotence. There is nothing in the text to prove Isaac was on the way, but if he was, and especially if he had not yet been conceived, such would have confused God's miracle in the minds of the people. There had to be no question that Isaac was the son of Abraham, not Abimelech.

Genesis 20 closes higher than it began. Abraham returned to his role as an intercessor. His prayer caused the restoration of fertility among Abimelech's household (see 20:17).

## ENDNOTES

[1]C. S. Lewis, *The Screwtape Letters,* letter VI, para. 1–2, pp. 28–29.

[2]In 12:1-9, God came to Abraham with a special promise after the unsettling orders to abandon all that had been familiar to him. In 13:14-17, the Lord spoke to Abraham "after Lot had parted from him." In 15:1-21, God came a third time, after Lot, freed by Abraham from captivity, decided to return to Sodom.

[3]G. Ch. Aalders, *Genesis,* vol. 2 (Grand Rapids, Mich.: Zondervan Publishing House; St. Catharines, Ontario, Canada: Paideia, 1981).

[4]Derek Kidner, *Genesis,* Tyndale Old Testament Commentaries (Downers Grove, Illinois: InterVarsity Press, 1967), p. 120.

[5]It could well be that Sodom and Gomorrah have been found, along with other cities that existed at about the same time. The most prominent of them, Bab edh-Dhra, is located about one mile east of the "tongue" on the east side of the Dead Sea. Some 20,000 tombs were found in which over a half million people were buried. At another of the towns uncovered in 1975, named Numeira, on the southeastern side of the Dead Sea, proof of a sudden destruction by fire is still visible at the site. The biblical record named three other cities as being located beside Sodom and Gomorrah: Admah, Zeboiim, and "Bella (that is, Zoar)" (Gen. 14:8). These may also have been found, though as yet no digging has been done on them. "As a result of . . . combination of data, Rast and Schaub [the excavators] . . . propose that Bab edh-Dhra and the four other sites may well be the remains of the five Cities of the Plain" (see *Biblical Archaeological Review,* vol. 6, no. 5, p. 33).

[6]Gordon J. Wenhem, *Genesis 16–50,* Word Biblical Commentary, vol. 2 (Dallas: Word Publishing, 1994), p. 62.

# Part Seven

# FOCUS ON ABRAHAM WITH ISAAC

## Genesis 21:1–23:20

The moment when Abraham realized that his wife Sarah was having difficulty conceiving a child is not clear from the text. The likelihood that Abraham went through the procedure for adoption of Eliezer, his servant, as a son and heir is strengthened by our knowledge of the practice current during that time. A genuine filial adoption of a slave by a childless couple was a common practice in a place called Nuzu in central Mesopotamia, where thousands of clay tablets have been found dating broadly to the time of the patriarchs. The arrangement gave the couple assurance that the adopted slave would look after them in their old age, and would have assured them of proper funeral rites in exchange for the new son's receiving their inheritance upon their deaths.[1] Abraham may well have taken this legal step before he left Haran.

Abraham had become aware that Lot was little interested in Abraham's plans for him. Lot went to Sodom because of the need for more grazing land for his animals (see 13:6-12), and decided to return to Sodom after being freed by Abraham's strategic attack on the kings who held Lot captive (see 14:15-16).

What were Abraham's alternatives? He had considered the adoption of his head servant, Eliezer (see 15:2-3). Categorically, God had let Abraham know that He had plans for a son to come forth "from your own body" (15:4). At Sarah's suggestion, Ishmael had been born to Hagar (16:15). Rather than fulfilling God's plan, this deviation interrupted it.

Though Abraham's faith had brightened during the twenty-five years that had passed, his hope of a son by Sarah had continued to dim. It seems probable when Ishmael was born, Abraham believed that Ishmael would be the promised son, for before Isaac's conception Abraham had pled with God that Ishmael would be this son (17:18).

The promise of Isaac had been made repeatedly (see 13:16; 15:4-5; 17:19; 18:10-15), but no one would have believed such a birth possible. No one, that is, but God, who by a miracle was going to make it happen! Though Abraham's faith had stumbled again and again, it was finally rewarded. The incredible occurred; the impossible was realized! There is little doubt that Abraham was more proud than any other father of his time could possibly be.

God would take Abraham through the heart-wrenching experience of making a human sacrifice of Isaac, but through it all Abraham would learn the true basis of his love for God—a love for who God is, not for what God does.

At the close of this section in Genesis, Abraham lost his wife Sarah. Since he had not prepared for her death by purchasing a burial plot for her, that task consumed his whole attention in chapter 23.

## ENDNOTE

[1]D. Winton Thomas, *Archaeology and Old Testament Study* (London: Oxford University Press, 1967), pp. 73–74.

# 18

# GOD'S WILL: ISAAC

## Genesis 21:1–34

enesis 18 informed readers that Isaac would appear within a year. That year has now passed; in fact, in 21:2 alone nine months have transpired, and Isaac has been born. God's will had finally been done God's way. Abraham was careful to follow God's command (see 17:19) by naming his new son "laughter" and, because of another command of God (see 17:12), at eight days of age Isaac was circumcised. A full century separated the ages of father and son.

Sarah was happy to name her son "laughter" for she said, **God has brought me laughter** (21:6). She did not see his name as a punishment for her laughing at the announcement of her giving birth (see 18:12). That was a laugh of disbelief; at this point, she laughed with joy and happiness. Some have thought maybe Sarah was fearful that when news of Isaac's birth spread, people would laugh at her having a child at such an advanced age. But she did not say, "The people will laugh *at* me"; she said, "They **will laugh** *with* me" (21:6). Sarah was sincerely thankful that God had made her lifelong yearning a reality, especially after her childbearing years.

When a child was weaned, it was a custom to honor the occasion by holding a special celebration. In our culture, children are generally weaned sometime during their first year. Such was not the case then. Weaning more likely happened near the age of three.[1]

Abraham held a feast **on the day Isaac was weaned** (21:8). Sarah could not have been happier. Long years ago, she had given up hope of bearing a child. Now the miracle had been realized, and her son's weaning was his first step toward becoming a man. What a joyous occasion! But what gave her joy gave Ishmael jealousy.

# 1. ISAAC AND ISHMAEL: THE SEPARATION (21:1-21)

Ishmael would have been sixteen years old at this point. And at the feast he **was mocking** (21:9). There is no reason given for this **mocking.** Perhaps he mocked Isaac's mannerisms at the celebration or Isaac's place in the family compared to Ishmael. Another suggestion is that Ishmael was making fun of God's sacred promise of a son for Abraham or of Sarah's age, or perhaps he was making a pun on Isaac's name. As might be suggested by Sarah's statement to Abraham—that Hagar's **son will never share in the inheritance with my son Isaac** (21:10)—Ishmael may have insinuated that because of age alone he should get the firstborn portion of the inheritance (two-thirds of the property) when Abraham died. Deuteronomy 21:17 states a later law that a firstborn son would get a double portion at the death of his father, even if that son had been born to a lesser wife.[2] Though this was yet to be made law, until Isaac was born, Ishmael would have been expected to inherit everything; once Isaac was born, Ishmael would inherit half as much. Whatever the cause for Ishmael's mockery, it is likely he was simply reflecting the attitude of his mother, Hagar.

Sarah's request to **get rid of that slave woman and her son** (21:10) deeply disturbed Abraham. Ishmael was his son also, and though Hagar was a lesser wife, she was still his wife. Sarah's reference to Hagar as a **slave woman** was obviously demeaning of Hagar's position. Sarah also refused to refer to either Hagar or Ishmael by name. A further understanding of Abraham's reaction to Sarah—**the matter distressed Abraham greatly** (21:11)—is revealed in the fact that the culture of the time did not allow Abraham to do what Sarah requested. And it was not until God told Abraham to follow Sarah's advice—because He would also make the son of the maidservant into a nation (see 21:13)—that he acquiesced and heeded Sarah's request.

**Early the next morning** (21:14), Abraham prepared Hagar and Ishmael with food and water for basic survival. A skin bottle could not hold more than three gallons of water, and if the food given was only what the two could carry, as John Calvin suggests, perhaps Abraham secretly intended to make it necessary for them to return.[3] He showed concern for Hagar's well-being when **he set them** [the food and water] **on her shoulders** (21:14). Abraham did not just leave the task to Hagar and Ishmael as he could have done. Then, Abraham **sent her off** (21:14). He did not drive her out.

It would not take long even today for someone unfamiliar with **the desert of Beersheba** (21:14), where Hagar and Ishmael were sent, to get lost. In that hot climate, with little awareness of direction, one can become disoriented rather quickly. When the supply of water was depleted, Hagar lost hope for survival (see 21:16). She felt sure that Ishmael would be the first to go: **. . . she thought, "I cannot watch the boy die. . ."** (21:16). Perhaps Ishmael had bravely given his mother part of his share of the water. The original Hebrew says that Hagar "cast the lad" **under one of the bushes** (21:15). The impression is that Ishmael was half-conscious, virtually unable to walk on his own. Hagar half dragged him to a nearby bush. She walked away from him, knowing she could not bear to stay close to him as he died. Her sobs reveal her utter despair (see 21:16).

**God heard the boy crying** (21:17). Why did God hear the crying of Ishmael instead of Hagar's? There is no record that Hagar prayed to God. Had she done so, God would have responded. It may well be that in God's opinion their plight was more the result of Ishmael's behavior (see 21:9), and God awaited his recognition of it.

God always hears the penitent's plea. As Ishmael's behavior led to their near-death experience, his prayer led to their salvation. How typical of God—always willing to rescue afflicted people even when their immediate plight is the direct result of their own behavior. But Hagar was not overlooked by God. Very soon after Ishmael's crying reached God, the voice of **the angel of God called to Hagar from heaven** (21:17). Why the angel did not descend to her immediate presence is not indicated. The same expression can be found later when Abraham was about to sacrifice Isaac on Mt. Moriah (see 22:11). In that passage especially, speed was needed to stop Abraham from killing Isaac. There was a sense of urgency. The first impression is that both were too near death to wait for the angel's descent, but distance would not likely pose a problem to the angel. In 21:17, the physical condition of Ishmael may have been a factor. He, too, was near death. Speed was crucial.

This incident with Ishmael, as well as other incidents where angels appeared to speak for God (see 18:9; 19:12; 1 Chronicles 21:15), reveals that angels do not have infinite knowledge. The angel asked a question in Genesis 21:17—**What is the matter, Hagar?**—that would not have been necessary if the angel had had infinite knowledge. Then the angel let Hagar know that he did have knowledge of the plight of Ishmael: **God has heard the boy crying as he lies there.** Hagar was then instructed to **lift the boy up and take him by the hand** (21:18). In her weakened physical condition, Hagar could not have lifted Ishmael. The meaning of the words is that "Hagar helped the boy to his feet."

Faith renewed was given a chance to act. When Hagar followed the angel's instruction, God opened her eyes, causing her to see a spring of water. Had it been there all the time? Likely, but because of Hagar's grief and despondency, she had overlooked it. Water sources in the desert are not always easily detectable. Only those who are aware of water's location can easily find it. Without God's help, Hagar likely would not have made the discovery.

When faith is applied in difficult situations, new options come to the eye or to the mind. "The episode tellingly portrays man's plight and God's grace: on the one hand, diminishing supplies, scant refuge and final despair; on the other, the abundance of the well (once it was revealed), the promise of life and posterity, and the presence of God."[4]

The miraculous deliverance of Hagar and Ishmael from near death was a turning point for Ishmael. He moved farther south to the Desert of Paran, located in the center of the Sinai Peninsula. With God's help, Ishmael became an archer, developing a skill in hunting that was necessary to Bedouin life. During this ancient period of time, it was normally the concern of a father to find a suitable wife for his son. However, in Hagar's last appearance in Scripture, she shouldered that responsibility in Abraham's absence. Having been born in Egypt, Hagar felt comfortable finding a mate for her son in her homeland.

God never creates culture; people do. It is God's desire to change people so they will in turn change practices of a culture that contradict His will. In the Genesis record, God inspires a faithful accounting of Abraham and Sarah's way of doing God's will, actions which gave rise to the birth of Ishmael. But God made sure that all who read this story learn of the jealousy, alienation, and separation that resulted.

## 2. ABRAHAM AND ABIMELECH: THE TREATY (21:22-34)

At least three years transpired after the events at the close of Genesis 20. Added to this would be the length of time since Isaac was born and Hagar and Ishmael had left. Also, some years had transpired in that the close of 21:21 reveals a married Ishmael.

Much had changed in Abraham's status. He had gained enough prestige that King Abimelech visited him and brought with him his army commander. In Genesis 20, Abraham was treated as a nomadic visitor to Abimelech's land. By Genesis 21, Abimelech considered Abraham as one of equal status and as one whom God had honored in everything he had done. Abimelech's change of opinion may have occurred because of Abraham's prayer and its results (see 20:17) as well as Abraham's increased herds, employees, and descendants.

Genesis 21:25 may suggest that there was some contention over water rights between the employees of Abimelech and Abraham. Though Abraham was willing to pledge himself immediately to a nonaggression pact suggested by Abimelech, Abraham wanted his well that had been seized by this king's servants to be released. Wells in the southern area of Israel were and still are vital to any living there. Irrigation was very important to growing grain. Abraham learned that Abimelech knew nothing about the seized well, having only heard of it from Abraham's mouth (see 21:26). To show his good intentions, Abimelech said in effect, "Why didn't you tell me before now?"

It appears Abimelech made the offer of a treaty, for it was Abraham who gave **sheep and cattle** as a gift to him. Normally, it was the weaker king who gave a gift to a stronger power to cement such a pact. Though Abraham was strong enough that Abimelech was motivated to make the pact, it may be that the peacemaking patriarch wanted to emphasize further his desire for nonconfrontation by offering a gift as if he were the weaker one.

After the verbal covenant was made, Abimelech noticed that Abraham had **set apart seven ewe lambs from the flock** (21:28). Abimelech's curiosity was peaked. He apparently could understand why the sheep and oxen had been given, but why were the seven ewes set off by themselves? Abraham let Abimelech know that the king's acceptance of the animals would testify to his claim that Abraham had indeed dug the well that had been seized, and that it, therefore, belonged to Abraham (see 21:30).

As a member of one of the two archaeological teams that worked in Beersheba in the 1970s, I am intrigued to think that the well discovered there may well have been the one dug originally by Abraham. Though some question such a claim, the well is located where the city of Beersheba later sprang up.

Abimelech agreed to the verbal claim of Abraham, apparently taking ownership of the lambs since their reception signified Abraham's repossession of the well he had dug. Though it is not specifically stated, it seems likely that Abimelech returned the well to Abraham at this time. The name given to the well—Beersheba, which translated means "well of oath"—attested to the agreement both leaders made. Having accomplished their objective, the visitors left to return to their land.

Where did they go? They **returned to the land of the Philistines** (21:32). This is the first mention of the Philistine race in the Bible, and it comes in connection with the patriarchs. The Philistines are mentioned again in 21:34. The people most commonly known by this title did not arrive as a whole in Palestine until after their defeat at the hands of the Egyptians at the beginning of the twelfth century, long after Abraham's time. Therefore, critical scholars declare this mention of the Philistines in Genesis 21 to be anachronistic, incongruous with what is known about Abraham's time. These scholars believe a later author inserted the phrase **the land of the Philistines** at a time after the Philistines had arrived in that area, in effect claiming the story to be untrue or only partially factual. To preserve the authority of the Bible, it is more likely that the Philistines mentioned in the text were earlier peoples of the same race that arrived centuries before the remainder came en mass. Otherwise, Isaac's encounter with the Philistines in Genesis 26 also would be unreliable information.

Abraham's reaction to the occasion of the treaty was to plant **a tamarisk tree** (21:33), a stately tree that has been known to reach a height of thirty feet. This tree is especially desirable in the Negev Desert, planted there by Bedouins for its valuable shade and foliage, which was needed by their flocks. But the actual kind of tree was not what was important to Abraham. Trees are mentioned repeatedly in connection with altars he built or places where he stopped or lived. Exactly why Abraham planted this particular tree is not mentioned, but the feeling one gains after reading the text is that to Abraham the treaty is a special occasion. He calls **upon the name of the LORD, the Eternal God** (21:33).

The reference to Abraham's prayer by calling God **Eternal** suggests that the occasion is proof to Abraham of God's faithfulness. God had kept His promises to Abraham from the time Abraham first received those promises in Haran until the present moment. Abraham made a covenant with Abimelech that would last for generations (see 21:23), and even if the well would not be returned to him, he was given legal rights to its waters. Abraham knew he could live in the land permanently. He had gained the reputation God promised, he had the descendant God miraculously gave him, and he felt ownership of the land. The delays were all behind him. He must have felt fulfilled in every sense. But he was about to be given a test that would try his faith to the utmost.

## ENDNOTES

[1]One archaeological find shows a mother nursing her son while both mother and child are standing on their feet. This son must have been more like six years of age.

[2]A lesser wife was either a servant girl to the first (main) wife, who would be available to the husband in the event his wife could not bear a child, or sometimes a woman given to him as a result of some treaty or agreement with another king, sheik, or other notable person.

[3]Gordon J. Wenhem, *Genesis 16–50,* Word Biblical Commentary, vol. 2 (Dallas: Word Publishing, 1994), p. 84.

[4]Derek Kidner, *Genesis,* Tyndale Old Testament Commentaries (Downers Grove, Illinois: InterVarsity Press, 1967), p. 141.

# 19

# GOD'S WILL: ISAAC OR NOT?

## Genesis 22:1–23:20

Very few students look forward to being tested on a subject they have studied, a book they have read, or an experience they have had. Yet there seems to be no better way to prove how much knowledge has been gained than through testing. Abraham was tested and, indeed, by a test of the most difficult kind that a loving parent would have to endure.

## 1. ABRAHAM AND ISAAC: TEST (22:1-19)

Not long before, Abraham had said good-bye to his older son, Ishmael. The words **some time later** at the beginning of Genesis 22 (see 22:1) do not give any definitive time measurement for the present events. These words could mean anything from months to years. Yet it seems improbable that more than a few years had passed since Ishmael's leaving. At this point, Abraham still referred to Isaac as a **boy** (22:5). The Hebrew word used here usually indicates a youth yet to attain manhood. Early Jewish tradition fixed the age of Isaac at thirty-seven. Josephus judged him to be twenty years old. A son of either age would not be addressed as a **boy**. The text seems to connect Ishmael, who at age sixteen was also called a "boy" when taken from Abraham (21:14), and Isaac, who may also be taken—through death in this case. If the boys were about the same age at these points of separation, Ishmael's departure first may have been a help to Abraham for the test of this now more difficult separation.

Child sacrifice was a common practice in Abraham's era. He must have known of these desperate practices on the part of the Canaanites to appease the fertility gods in order to receive rain in due season. Skeletal remains of children of all ages have been discovered in archaeological excavations, some of which I personally have found. From these, it has been revealed that burials of children under foundations were common to ensure that a wall or a building would not collapse through an earthquake caused by some angry deity. Two things supported the idea that these children did not die natural deaths. First, one burial was intentionally put in the ground and then the wall constructed above it; second, numerous burials were found beneath a four-inch plastered courtyard of a palace, and other children were buried in a room just beyond. The skeletal remains of the children ranged in ages from three months to teenage years at their deaths.

It is important to note two things about the story in Genesis 22.

First, in the initial few usages of the name **God** (22:1-3, 8-9) in the original Hebrew, this title is preceded by the definite article "The." We would expect the name "Lord" to be used, but it does not appear until 22:11, and then only as **the angel of the LORD.** Perhaps this is explained by Exodus 6:3 where God told Moses, "I appeared to Abraham, to Isaac and to Jacob as God Almighty, but by my name the LORD I did not make myself known to them." The Hebrew word for God *(Elohim)* is also used when a pagan god is indicated. Therefore, using the definite article "The" before God's name allowed the author to indicate to his readers that this message being given to Abraham, which might be thought to come from a pagan god, was really coming from the one and only God.

Second, in normal Hebrew sentences, the verb comes before the subject if the verb is considered more important. Therefore, 22:1 would read "tested God Abraham," but it doesn't read this way. It reads, "The God— He tested Abraham." This word sequence indicates that God was entirely responsible for the heartrending experience Abraham was about to have.

At first glance, it is easy to wonder why God tested Abraham at all. Didn't God know everything He needed to know about Abraham? God did, but Abraham did not. Through my years as a professor, I have given thousands of tests. This is because I cannot know precisely how the student is doing until I see the results of an exam. My knowledge is limited. But God's is not! So the test in Genesis 22 was entirely for Abraham. God wanted him to see the main object of his spiritual loyalties.

God could have given His instruction without pausing after calling Abraham by name (see 22:1). But God wanted to give Abraham a chance to respond with evident attentiveness. And indeed, Abraham did respond with a special openness. Had God come to him when he was devising his plan to pass off Sarah as his sister, either to the Pharaoh or to Abimelech, Abraham likely would not have answered as he did in Genesis 22. Perhaps those two incidents had made him realize how futile it is to try to hide from God. Essentially, Abraham's reply was, "Behold me, God! Here I am!" (22:1).

God knew His request would be the most difficult one Abraham would ever receive, so He softened it with a plea: "Please take . . ." (see 22:2). Unfortunately, this politeness does not come through in the translation, but it is there in the Hebrew. Then God followed with **your son, your only son, Isaac, whom you love.** God wanted to show Abraham that He knew of the intimate relationship between Abraham and his son Isaac, but God still told Abraham to take Isaac **to the region of Moriah [and] sacrifice him there as a burnt offering . . .** (22:2).

It might seem normal for Abraham to object verbally with something like, "No God! You can't mean that! You promised me; you gave him to me! What kind of a giver are you, anyway?" But there was none of that, apparently not even in his thoughts. And his silence was not because he was callused and hardhearted. God knew this not to be the case, acknowledging the relationship between father and **son . . . whom you love** (22:2). Through the years since Abraham's call at Haran, though he sometimes had strayed a bit from the true direction of God's will, he had learned. Abraham now trusted God enough that though he did not fully understand the reason for this divine request, he knew he must obey God fully. "The story functions to make crystal clear the depth of Abraham's devotion to God. His loyalty to God conditions every other loyalty."[1]

One might imagine that Abraham had a sleepless night, perhaps making it easier for him to get up **early the next morning** (22:3) and prepare for the journey. The reason the father and son took two of their servants is not apparent. It is likely Abraham could have cut wood near the spot, for the land of Israel in his day was heavily wooded, and yet he chose to take care of the wood before he left Hebron (he got the wood after he saddled his donkey; see 22:3). Perhaps Abraham wanted Isaac to grasp the purpose of the trip without knowing that he was the intended "animal."

It took the party three days to arrive at Moriah. Where is the mountain **in the region of Moriah** located (22:2)? Though the author of 2 Chronicles does not mention the incident of Abraham and Isaac, he does locate Moriah as the place where Solomon later built the Temple (see 2 Chronicles 3:1). This would make the place even more significant, for God knew that the Temple would be built there. It was also a place where later pavements would run red with the blood of innocent sacrifices to atone for the sins of guilty people. And God was asking Abraham to do something that He himself had planned to do for eternity—sacrifice His own son. Indeed, the whole episode was a picture prophecy of what was to come. Isaac was dead in Abraham's mind for three days, and there was a substitution of a ram so that his son would not have to die. For Isaac of course, there was a ram; for all people since Jesus' death, He was and is the sacrifice.

That Abraham received more specific directions about where to go is hinted in the phrase stating that Abraham **set out for the place God had told him about** (22:3). And before Abraham arrived, he looked up and saw the place in the distance (see 22:4). Not wanting his servants to witness the sacrifice at close range, and desiring to be alone with his son at this most delicate moment, Abraham told his servants to remain at the spot with the animal. Then he added, **. . . while I and the boy go over there. We will worship and then we will come back to you** (22:5).

Did Abraham think God would supply a substitute? It seems unlikely. Abraham did know he had been told by this very same God that He would establish His "covenant with him [Isaac] as an everlasting covenant for his descendants after him" (17:19). We also read in Hebrews 11:19 that "Abraham reasoned that God could raise the dead." However, though Abraham reasoned that God "could," there had to be doubts surfacing in his mind, such as "Would God do it?" There seems a hint here in Genesis that this situation was so tough for Abraham that he tried to prepare himself by distancing himself a bit from Isaac, for he did not refer to Isaac as "my son," as we might expect, but rather as **the boy** (Gen. 22:5). And it may have been another small indication that Abraham was hinting to Isaac what was soon to come.

As the old patriarch moved the wood from the donkey to the back of Isaac, as Abraham picked up the pot of smoking embers and the knife, and as Abraham and Isaac walked up the mountain together, the curiosity of Isaac surely had to have needed an explanation. Isaac spoke. In Hebrew he said, "My father," which was a most tender address. This is about the equivalent to "Daddy" in today's English. Abraham had to have been expecting Isaac's question: **The fire and the wood are here, but where is the lamb for the burnt offering?** (22:7).

Through the lines of the text, one can almost hear the tear that ripped the heart of Abraham. What could he say but, **God himself will provide the lamb for the burnt offering, my son** (22:8). To this author of Genesis, the real sense of the text here is not that Abraham expected to find a lamb on the mountain but rather, "Isaac, you are the lamb God has provided." What was implicit was now explicit. Abraham was prepared to go all the way with God's command, but he still could not bring himself to tell Isaac directly.

The close relationship between Abraham and Isaac, and yet the silent isolation from each other in their slow climb is emphasized twice in this Scripture passage (see 22:6, 8) with the words **the two of them went on together.** Not yet fully aware what it was all about, Isaac walked on in the curiosity of his thoughts, while Abraham's spirit was bleeding profusely. Abraham's feet no doubt became more leaden as he lifted each one ahead of the other to move farther up the hill.

When they arrived together, no recorded conversation occurred between them as **Abraham built an altar there and arranged the wood on it** (22:9). Still no words as Abraham bound his son, then hoisted him up onto the wood. Who could help but imagine the tears streaming down the cheeks of Abraham as he lifted his knife to slay Isaac. If Isaac was a strong teenager, and given that Abraham was old and weakening physically, Isaac might easily have resisted and run away. Scripture does not say, but it appears Isaac had great faith in his father and trusted him completely, no matter what he did, just like Abraham trusted God so completely no matter what He required.

The knife in the hand of Abraham was ready to move toward Isaac's jugular vein. Suddenly, at the last half second, from heaven rang the call, **Abraham! Abraham!** His arm froze in movement. **Do not lay a hand on the boy**, God told him (22:12). **Now I know that you fear** [reverence] **God, because you have not withheld from me your son, your only son.** One gets the impression there was something about Abraham's faith that God did not know thoroughly enough and could only know by means of this test. This cannot be God's intent. He knew more about Abraham than Abraham knew about himself. God wanted *Abraham* to learn what he could learn only by such a test. It made Abraham come to the point of decision, to the most critical question anyone has ever faced in assessing his or her relationship with God: What is the *basis* of my relationship with Him?

For Abraham the question was, "Do I love God because of what He has done for me (miraculously given me this son), or do I love Him because of who He is?" Any love one has for another that is performance based is inadequate at best. Love, to be genuine love, must be rooted deeply in the character of the one loved. Performance-based love stops when performance stops, but love based on who a person is does not die even if the anticipated service is no longer rendered. Many serve God only while things go the way they expect them to, and when God does not do for them what they want or think they need, their love turns cold.

True worship demands a sacrifice, but an appropriate sacrifice. Isaac was never intended to be a physical sacrifice. God already had provided **there in a thicket . . . a ram caught by its horns** (22:13). Abraham's face aglow with relief, his tears having turned to an expression of joy, he cut the ties binding Isaac, and together the two took the ram, slew it, and laid it on the altar. Never did Abraham or Isaac appreciate a sacrifice more than that one!

How much of a difference did this story make in the biblical account? One indication might be the amount of material in the biblical record given to Abraham, Jacob, and even Joseph compared to Isaac. The other three get an average of thirteen chapters, compared to Isaac's four chapters. Why the pronounced difference? Could it be that Isaac's life was spared more traumas because of the witness of Abraham's strong faith during Isaac's childhood? This one incident surely had the most impact on Isaac. He saw how deep and unconditional his father's love was for God. Abraham was willing to forfeit all—even his most cherished son. Imagine Isaac's frequent prayer after this incident: "Oh, God! Make me a man like my dad!" A father's acts of faith influence his children immeasurably.

God provided a substitute for Isaac in a way scarcely dreamed of by Abraham. Abraham joyously decided to name the place. He might have named it "The place where I obeyed" to commemorate his most difficult moment. Instead, he honored God's timely intervention with this name: **The LORD Will Provide** (Gen. 22:14). Notice that the name is not in the past tense. It is in the future tense. The name spoke not only to what had occurred there, but also to Abraham's belief that God would come through for him in the future whenever and whatever the need would be.

As the influence of this occasion permanently altered Isaac, so also it proved to have a long, powerful influence on Abraham's descendants. These descendants not only would be **as numerous as the stars** and **take possession of the cities of their enemies** (22:17) but also would cause blessing to come on **all nations on earth** (22:18). "[All this, Abraham,] **because you have obeyed me**" (22:18). There is never a viable substitute for obedience, never an authorized alternative to doing exactly what God commands. And how often are blessings not only denied to the one who disobeys but also, because of that one's disobedience, withheld from others for generations to come? Can there be a more emphatic reason to underscore the indelible influence even one obedient act can have on others?

It is very noticeable that Isaac is not mentioned in 22:19. That he is not has caused some to conclude that he was actually sacrificed. Such a conclusion is unwarranted. The emphasis of the account is on Abraham's obedience and the blessings that resulted for all humankind. The author did not feel it necessary to mention Isaac's returning with Abraham to the place where the servants were waiting, or his return with the group to the area of Beersheba. Think how different—to both father and son—the trip back home must have been, compared to the trip to Moriah. It surely seemed half as long and twice as meaningful.

## 2. ABRAHAM AND NAHOR: LINEAGE (22:20-24)

In the time of Genesis, nomadic life tended to cause the lives of family members to be more isolated, with less contact than might be expected. Travel over even short distances was laborious and time consuming. Animals to be tended and ground to be worked further restricted visits. Sometimes years passed before one could be informed of all that had transpired in the family. Abraham had not heard from his brother, Nahor, since Abraham had left Haran at least forty years before.

Genealogies or family trees may make dull reading for the modern reader, but they were considered very important in biblical times. "I lack roots if I don't know my ancestors by name" appears to have been their mind-set. Then, too, there was the practice of giving a child only one name and connecting it with the father or mother, as with our Lord Jesus: "the son of David" (Matthew 22:42). While the genealogy in Genesis 22:20-24 might seem more appropriately placed in Genesis 24, where we are given more information about Rebekah, it here gives a glimpse of the development not only of Abraham's brother's family but also of Rebekah, Isaac's future wife.

## 3. ABRAHAM AND SARAH: DEATH (23:1-20)

By the time of Genesis 23, much time had transpired since the return of Abraham and Isaac from the incidents of chapter 22—at least fifteen to twenty years. Those years were passed in silence. The last information provided on Sarah dealt with her expulsion of Ishmael and Hagar, which had taken place more than thirty years earlier. It is easy to wonder what Abraham told Sarah about the trip to Moriah, how she reacted, how she received the news upon his return with Isaac, what had occurred since that time, how she had fared physically, and what now caused her death. That information was not important enough to have chronicled. The text merely states that **she died at Kiriath Arba** (an earlier name for Hebron; 23:2) at the age of **a hundred and twenty-seven** (23:1). Because she and Abraham had lived together many years, her loss caused Abraham **to mourn . . . and to weep over her** (23:2).

This grief could not be expressed long, for in that hot, dry country, decay set in quickly, and Abraham had not yet obtained a place to bury Sarah. Did she die so suddenly that Abraham had no time to plan properly? Perhaps, but he needed to obtain a place for her burial quickly.

Near Kiriath Arba was a settlement of **Hittites** (23:3). They are often called "children of Heth," as it reads literally in 23:3. They were known to have had a very large concentration of their people in what is now Turkey. They appear to have moved south to facilitate trade for their extended empire. They had not only moved there but also purchased much of the land.

Abraham appeared before a committee of leaders, among which was the owner of a cave he desired to purchase. Abraham may have been aware of the presence of this man—Ephron—but protocol demanded a specified recognition of the Hittite leadership first. Recognizing himself as **an alien and a stranger among** them, Abraham requested **some property for a burial site** (23:4). The leaders recognized Abraham's status as **a mighty prince among us.** They told him he could have his choice of their best tombs (see 23:6).

It appears likely that Abraham had been sitting among them. This would have been a recognition of his status and acceptance, and of Abraham's observance of proper courtesies. He now rose to make his more specific request (see 3:7). He respectfully bowed in recognition of their graciousness and generosity in offering the tomb of his choice. He then let them know that he specifically wanted to buy **the cave of Machpelah,** owned by Ephron, which was **at the end of his** [Ephron's] **field** (23:9).

Ephron, upon being brought into the conversation, now could speak directly to Abraham, and in a typical Near Eastern bartering procedure, Ephron offered to **give** not only **the cave,** but also **the field** in which the cave was found; three times Ephron offered to **give** Abraham what he wanted (23:11). But Ephron had no intent to hand over the field and its cave without payment. He simply was opening the negotiation.

In the early 1900s, excavations conducted in present-day Turkey confirmed some customs that clarify the Scripture text's meaning. When a Hittite sold only a part of his field, it then belonged to the owner free and clear. But when he sold the entire field, there were certain continuing services the buyer had to render to the seller. Ephron let it be known that the cave alone was not for sale; the cave went along with the entire field. Additionally, mention is made of Abraham's buying the field **and all the trees within the borders of the field** (23:17). Hittite law also required the listing of trees on a property when it was sold.[2]

Abraham agreed to the conditions that were set out. But as yet no price had been stated. Abraham stated his wish to **pay the price of the field** (23:13). Ephron accommodated Abraham's request by informing him that **the land is worth four hundred shekels of silver** (23:15). Now, to stimulate the generosity of Abraham, Ephron added, **but what is that between me and you? Bury your dead.**

**Abraham agreed to Ephron's terms and weighed out for him the price he had named . . .** (23:16). The value of four hundred shekel weights of silver is difficult to grasp, but we know the weight in metal was the equivalent of one hundred sixty ounces of silver, a large sum. A common laborer would have had to work for a period of almost three years, saving nearly every ounce of silver he earned, to negotiate such a sale. David bought the Temple site for fifty shekels (see 2 Samuel 24:24), and Jeremiah paid but seventeen shekels for the field of his cousin (see Jeremiah 32:9). In Judges 17:10, ten shekels was considered an annual wage, which included clothing and food. Earlier, in the time of Hammurabi—a Babylonian king who lived sometime near the time of Abraham—six shekels was a standard annual wage.

Even if the field was a very large one, only someone of significant wealth could have purchased it. Abraham's flocks would likely have numbered in the hundreds—perhaps thousands—making him very wealthy. We know, too, that he had been given a thousand shekels of silver as a gift from Abimelech (see 20:16), some of which he likely still carried.

This piece of land that Abraham purchased was the only piece of land Genesis says he owned, but his descendants would ultimately own the entire region. With the quick purchase of the field, presumably the same day as the death of Sarah, Abraham was able to lay her to rest. The cave also would become the burial place for Abraham, as well as that of Isaac and Jacob and their two wives.

### ENDNOTES

[1]Christian E. Hauer and William A. Young, *An Introduction to the Bible* (Upper Saddle River, New Jersey: Prentice Hall, 1998), p. 71.

[2]Roland Kenneth Harrison, *Introduction to the Old Testament* (Grand Rapids, Michigan: Wm. B. Eerdmans Publishing Company, 1969), pp. 111–12.

# Part Eight

# FOCUS
# ON ISAAC

## Genesis 24:1–27:46

braham lived another thirty-eight years after Sarah's death. The only incident mentioned that occurred during this period is the choosing of a wife for Isaac, unless Abraham's marriage to Keturah is from this period also (see Genesis 25:1). But if indeed Isaac came along after Abraham could no longer father a child, then Abraham's marriage to Keturah preceded Isaac's birth. It appears that this remaining period of Abraham's life, though not uneventful according to what is chronicled in Scripture, must have had more to do with Abraham's peaceful end than it did with the flow of revelation. The writer of Genesis turns his attention in Genesis 24 to Isaac's part in the extended promise God had made to Abraham.

As the curtain rises in Genesis 24, Abraham is pictured as quite concerned that his son of promise might find a proper marriage partner. The fact that Abraham is **old and well advanced in years** (24:1) points to one aspect of God's fulfilled promise—that of a long life (see 15:15). Other aspects of God's promise were Abraham's prosperity (24:35-36), his military victory over kings from the East (14:15), his deliverance from tough situations of his own making (12:11-20; 20:2-13), his and Sarah's ability—with God's help—to have a child (18:14), and finally Isaac's birth and survival (21:1-5).

# FOR ISAAC: A WIFE

## Genesis 24:1–25:18

It seems likely the events of Genesis 24 came late in the last thirty-eight years of Abraham's life. Perhaps Sarah's death caused Abraham to think more about Isaac's mate; Abraham's advancing age meant that his last chance to help his son in this very important matter was soon to vanish completely. Though Abraham knew Sarah's death would come, he may not have had much warning or time to prepare, for he had apparently not given any consideration to a burial place for her until after she died (see comments on Genesis 23). But there may have been weeks, even months, or possibly years during which Abraham developed a growing concern for an eventual mate for his son of promise before voicing his apprehension concerning whom Isaac would marry. Some think Abraham was actually on his deathbed when he finally called his servant to undertake the selection of a wife for Isaac.

We will read of Abraham's taking his last breath at the advanced age of 175. His life contained the trauma, excitement, suspense, and yet fulfillment of all he and Sarah had most desired. He died satisfied and happy (see 25:8).

At the conclusion of this section in Genesis, we are given the names of the twelve princes God promised Abraham his son Ishmael would father (see 17:20).

## 1. THE RIGHT MATE DESIRED (24:1-49)

The writer introduces **the chief servant** in Abraham's household without telling the servant's name (24:2). It may be assumed from what Abraham had said (see 15:2) that the servant was Eliezer. No other of Abraham's servants was named. Perhaps Eliezer had died and another had taken his place, but if so, one would think this man's name would appear. However, if it was Eliezer, his name was purposely ignored, perhaps to give more emphasis to his relationship with Abraham and to God's part in the finding of a wife for Isaac.

The land of Canaan was generally filled with religiously depraved people. Abraham knew that a wife for Isaac who had been brought up to pray regularly to gods of wood and stone, and whose worship involved all types of sexual immorality, would most likely be unsympathetic to God's designs. Abraham had decided there was no other recourse than to find a mate for his son from among his own people. Perhaps he had searched for suitable candidates among eligible Canaanite, Philistine, and Hittite women, but finally had given up the search. Isaac had reached his fortieth year (see 25:20).

Abraham knew Ishmael had married an Egyptian woman (see 21:21), and he remembered the deviation caused by his nearly losing Sarah to a pagan Pharaoh and later a foreign king. Abraham wanted a daughter-in-law from his own race (see 24:4).

Abraham knew he himself could not return to Mesopotamia (literally, "Aram of the two rivers"), so he called his servant. The mission the servant was asked to take required much solemnity. The patriarch required something that would appear very strange today (see 24:2). The act of putting a hand under a man's thigh when a pledge was made was a way of saying that if the instruction and assignment were not fully followed, the servant would have to answer to all of Abraham's descendants. It is especially significant that the pledge was made about obtaining a wife for Isaac with reference to the seat of procreation from which Isaac came.

Into the mind of the servant immediately came a question, and he posed it to Abraham: **What if the woman is unwilling to come back with me to this land?** (24:5). A typical first concern today would be how to choose the right woman for a wife, and the servant did consider that later, but his initial anxiety was the possible reluctance of the woman chosen to return with him. The servant probably knew firsthand how difficult it had been for Abraham to uproot himself, totally abandon his family, and go to a strange land. He also was apparently not fully aware that the promise God gave to Abraham He intended to carry over to Isaac. Thus, the alternative that came into the mind of the servant was, **Shall I then take your son back to the country you came from?** (24:5).[1]

Abraham knew that nothing could be more disruptive to the divine promise to him and his descendants than for Isaac to leave the land God had given to him and his descendants. He knew Isaac could not be an absentee landlord. As emphatic as Abraham could be, he said in effect, "Under no condition whatever are you to do that!" He repeated the warning (see 24:8). Then Abraham brought to mind his own odyssey from his homeland, ending with an exact quotation of the promise God had given him (see 12:7): "To your offspring I will give this land." With a faith measured, firm, and rooted by past experiences, Abraham assured the servant he would not be going alone. "God **will send his angel before you** [so that you will be successful in your search. But if she still does not want] **to come back with you,** [then you have done your part, and] **you will be released from this oath of mine** (24:8-9).

It is interesting that during this time when marriages were arranged by fathers, as was being done by Abraham for Isaac, the consent of a chosen woman was not ignored. Even with angelic direction and divine selection, she could undo the choice. If she would not consent, Abraham told the servant, he had done his part. With that assurance, the oath was taken.

Ten camels laden with luxuries made up the "bride price" (24:10). In that day, the father of the groom "paid for the wedding," so to speak, by giving the father of the bride numerous gifts. The number ten may have had some significance (see 32:15; 45:23; 1 Samuel 17:17; 1 Kings 14:3; 2 Kings 5:5). Camels were rare and extremely valuable at the time. The camels and the valuables they carried speak to Abraham's great wealth.

The journey ahead of the servant was close to five hundred miles. If he pressed ahead every day, it would have taken him four to six weeks to complete it, but the journey is barely described. The destination was **Aram Naharaim,** more specifically the town of **Nahor** (Gen. 24:10). Since Abraham had a brother by the name of Nahor, the suggestion is that the town intended was where Abraham's brother lived, likely in Haran, where Terah had settled with Abraham after leaving Ur (see 11:31).

However long the camel caravan traveled before their arrival, they were tired and thirsty enough for the servant to have his camels kneel down at the well outside the city. Nearly all towns had water sources outside the city walls at a low spot in a valley, and at that time it was the customary task of women to obtain the water required for everyday needs. As if God were already involved in the whole process, the time of day that the servant arrived at the well was **toward evening, the time the women go out to draw water** (24:11).

From the phrase in 24:13—**the daughters . . . are coming out to draw water**—one gets the impression that the women could be seen coming in the distance. The servant was worried about how to determine which one should be selected for Isaac. He knew that both he and his camels were very thirsty. In a quick prayer to the Lord, he asked that the one who, when asked to give him a drink, would respond, **Drink, and I'll water your camels too,** would **be the one you have chosen** (24:14).

This test was not haphazardly selected. It was not something like, "Let her have a dimple on her right cheek," or "May she be about my height." It surely would have seemed presumptuous to expect a reply to such a request. Yet it was an artful strategy to determine the depth of character the girl possessed. The question he had was, "Would she be willing to offer me a drink and then, of her own initiative, draw close to five gallons of water for each of my ten camels, a normal amount thirsty animals would drink after a long, hot day of travel?" If so, he would know she possessed a most humble and generous servant's heart. Such a reaction would not be typical. The reply more likely to be heard would have been, "Sure, I'll be glad to!" and the reply would have ended there.

How quickly God answered the servant's request is indicated by the fact that the prayer was still in process when Rebekah, granddaughter of Abraham's brother, arrived at the well. The servant had no idea of her identity. In a sense, readers find out before he does. The text reveals her identity, her lineage, her physical beauty, and her chastity — a condition of great honor in that day — before she even had a chance to obtain water. As she went down to the spring and returned, Eliezer, watching her closely all the time, quickly approached her with his searching request (see 24:17). Rebekah responded with an offer for a drink, without hesitation, as any girl would have been expected to do for a thirsty stranger. But, would she go beyond what was customary? As Eliezer consumed the water, his ears were anxiously waiting for the right words. The words came. And they weren't in the form of a question, such as, "Would you also like for me to water your camels?" She said what she would do and she did it.

Rebekah was the first girl to arrive, so Eliezer did not have to make the suggestion to other girls and have them fail the "test." This reveals how closely God was working with the servant to confirm Rebekah as the intended wife for Isaac. The servant had had great apprehension about the success of his mission, which likely remained and intensified during the long journey. Though his way of determining the right mate for Isaac involved a test that would have been generally difficult for a young girl to pass, in all of this God was working "for the good of those who love him, who have been called according to his purpose" (Romans 8:28).

The servant waited until the camels had finished drinking. Perhaps he wanted to make sure Rebekah would complete the difficult task of drawing enough water for all ten camels. He then presented her with three pieces of valuable jewelry. Their weight in gold would be valued today at more than one thousand dollars. These appear to be generous gifts merely for the selfless spirit she exhibited, not intended as bridal gifts, for Eliezer still did not know her name, let alone her background.

With his criteria for a suitable wife having been met, Eliezer asked her father's name and, with the same breath, if there was lodging available for the night. Her magnanimous spirit was expressed not only in her willingness to do hard labor for this man but also in her response to provide information beyond what was requested. She made it clear that she was a relative of Abraham on both sides of her family (see 24:24) and that there was ample room for the servant and plenty of straw and fodder for his camels. That information, together with what had just occurred, was enough to assure the servant that God had worked more perfectly than he could have imagined. He immediately bowed down (literally in Hebrew, "prostrated himself") **and worshiped the LORD** (24:26). It appears he was so overwhelmed by how God had worked that he had to worship God immediately, on the spot.

Rebekah was so excited about the expensive gold gifts she had been given by the generous stranger (see 24:22) and his devotion to the Lord (see 24:27), she could not contain her joy. She hurried home to **tell her mother's household** (24:28). We can determine from the statement in 24:50 that her father was still alive, so it is curious why the household is not considered his. It normally would have been designated as such. However, Rebekah's brother Laban was the main spokesman, which might suggest that her father, perhaps due to impaired physical condition, had had to relinquish leadership to his son and that the mother was really the one in charge of the extended family.

The author may be saying that Laban was somewhat motivated by money in that he was impressed by the expensive jewelry given to Rebekah (see 24:30); as soon as he saw it, he hurried out to meet this man who had remained near the spring. It may be that Laban's generous hospitality was somewhat based on his covetousness and the wealth of the visitor. Nevertheless, the servant accepted the offer of a room and a sumptuous meal for him and his men (see 24:32). But he could not sit down to eat until he had related all that had happened, beginning with his connection to Abraham and Sarah, the birth of Isaac, and his assigned mission to find a suitable wife for this son. He included God's part in giving him divine guidance at the spring of water. He ended by asking permission from Rebekah's family to allow her to accompany him when he returned.

## 2. THE RIGHT MATE CHOSEN (24:50-67)

After the long recitation of events had concluded, whether in unison or with one speaking and the other nodding in agreement, both Rebekah's brother and father said, **This is from the LORD** (24:50). The statement shows that at some point the family had started recognizing the Lord, perhaps subsequent to Abraham's departure. They were so awed by the way God had put everything together that they felt they **could say nothing to you one way or the other** (24:50), meaning that since the Lord had orchestrated everything, He needed to be unhindered in His purposes. They consented to Rebekah's becoming the wife of Isaac (see 24:51). The bride price was then paid in gold and silver jewelry, fancy clothes, and other costly gifts (see 24:53). After the meal, the day having ended, they all retired for the night (see 24:54).

No sooner had the servant arisen the next morning than he requested permission to be sent **on my way to my master** (24:54). The family preferred to allow Rebekah **ten days or so** (24:55) at home before she left, but since the Lord had so perfectly blessed the mission, the servant was anxious to return immediately so he could inform Abraham of the good news. The ten-day waiting period appears to have been in Rebekah's interest, for the decision was made to let her decide if she should go immediately or wait for a period of time to ease her departure (see 24:57). Rebekah had no hesitation about leaving as soon as preparations could be conveniently made (see 24:58).

As the group was about to depart, two blessings were given to Rebekah. The first was what young women wanted in that day—many children; the second was that her offspring would be victorious over any enemy (see 24:60). Rebekah and her maids mounted the camels, and the entourage began the long journey back with the servant.

Again no details are given about the weeks that follow. The text moves immediately to Isaac, who it seems had moved to Beer Lahai Roi, somewhat south of Hebron (see 27:62). Had Abraham died? Possibly, for Rebekah, seeing Isaac at a distance and inquiring as to his identity, was told, **He is my master** (24:65)—**master** being the title that had been reserved for Abraham previously. And the servant reported to Isaac (see 24:66); the text makes no mention of Abraham. However, if Abraham had died during the time the servant was away, it would seem that the servant's surprise and grief would have been mentioned. Yet, the oath could have been taken earlier on Abraham's deathbed, in which case the servant might have already adjusted to Abraham's death.

Rebekah certainly had been told when they were nearing the end of their journey. When she saw Isaac at a distance, perhaps suspecting it was he, she dismounted. She then inquired as to his identity. Told that it was her future husband, she raised a veil over her face (see 24:65).

When Isaac and Rebekah met, the servant told **Isaac all he had done,** undoubtedly recounting God's providential guidance. With Isaac now assured enough, the couple entered Sarah's tent, an event that was then part of the ceremony, and the marriage was performed. How significant it is that Isaac already **loved** Rebekah (24:67); they had just met! That would seem impossible in our day, but though she was indeed "very beautiful" (24:16), Isaac's love really shows Isaac's acceptance of God's part in bringing the two together.

# 3. ABRAHAM: DEATH (25:1-11)

Was Keturah a wife of Abraham (see 25:1) or a concubine (see 1 Chronicles 1:32; also Genesis 25:6)? The former title might suggest that Abraham married her after the death of Sarah. But the title "concubine" would suggest otherwise (see Genesis 25:6). This title might point to Abraham's marriage to her during Sarah's barren period; this is what had led to his marriage to Hagar. Genesis 25:6 describes how Abraham had more than one concubine. Like Ishmael, other sons were sent away after having been given gifts (see 25:6). Nothing must interfere with Isaac's faith and development—not the wrong wife nor contentious brothers.

Abraham lived not only a long life but a life **full of years** (25:8)—a Hebrew phrase indicating a happy, contented life. Abraham was **gathered to his people,** possibly indicating typical burial practices at the time involving entombment in the same cave as earlier generations buried there. We know in Abraham's case, though, that this cave had not been used before Sarah's burial (see 23:17-19). Note that both Ishmael and Isaac together buried their father in the same cave. Probably Isaac had sent messengers informing Ishmael that Abraham's death was near. That the two were together for Abraham's burial suggests that a reconciliation had occurred between the brothers, either on this occasion or possibly at some earlier point after Ishmael and Hagar were forced to leave.

# 4. ISHMAEL AND FAMILY (25:12-18)

In this short section of Genesis is given a rather brief family tree of Ishmael. His descendants were at times at peace with the descendants of Isaac. They appear as tradesmen on the way to Egypt (see 37:25). They were the means for Joseph's being taken there. At other times they were engaged in battle, as is mentioned in connection with Gideon (see Judges 8:24). Though Ishmael was not more prominent in the divine fulfillment of prophecy, this brief summary in Genesis 25:12-18 does reveal that God did include Ishmael in His plan. Abraham loved Ishmael, and if Abraham had had his way, his oldest son would have been his heir (see 17:18). Knowing this, God promised that He would bless Ishmael. Ishmael also would become the father of twelve rulers whose descendants would become a great nation (see 17:20). Those twelve are named in 25:12-18. By contrast, this section prepares readers for the greater fulfillment of God's promises in the life of Isaac.

There was a time when Sarah had believed that God's will was to be fulfilled by her having a son through Hagar, and Ishmael was born (see 16:1-4). For thirteen years, Abraham had believed this too. When God had told him that Sarah was to mother a son by him, it was so inconceivable that he had exclaimed, "If only Ishmael might live under your blessing" (17:18). But through faith Abraham finally was able to grasp God's promise, and now he knew Isaac was to succeed him. So it was now time for Abraham's first son, Ishmael, and his descendants to be taken from the mainstream of God's covenant people.

## ENDNOTE

[1]Where exactly was "Ur"? The location of Abraham's Ur is in doubt. In this chapter, Abraham repeatedly refers to his homeland as being far to the north of Ur of the Chaldeans (see 11:31). Aram, or present-day Syria, is where Rebekah lived and where Jacob worked for Laban. Haran is 1000 miles north of the traditional site in lower Mesopotamia. One clay tablet found in northern Syria at the site of Ebla confirms that there was also an Ur located near Haran. It might well be that Abraham's clan moved from this "Ur of the Chaldeans" to another Ur in the north, near Haran. Perhaps it would be something like a person's moving from Marion, Indiana, to Marion, Illinois (see *The Interpreter's Dictionary of the Bible* [Nashville, Tennessee: Abingdon Press, 1962], pp. 735–38; also see *The International Standard Bible Encyclopedia, vol. 4* [Grand Rapids, Michigan: Wm. B. Eerdmans Publishing Co., 1988], p. 955).

# FOR ISAAC: TWINS AND TROUBLE

## Genesis 25:19-27:46

A t this point, the writer of Genesis turned his full attention to Isaac. **This is the account of Abraham's son Isaac** (25:19). "The account of Esau" does not occur until 36:1, and not until 37:2 is found "the account of Jacob." Though Isaac is little mentioned after Genesis 27, the title **the account of Abraham's son Isaac** is meant to cover the time Isaac was at least the nominal head of the patriarchal family. His two sons' activity came at the time when he was technically in authority.

At 25:19, the author enters a new phrase of patriarchal history. With Abraham's death, the focus of the promise was passed to Isaac.

There are times when the chronicle of God's movement with the patriarchs slows down so as to allow a microscopic look at one incident, such as we read in Genesis 24. Genesis 25:20 informed us that Isaac was forty when he married Rebekah, but just six verses later we learn that twenty years passed before Jacob and Isaac were born (see 25:26).

## 1. THE STRUGGLE BEGINS (25:19-26)

Initially, Rebekah was barren. She appeared to have struggled to have children for twenty years (see 25:26), but as a result of Isaac's prayer for her, she became pregnant. Within a few months, the babies, hyperactive within her, distressed her greatly. When she went to the Lord she was told, **Two nations are in your womb . . . one people will be stronger than the other, and the older will serve the younger** (25:23). The revelation gave Rebekah three bits of information that surprised her: (1) the two sons to be born would be the founders of **two** separate **nations;** (2) they would be of unequal strength; and (3) the one born second would be given priority.

195

The last bit of information must have been the most surprising, for during Old Testament times there was an expressed favoritism of the older child over the younger. This bias was part of pagan practices at the time, and at best it was a culturally stifling custom. God gives everyone individual gifts (see 1 Corinthians 7:7); these cannot be determined by birth order. Throughout the Old Testament, whenever it can be determined, generally it appears that God does not choose the eldest child for a leadership role unless, like Joshua, no mention is made of brothers and sisters. Leadership roles must be based on the abilities God gives each person.[1]

Was Rebekah stunned by the news from the Lord about **two nations** within her? Until that point she likely did not know she had been carrying twins, but after God spoke to her she must at least have suspected it. Having twins would be difficult enough to ponder, but **two nations,** one **stronger than the other?** She offered no rebuttal of any kind. It is likely that her condition did not improve. The struggle within continued, but no doubt the knowledge of the cause helped her to endure the pain.

After Rebekah's full term, the first child born was **red** ("ruddy" in Hebrew). This referred to his skin or his hair. The same description was used twice of David (see 1 Samuel 16:12; 17:42), suggesting that this condition was a bit unusual, either at birth or later. Additionally, this first child uncharacteristically had a predominant growth of hair, so thick that his whole body was like a hairy garment (see 25:25). Through a word play in the original Hebrew, the name given this first child was Esau.[2] Before he was completely free of his mother, a hand of the second son emerged, grasping Esau's heel. The second son was named "heel grabber": Jacob. The contrast is noticeable, Esau was named because of the way he looked; Jacob was named according to what he did. "The symbolism is everything. Here the second twin is seen trying desperately to catch up with the first. The struggle in the womb is obviously going to continue outside. The pattern for the rest of the story is set."[3]

## 2. BIRTHRIGHT BARGAINED AWAY (25:27-34)

The phrase **the boys grew** (25:27) gives no hint as to their ages, but for Esau to have become **a skillful hunter** suggests much practice. Both are referred to as men. It appears that Isaac put his own tastes ahead of propriety with respect to his sons, for he **had a taste for wild game** (25:28). It loomed large in Isaac's preference of Esau. Naturally, to please his father, Esau majored in hunting wild game. And the more

Isaac favored Esau, the more Rebekah favored Jacob. Isaac's growing one-sided bias for Esau, of course, caused Rebekah to come to the defense of Jacob, whom she must have felt was being slighted by his father. The younger boy tended to stay close to his mother, **staying among the tents** (25:27), and it is probable that he was active in raising the cattle Isaac owned.

Because of the pagan custom of what is called primogeniture, the eldest son was supposed to get a double portion of the father's estate presumably upon the father's death, while the other son(s) would receive a single portion. So in Jacob and Esau's case, while Esau would be expected to gain two-thirds (a double portion) of Isaac's estate, Jacob was supposed to inherit only one-third (a single portion). Jacob could, of course, barter craftily for half of the double portion Esau would get. Rebekah surely told Jacob of the revelation God had given her about "the older serving the younger," so Jacob was looking for the right time to usurp Esau's place. Jacob's opportunity came one day while he was cooking some lentil stew. Speculation is that in the stew with the lentils was added onions, rice, olive oil, and probably some cuts of meat.[4]  As its savory scent wafted in the air, an exhausted, ravenously hungry Esau approached Jacob requesting some of his **red stew,** because Esau was **famished** (25:30). Here is a description of a man who was controlled more by immediate appetite than long-term promise. It was a crisis moment in the life of Esau. How unfortunate for him that he did not rise to meet the challenge. The incident shows that character is not created in a crisis; it is only exhibited. Jacob knew his opportunity had arrived.

Even before offering a bite, a cagey Jacob replied, **First sell me your birthright** (25:31). A caring brother would have offered the soup requested. Jacob was not caring. He was callused and calculating. And Esau, with little concern for the future, had more anxiety about his current appetite. How could anyone be so hungry that he would willingly surrender his birthright, especially when that meant losing half of his inheritance? In our day, this idea seems fanciful at least, and absurd at most. In a city of the northeast part of Mesopotamia, about one hundred miles due east of the Assyrian city of Asshur a clay tablet was found, from just after the time of the patriarchs, of a contract of a younger brother trading his birthright for only three small lambs.[5]  Property was evidently not considered as important as it is today. Tent dwellers did not change their lifestyle no matter how many animals they owned. And there were no twenty-five-thousand-dollar tents as opposed to one-hundred-fifty-thousand-dollar tents.

Esau exhibited a disrespectfulness of his elder status. He flippantly agreed to Jacob's requirement for food, turning his back on what should have been treasured family rights. Esau certainly did not have an impressive outlook on life—careless and indifferent about things of importance, always interested in the immediate reward, undisciplined, erratic, and wayward. He became the antithesis of the saints of Hebrews 11, because "for a single meal [Esau] sold his inheritance rights as the oldest son. Afterward, as you know, when he wanted to inherit this blessing, he was rejected" (Heb. 12:16-17).

On the other hand, Jacob was devious and deceptive, determined to ignore convention. One must be careful not to justify Jacob's action simply because of his knowledge that God had ordained that he be over his brother. While this would have happened as prophesied, Jacob should not have taken advantage of his brother's condition. There is no immediate censure of Jacob in the Scripture text, but he later spent many anxious hours, even years, regretting what he had done, for in many ways his actions returned to haunt him.

The transfer of inheritance rights only took an oath—no notarized document, no change of Isaac's will, just a verbal agreement—for it was a society based on the spoken word. Since few knew how to write, little effort was made to have written records. A man's word was his bond. It was all that was needed. Esau's consent could not be reversed; he was totally indifferent to what he had just done.

## 3. THE FAMINE BEGINS (26:1-6)

For whatever reason, the author of Genesis did not always put his information in chronological order. It seems apparent that the events of chapter 26 did not actually occur between chapters 25 and 27 where they are placed. In chapter 25, Rebekah had twin sons, but there is no hint that they even exist in chapter 26. They return to the record in chapter 27. It is unlikely that Rebekah could be considered unmarried by so many men in Philistine country for so long a period of time (see 26:8), and if Jacob and Esau had been left in the home area, the famine there would have made it as difficult for them to remain there.

Likely, the events of Genesis 26 took place before Jacob and Esau were born. (Similarly, as we will see, Genesis 34 was purposely placed out of chronological order by the author.) Though King Abimelech (see 26:1) and Phicol, a military commander, are mentioned (see 26:26)—and their names are identical to men who earlier confronted Abraham (see Genesis 21)—these cannot be the same men. Looking carefully at ages given for Abraham and Isaac, and when their encounters occurred with Abimelech and Phicol, there were at least seventy-five years between the Abimelech and Phicol of Abraham's time and those of Isaac's time. Likely "Abimelech" was a title of office similar to "Pharaoh," a king in Egypt; "Phicol" was likely a military title such as "Captain." Added evidence of this is to be found in the superscription of Psalm 34, where the Philistine King Achish is called "Abimelech."

In times of famine, it was customary for people from Canaan to go to Egypt. It seems Isaac was planning to go there. With the plenteous fresh water of the Nile to irrigate the land, famines seldom occurred in Egypt. The famine mentioned in Genesis 26:1 is compared to the famine experienced by Abraham, but this one was likely not as severe, for Gerar was relatively close to where Isaac and Rebekah lived, and they did not have to travel far to be removed from its effects.

Isaac may well have been preparing to go to Egypt as his father had done (see 26:6), causing the Lord to preface his remarks to Isaac with, **Do not go down to Egypt** (26:2). During Isaac's time of stress, God repeated the covenant He had made with Abraham (see 26:3), telling him he would have **lands** (26:3), **descendants,** and a ministry to **all nations on earth** (26:4). That was enough to reassure Isaac, so he **stayed in Gerar** (26:6).

## 4. ISAAC DECEIVES ABIMELECH (26:7-11)

In time, like Abraham, Isaac thought his life in danger, and again, like his father, he resorted to a scheme of "the end justifies the means." The pagan culture of the day stated that women were the property of men, and they were used to seal treaties and agreements, to advance social relationships, and ensure good political relations. These ideas did not come from God. Women were created to be "comparable to" or to "complete" their mates (see Genesis 2:18). Through Moses, "in the fullness of time" God would give the Law at Mt. Sinai, but had God tried to give too much of His Law to Abraham or Isaac, they might well have perceived it as not coming from God. The Bible often reveals the results of pagan customs that people took as normal practice but which led away from God's grand design.

When the men approached Isaac in Genesis 26:7, they simply wanted information about Rebekah. There appears to have been no threat at all on their part, but Isaac assumed there was. Perhaps there was a practice among different peoples to do away with the husband of a beautiful wife in order to make her more available. Otherwise, Isaac's fear of such a thing would have been unfounded. The fact that the true relationship between Isaac and Rebekah was discovered some time after the time of questioning shows that Isaac's fear was unwarranted, for there had been no threat mentioned involving him.

We do not know where Isaac and Rebekah were when Abimelech observed them **from a window** (26:8). Since he looked down, one gets the impression that he may have been viewing them from an upper floor of his palace. Maybe they were in a secluded place in a garden where they thought no one could see them. The Hebrew word for **caressing** (26:8) is found a total of seven times in the Old Testament. In four places, it indicates behavior leading to sexual activity. Whatever it involved, Abimelech knew that Isaac and Rebekah could not have been brother and sister and do what they were doing. He immediately summoned Isaac and simply stated, **She is really your wife!** (26:9). Then he wanted to know why Isaac had deceived him. Isaac responded, **Because I thought I might lose my life on account of her** (26:9).

Abimelech's rebuke of Isaac shows how serious he viewed the deception, for if **one of the men [had] slept with your wife, you would have brought guilt upon us** (26:10). How ironic that a pagan king needed to rebuke a patriarch of the faith! Abimelech actually had more moral sensitivity than did Isaac. If ever a "sinner" is more concerned about guilt, or is more just, honest, or responsible than one who thinks he or she follows God, the witness principle is reversed, and God's cause suffers.

Abimelech ordered that no one would **molest** either Isaac or Rebekah (26:11), lest in doing so their punishment would be death. Although the Philistine king was very angry with Isaac for his deception, both Isaac and Rebekah were given protection.

# 5. ISAAC PROSPERS (26:12-25)

After the resolution of the Rebekah issue, Isaac felt safer. He planted crops in the land. This area today can be most nonproductive if there is not enough moisture, so irrigation is essential. Isaac's reaping **a hundredfold** suggests that the Lord had blessed him. It also suggests that Isaac had learned how to use water from the wells Abraham had dug to water his crops, which led to Isaac's becoming very wealthy with **flocks and herds,** causing envy among his hosts (26:14). The Philistines then resorted to **filling** the wells **with earth** (26:15). Finally Isaac was asked to move. He did, but immediately reopened the wells that had been made inoperable.

Isaac did not have enough water for his farming, perhaps because some wells had gone dry. Isaac's servants **discovered** (26:19) a new source of water, and dug three more wells (see 26:19, 21, 22). At that point, the Philistines claimed, **The water is ours!** (26:20). Perhaps they had discovered the secret of Isaac's productivity and, rather than filling the wells, they simply claimed them, requiring Isaac to move and find new sources of water. The first new well dug was named **Esek,** meaning "contention" or "challenge;" the second was called **Sitnah,** meaning "opposition." After the third well was completed, the Philistines made no attempt to claim it, so Isaac named it **Rehoboth,** meaning "wide places." Isaac stated the reason for this third name: **The LORD has given us room and we will flourish in the land** (26:22). Isaac may well have had the muscle to successfully overpower the Philistines, but on each occasion he chose to move on. His peaceable nature was evident.

When the famine ended, Isaac returned to his home in Beersheba (see 26:23), where God gave him a renewal of the promise Isaac had received earlier (see 26:2-4). Isaac had expressed a fear for his life (see 26:7), so to the promise was now added, **Do not be afraid, for I am with you** (26:24). When both Isaac and Abraham got into situations where they feared for their lives, they prepared to sacrifice their wives' honor for their own safety. In so doing, they got into trouble. Fear should always find its resolution in faith and trust, not in an act of self-preservation that uses others and tends to ignore God. Perhaps Isaac had come to recognize his error, for he **built an altar there and called on the name of the LORD** (26:25).

Now with less fear, and a greater resolution of faith, not only did Isaac pitch **his tent,** but **his servants dug a well.** It seems from then on he had more confidence God would run interference for him.

## 6. ISAAC'S PEACE PACT (26:26-33)

To this point, it would appear Isaac was rather timid in his relations with the Philistines. They pushed him around. And since he tended to avoid confrontation, they took advantage of him. But the Lord had prospered Isaac in spite of this, and His promise to Isaac had given Isaac more courage. Abimelech and two of his advisors decided it was time for amends to be made. They went to Isaac in Beersheba. He expressed surprise at their appearance and asked, **Why have you come to me, since you were hostile to me and sent me away?** (26:27). They assured him of their desire for peace and good relations in the future. This would have been somewhat apparent to Isaac in that there were only the king and two advisors present—no threatening army of soldiers. There was in their decision a realization **that the LORD was with** Isaac. They mention this fact twice (see 26:28-29).

Had Isaac realized he could more completely trust God with his fortunes? He does not appear to have been vindictive in any way, though in the eyes of the Philistines he had the power to harm them (see 26:29). Rather, Isaac **made a feast for them, and they ate and drank** (26:30). They then stayed the night, a confirmation that Isaac was a gracious host and was considering their request. Early the next morning, oaths were taken between the leaders, and then the guests were **sent on their way . . . in peace** (26:31).

Later, but still on the same day the oath was made, Isaac's servants went to him with the exciting news that they had found another source of water. Isaac named the well **Shibah** (26:33), which in English means "oath." Isaac saw God's hand in both situations. He knew that "when a man's ways are pleasing to the LORD, he makes even his enemies live at peace with him" (Proverbs 16:7). He had earlier left the Beersheba area because of a lack of water. Now Isaac felt a sense of greater security, both from the earlier foe of nature, as well as his former Philistine enemies.

## 7. ISAAC'S GRIEF (26:34-35)

Apparently a large segment of time passed between the events of Genesis 26:33 and verse 34. This is indicated by the opening phrase of verse 34: **When Esau was forty years old.** Genesis 26, an interlude, almost certainly occurred before Jacob and Esau were born, but the events of chapter 25 had to have happened as much as twenty years earlier than the events recorded in the verses following 26:34. The quiet war between the twins continued with devastating effect.

Esau chose not just one wife but two. This and the fact that they were of the pagan Hittite race, perhaps bringing some of their pagan symbols and practices with them, caused Isaac and Rebekah much grief. Either Isaac was not as concerned as Abraham had been that he find daughters-in-law from his own people, or Esau was deliberately turning away from the faith of his fathers. His careless approach to life and his shallow regard for the responsibility of his position made him take himself away from inheriting the patriarchal blessing.

Compare Esau with King Saul, who later improvised and altered instructions from the LORD. Saul may have lost the possibility of being the ancestor of the Messiah. Samuel told him, "You have not kept the command the Lord your God gave you; if you had, he would have established your kingdom over Israel for all time" (1 Sam. 13:13). The influence of decisions made today cannot always be divorced from their future effects.

## 8. ISAAC DECEIVED (27:1-40)

Genesis 27 opens with an aging Isaac with impaired sight. He knew his death was approaching. He decided it was time to pass the covenant blessing to Esau. One has to wonder why he did not invite Rebekah and Jacob. When Jacob neared death, he called all of his sons to hear his last words (see Genesis 49). That was the normal procedure.

It seems Isaac planned a meeting between only Esau and himself, purposely ignoring Jacob and Rebekah. Could it have been this way because the message Rebekah received from God while carrying her sons was not to his liking? He wanted Esau to be over Jacob, to take his place as clan leader when he died. Did his taste for wild game (see 25:28) color his rationale even more?

Esau was called and instructed to hunt and kill the game, and **prepare . . . the kind of tasty food** Isaac liked (27:4), so the blessing could be given to Esau before Isaac's death. Literally, Isaac said, "that my soul may bless you before I die." There seems in this statement a deliberate choice to overlook both his oldest son's disregard for propriety and God's plan for Jacob.

Tent dividers are not as secure as doors, and Rebekah overheard what Isaac had told Esau. The parental favoritism is revealed in the reference to Esau as **his** [Isaac's] **son** (27:5) and the reference to Jacob as **her** [Rebekah's] **son** (27:6). Instead of leaving matters in God's hands, Rebekah decided she must intervene.

Rebekah waited until Esau left, then called in Jacob and informed him of all that had transpired. But she slightly altered what Isaac had said to Esau. She did not mention Esau's being told to **get your weapons** (27:3). She also changed the "that my soul may bless you" (27:4 NKJV) to "that I may . . . bless you" (27:7 NKJV) and added **in the presence of the LORD before I die** (27:7). All of this may have been calculated to persuade a reluctant Jacob to follow her advice to pretend to be Esau in order to receive the blessing Isaac intended for Esau. Jacob knew deceiving his father would be most difficult (see 27:11-12).

Why did Rebekah resort to this scheme of deception? This was so uncharacteristic of the gregarious young woman at the well of Haran (see

24:19). There she was giving; here she is grasping. There she was submissive; here she is domineering. Perhaps she had been kept from knowing Isaac's exact plan until now, but she had surely been fearful of what was about to transpire. She had to think that God's will was being circumvented; she decided she would help God do what needed to be done, lest Jacob forever lose his divinely appointed place in life.

When Jacob was told of the scheme, he showed great concern for the fact that he lacked the dense body hair of Esau, and though he knew the blind Isaac could not see him, Isaac might determine his son's identity by a touch of his **smooth skin** (27:11). Furthermore, Jacob showed less concern for taking advantage of his aged father than he did about a **curse** falling on him instead of a **blessing** (27:12). Rebekah minimized Jacob's concern by offering to take the curse on herself. Then she ordered him to **just do what I say** (27:13).

Had Jacob's fears increased Rebekah's uncertainty about her plan? Perhaps she thought she must make sure the plan succeeded. She cooked the food as planned, but then she decided to take **the best clothes of Esau . . . and put them on . . . Jacob** (27:15). In the event Isaac's sense of touch was a bit keener than she anticipated, Rebekah provided goat's skin to cover Jacob's arms and the back of his neck. As Rebekah performed all these tasks, Jacob remained at best a reluctant participant. Every attempt having been made to work out the deception, the mother put the **tasty food and the bread she had made** (27:17) into the hands of Jacob, who then entered Isaac's quarters. There was no recognition until Jacob addressed Isaac as **My father** (27:18).

Jacob knew his last opportunity to back out of the scheme had transpired. He went farther in his speech than he might otherwise have done out of his fear of failure, but his actions seemed to raise more suspicion on Isaac's part. Isaac asked, **How did you find it so quickly?** Jacob showed his fear and apprehension by lying: **The LORD your God gave me success** (27:20). Isaac was not convinced. Jacob's voice did not sound like Esau's. Suspecting that something may have been amiss, Isaac told Jacob to come close enough so he could touch his arms and neck. One can easily imagine the anxiety pervading Jacob's thoughts as he stepped forward and held out his hands. Would Isaac discover his true identity?

Feeling the goat hair on Jacob's arms, Isaac must have thought, "Not only is my sight gone, but I can't depend on my ears either. I can't distinguish between the voices of Esau and Jacob!" Surely Jacob was doing everything in his power to sound like his brother. Momentarily, the aged patriarch laid aside his misgivings, but they quickly surfaced again.

**Are you really my son Esau?** Isaac asked. Jacob found it necessary to lie again. He replied, **I am** (27:24).

The food was eaten and the meal finished. All the time, Jacob had kept as much distance as possible between him and his father. Isaac needed one more proof of Jacob's identity. He asked him to come and kiss him. His sight gone, and believing his ears and touch failing him, he wanted to call upon his sense of smell. He would recognize the undeniable scent of Esau's clothes. Smelling them, he concluded that the man before him truly was Esau. Isaac gave Jacob the blessing (see 27:27-29).

Jacob left the tent just moments before Esau entered (see 27:30). This may suggest that there had been an unexpected delay in Jacob's convincing Isaac that he was Esau. Esau knew nothing of what had transpired, so he brought Isaac the food he had prepared and requested the blessing (see 27:31). Isaac asked his identity. Under normal circumstances, he would have recognized Esau easily, but after being convinced his senses were failing him, he asked the identity of this new visitor.

When he was told the true identity of Esau, **Isaac trembled violently** (27:33). At that point, he did not know the identity of the one he had blessed and asked who it was, adding, **I blessed him—and indeed he will be blessed.** Behind that statement was the prevailing belief that words, once spoken, could never be reclaimed. In our day, Esau might have responded, "I'll take him to court and sue him! He got the blessing under false pretenses. I will regain it!" But no, Esau recognized that the original blessing could not be his. He begged (the Hebrew indicates that he "screamed"), **Bless me—me too, my father** (27:34)! Behind these events, we now know by the discoveries of clay tablets from Nuzu, was a judicial respect for a death-bed affirmation.[6] Once said, they were binding on all concerned.

Cyrus Gordon tells of one clay tablet found in Nuzu, identified by P56, that mentioned a lawsuit involving three brothers, two of which contested the third's right to marry a certain lady. The would-be groom won the case by arguing that his father had given him permission while his father was on his deathbed.[7]

Isaac knew the identity of the impostor. He told Esau that his blessing was taken deceitfully by his brother. Esau replied that Jacob was rightly named **Jacob** ("deceiver"). He claimed that Jacob had "cheated" him twice (27:36). Then again he pled, **Haven't you reserved any blessing for me?** Isaac's reply to Esau, **So what can I possibly do for you, my son,** hints at his acceptance of the idea that God himself had overruled his plans to give Esau the blessing he had expected.

Had that been a normal situation, Isaac would have had a blessing for Jacob, too, which would have been still undelivered. But it may be that Isaac had planned to leave his younger son without a blessing, so there was no blessing left even for Esau. Thus the reason for Esau's remark: **Do you have only one blessing, my father?** (27:38). From Isaac the answer came that—because of the social customs of the time—could only be expected: "No!" What else was left for Esau to do but weep aloud?

From the beginning, Isaac had wanted to give his blessing **in the presence of the LORD** (27:7). This surely would have included Jacob's presence and maybe Rebekah's, too. Perhaps Isaac had come to realize that God wanted Jacob to have the blessing, and it belonged to him even though Isaac had planned otherwise, and even though Jacob obtained it deceitfully (see 27:35).

God could not have been pleased with the way this family was scheming to help Him work out His will. God would have accomplished His plan without Rebekah and Jacob's craftiness if they had only waited on God's timing. Instead, they preferred to do God's will their own way. This always brings added grief and pain.

The use of the word **father** is found no less than thirteen times in eleven verses (see 27:30-41). One can easily sense the deep desire and desperation that Esau had to turn back the calendar. How he would have loved to once again cherish his birthright, but that opportunity was gone forever. He had lost not only that birthright but also the future leadership rights of the family.

The words Isaac spoke to Esau (see 27:39-40) were more of a curse than a blessing. It was as if his sins that brought him to where he now was—anguished and still unrepentant—had destined him to a future away from **earth's richness** where no **dew of heaven** would fall and where he would live a life **by the sword** (27:39-40), unblessed and untamed. It was to Edom that Esau eventually went, where a lack of moisture made the land unfertile. There he and his descendants lived primarily by raiding and looting the caravan traffic that traversed its borders and, when they felt it necessary, pillaged from more productive neighbors.

The author of Hebrews tells us that Esau was "rejected" by God (12:17). The Greek word used in that verse described one who was disqualified. Esau had left his faith to the point where he was on a hell-bent course to a life alienated from his Maker.

## 9. ESAU'S GRUDGE (27:41-46)

Esau was unrepentant. He **held a grudge against Jacob** (27:41). And that grudge deepened into a plot to murder Jacob as soon as their father Isaac died and the period of mourning passed. Esau was so bitter that, unable to keep it inside, he voiced his plan to some confidant, who then passed the word to Rebekah. Knowing well her rebellious son, she immediately developed a plan to prevent the death not only of Jacob, but also of Esau when justice would be rendered for his premeditated act (see 9:6).

Rebekah's plan was simple. She would send Jacob away to her brother Laban's house **for a while** (27:44) and then call him back when Esau was **no longer angry with** him (27:45). Little did she realize the little **while** would stretch into twenty years and that her conniving to save Jacob would take him away from her forever. She did not see him again before her death.

After preparing Jacob with good cause to leave home, Rebekah needed to set the stage with Isaac to agree to Jacob's trip. Astutely, she did not mention Esau's murderous intent. Isaac might not have believed that Esau would do such a thing and likely would have settled for reprimanding his favorite son. Instead, Rebekah mentioned the grief that the Hittite wives had caused and cunningly suggested that if Jacob remained he might also marry a Hittite. The remark was calculated to make Isaac remember the caution that Abraham had uttered to his servant to keep Isaac from marrying a Canaanite (see 24:3) and the plans that had resulted in Rebekah's becoming Isaac's wife.

Rebekah's argument produced the desired result. Isaac called Jacob and told him to leave **at once** (28:2) for Isaac's homeland.

How sad is the odyssey of Rebekah. She enters the pages of Scripture as a beautiful and pure young woman (24:16), hospitable and courteous (24:18), even unselfish and generous (24:19-20). Determining God's will in marriage was not difficult (24:58), even though she had no previous contact with her groom and could not recognize him by sight (24:65). A significant change occurred after the birth of Jacob and Esau. She resented the fact that Isaac was giving more attention to Esau than to Jacob. Instead of going to the Lord in prayer and seeking His wisdom, she allowed a deceptive spirit to pervade her thinking. Deceiving her own husband became an easy way to remedy the situation. She won the coveted place she sought for Jacob, but in doing so she lost him for the rest of her life. Scripture is silent about her final days, but they must have been filled with grief and regret.


## ENDNOTES

[1]Think of the incidents of God's choosing Isaac over Ishmael (21:12), Jacob over Esau (25:23), Joseph over his older brothers (39:1–45:15), Ephraim over Manasseh (48:12-18), Moses over Aaron and Miriam (Exodus 4:16), Samuel over his older brothers by Peninnah (1 Samuel 1:2, 19-20, 26), David over his brothers (16:5-13), and Solomon over Adonijah (1 Kings 1:17, 37, 43). It is also of note that this primogeniture system was deeply rooted in Egypt, and it was only the death of the firstborn, the tenth plague, that made the Pharaoh finally allow the Hebrews to escape in the Exodus (Exodus 12:31-32).

[2]Esau's other name Edom is a derivative of the color red. "Like a hairy garment" relates to the term Seir, the name of the territory of Edom.

[3]Gordon J. Wenhem, *Genesis 16–50,* Word Biblical Commentary, vol. 2 (Dallas: Word Publishing, 1994), p. 177.

[4]G. Ch. Aalders, *Genesis,* vol. 2 (Grand Rapids, Mich: Zondervan Publishing House; St. Catharines, Ontario, Canada: Paideia, 1981), p. 81.

[5]G. Ernest Wright and David N. Freedman, eds., *The Biblical Archaeologist Reader,* vol. 1 (Garden City, New York: Doubleday, 1961–64), p. 23.

[6]Cyrus Gordon, "Biblical Customs and the Nuzu Tablets," *The Biblical Archaeologist,* Feb. 1940, p. 8.

[7]D. Winton Thomas, *Archaeology and Old Testament Study* (London: Oxford University Press, 1967), p. 76.

# Part Nine

# FOCUS ON JACOB

## Genesis 28:1–31:55

J acob had been born with a driving propensity to get ahead, even at the expense of others. As a "heel grabber" (Gen. 25:26) with the innate ability of being artful, Jacob allowed himself to be turned into a manipulator who calculated ways he could reward himself, even at the expense of others. He exploited his own brother at a time of weakness (see 25:31). But he reached a new depth when, with his mother's encouragement, he deliberately picked on his own aging father.

Jacob paid dearly for his deceit. In acquiring Esau's birthright, he thought he would double the amount of his inheritance (see Deuteronomy 21:17)[1] and take over the honored place of head of the family upon the death of Isaac. That put him on a collision course with Esau. While careless about his birthright, Esau still coveted the deathbed blessing of Isaac, which would give him control over all the family assets, even Jacob's inheritance, including that which Esau had lost in the sale of his birthright. Esau had waited many years and looked forward to that special once-in-a-lifetime moment when in effect he would "replace" his father.

When told by Isaac that the time had arrived (see 27:4), Esau had happily set off to acquire the desired "wild game" (25:28) and cook it into a dish of Isaac's favorite "tasty food" (27:4). After Jacob again made Esau the indirect victim of his deception, Esau planned to wait until Isaac's passing to get his ultimate revenge upon Jacob (see 27:41).

At least there were some redeeming qualities in Esau, one being patience. "He said to himself" that he would wait to "kill my brother Jacob" until Isaac died and the mourning period was past (27:41). Fortunately for Jacob, Esau had apparently disclosed his plan to a close friend, who in turn informed Rebekah. With quick thinking, she devised a plan that gave Isaac a credible reason for sending Jacob away. Esau's Hittite wives had vexed Isaac as well as Rebekah. The possibility that Jacob might also marry a pagan Canaanite wife would make her life not "worth living" anymore (27:46). Since she knew Isaac would remember how she had become his wife, she correctly assumed he would be motivated to send Jacob back to her family.

Rebekah's and Jacob's actions made it necessary for Jacob to have to leave quickly and with nothing—no herds, no caravans of camels, virtually penniless—with no inheritance at all! And though he did not know it, the rest of his life would be fraught with being deceived as he had deceived. He had gladly let his selfish nature consume others. In the end, it not only consumed him, but it caused him to be separated from all of his nuclear family. Fortunately, God did not abandon him. God waited to meet Jacob until the "deceiver" had come to the end of his manipulative contrivances.

### ENDNOTE

[1]The law given here was intended to regulate, not sanction, the cultural practices to avoid where possible the very divisive, alienating, and destructive behavior exhibited by Isaac and his family. But in this case Esau was not gifted for the position the customs of the time believed he should have. That was to be the God-ordained lot of Jacob. In a similar situation, slavery was not God's first option for society, but sin-stained hearts of people caused it to be. Therefore, laws were given to regulate it until, in more enlightened times, it would be abolished.

# 22

# FROM DECEIVER TO DECEIVED

## Genesis 28:1–30:43

A Russian proverb goes, "He who digs a hole for another may fall in himself." Could this proverb have come from someone who had read the story of Jacob? It may well be. As Jacob fled for his life, he finally realized the truth of this proverb, that as he had carefully plotted his strategies as to how he could swindle the gullible, the end result had never entered his mind. In a sense, Jacob was caught in his own trap. And this trap ensnared him the rest of his life.

After one has read the accounts of Jacob's deceptive tactics to get what he wanted, it is typical to ask, "Why would God bless a rogue like Jacob? Did God approve of his actions?" Howard Vos has responded to such questions.

> It should be remembered that God never chose followers for what they were but for what they could become by His grace. The story of Jacob's life would not be looked upon as an account of God's blessing on wickedness, but rather as an account of God's patient dealing with a sinful man until he became Israel, "fighter for God," or "striver with God." His new name bears out the tenacity and perseverance of his character. Jacob was not without punishment either. For example, he was exiled from home for twenty years, himself a victim of deception.[1]

## 1. JACOB MEETS GOD (28:1-22)

The biblical record turns here (see Genesis 28:1) to the second phase in the life of Jacob. He left home with his father's blessing, which gave

Jacob a shield of protection from Esau's interference. Isaac made no mention of the way Jacob had taken advantage of his failing sight and touch to snatch the blessing that ultimately in God's timing would have been his anyway. Perhaps Isaac had come to realize that God had wanted him to give Jacob the blessing (Rebekah surely had shared with Isaac her revelation; see 25:23). Isaac's wish to give the blessing to Esau instead had been wholly his own desire.

Isaac's instructions to Jacob began with a very strong prohibition: **Do not marry a Canaanite woman** (28:1). He was then told he must immediately leave for Rebekah's home, **the house of . . . Bethuel,** and marry within Rebekah's family (28:2). The exact relationship between Rebekah and Isaac was that Rebekah was a first cousin once removed from Isaac; stated another way, Bethuel—Rebekah's father—and Isaac were first cousins. Such marriages are not advisable today but were widely practiced in patriarchal times. And within God's people, especially when paganism was so prevalent everywhere, marriage within the family unit was common. A marriage of close relatives was prohibited later in the Law given to Moses on Mt. Sinai (see Leviticus 20:17, 19-20).

In his blessing on Jacob, Isaac for the first time in the Genesis record mentioned Abraham (see 28:4). Isaac's God was the same as Abraham's God (see 26:24). Isaac now transferred the blessing Abraham had given him to Jacob. Isaac's realization that he was the vital link in God's plan for His covenant people would have been dim at best, but he was aware of his and Jacob's part in taking **possession of the land where you now live as an alien, the land God gave to Abraham** (28:4).

It was not until after Jacob left that Esau realized his actions in marrying Hittite wives had brought grief to his parents (see 28:8), further evidence of his insensitivity toward their feelings. Belatedly, he hoped to redeem himself by marrying his cousin, the daughter of Ishmael, Abraham's firstborn son by Hagar. It appears that his only concern was blood relationship, for there was no mention that his new wife, Mahalath, had any more of a relationship with God than did his Hittite wives. That would not have mattered to Esau anyway. So he did not—probably could not—understand the true basis of Isaac's grief.

At this point (see 28:10), the scene leaves Beersheba and moves with Jacob as he trekked to the homeland of his mother to find a wife. Jacob likely felt depressed and fearful as he left home. He had always preferred his home (see 25:27). Now he was forced to leave home because he had taken advantage of his brother and deceived his somewhat handicapped father. He needed to travel several hundred miles; he must have been on the road for at least three days before he arrived at Bethel, for it was some sixty miles away from his starting point.

Genesis 28:11 begins, **When he reached a certain place. . . .** The wording in the Hebrew gives the impression that Jacob chose that place at random. It was not a place he sought out, and since he did not seek lodging in some house, which he might be expected to do, it may be that he was too fearful to seek sheltered lodging for the night. Or it could be that he was so tired when he arrived at the spot that he did not desire a more comfortable place to sleep. But there was a providential involvement that made him choose that particular spot for his resting place, for God wanted to meet him while he slept and when he was alone.

What a dream Jacob had! He saw a **stairway** (28:12) which linked **heaven** to **earth,** and its base was near where he was lying. Up and down the stairs moved angels, who may have been intended to impress Jacob with their busy activity looking after him and protecting him, for God, standing at the top of the stairway, told Jacob that this was what He would do for him (see 28:15).

It may seem a bit surprising that God had nothing to say about the deceptive actions that had taken Jacob on this journey. God's will had been done, albeit not in the best way. The Lord was most interested in starting afresh with Jacob, accepting what had happened. Then, too, censure may have been difficult for him to sort out. Had God not told Rebekah this would be the end result? But there was an indirect reproof in God's first remark to him. He was told, **I am the LORD, the God of your father Abraham and the God of Isaac** (28:13). This statement had to stab Jacob's heart. What was said could have come to Jacob this way: "I am the God of the man you deceived, the God of the man you victimized, the God of the man to whom you were convincingly dishonest."

Then, in effect, God quickly said, "I want to be your God, too. And here is what I want to do for you. . . ." Following this were six promises that had Jacob as the recipient: **I am the LORD . . . , I will give [this land to you]** (28:13), **I am with you . . . and will watch over you . . . , I will bring you back . . . , I will not leave you** (28:15).

How uniquely like God! Always forgiving, always available, always ready to pick us up where we are, and always be with us. Jacob needed acceptance and assurance for he had lost his home, his possessions, his inheritance. Esau had threatened his life, and for all he knew Esau might be pursuing him. Jacob needed direction for the future. God was there when Jacob needed Him most.

When he awakened, Jacob reacted to all this by demeaning himself for not recognizing God (see 28:16). He felt a reverential fear because of the awesomeness of the place (see 28:17). He moved from surprise, through fear, to awe, a pledge of faith, and an affirmation that **the LORD will be my God and . . . I will give . . . a tenth** (28:21-22) of what he received. God's love was not conditioned by what Jacob had done before his arrival. But God, as always, wanted a response from Jacob. It came. Jacob's affirmation of the Lord being his God was a dramatic conversion experience. He summarized the full impact of his experience by naming his location **Bethel,** meaning "House of God."

Many people choose not to admit their transgressions until they stand in the presence of a holy God, before whom they cannot hide their sin-stained consciences. And despite Jacob's intent to run from home, he ran into God. Jacob could have turned from God, but he chose to turn toward Him. Who could offer Jacob more? God promised him **land** (28:13), **descendants . . . like the dust of the earth . . . all peoples on earth will be blessed through** him and his **offspring** (28:14), and God would take him **back to this land** (28:15). Recall the words of Peter when Jesus, after seeing some of His disciples turn from Him, asked, "You do not want to leave too, do you?" Peter responded, "Lord, to whom shall we go? You have the words of eternal life" (John 6:67-68). There are always alternative routes to traveling with God, but none leads to anything comparable to the blessings of this life or gives the certainty of eternal existence in the next life.

One must be careful not to read into Jacob's closing statement (see 28:20-22) an attempt to bargain with God. In reality, it was not that Jacob was so much choosing God at this time as God was choosing him! Jacob likely felt that his actions had disqualified him. With that in mind, he said, "**If God will be with me** (in spite of what I have done) this I will do. . . ." Jacob was throwing himself before God's mercy. He addressed God directly: **Of all that you give me I will give you a tenth.** Though Jacob was experiencing a strong emotional reaction to an overwhelming experience, one can sense the growing commitment on his part. He first addressed God, then pledged himself directly to God, emphasizing his commitment with a promise of his tithe.

# 2. JACOB MEETS RACHEL (29:1-12)

The Genesis account quickly passes over the remainder of Jacob's long journey. It merely says that he **came to the land of the eastern peoples**

(29:1). (The desert to the east was at that time a forbidding barrier to travel. Nearly always it was necessary to go north to Damascus before one could go east. Indeed Haran, Jacob's destination, was northeast of Damascus, but the desert caused people to think of this as east.)

Ancient roads often passed near wells where water, a most precious and scarce commodity, could be obtained without having to carry it a great distance. From afar, Jacob noticed **three flocks of sheep lying near** a well (29:2). Every person's continual need for water made a well a frequent meeting place where people could be found and the latest news could be heard. At least three shepherds had gathered, but were waiting for another to arrive so together they could remove the heavy stone covering to make the water accessible.

Jacob's initial concern was to learn the welfare of Laban. Again the providential acts of God are shown. First, the shepherds at the well knew about Laban and his welfare. Second, at the moment Jacob was talking to them, Rachel—Laban's daughter—was on her way to the well to water her father's flocks. The promises that God had given Jacob at Bethel were already coming to pass (see 28:13-15).

Jacob was also concerned about the lateness of the shepherds in watering their flocks (see 29:7). The impression given is that flocks were watered early in the morning before they went to graze. **High day** indicated they had been delayed for some reason. Jacob knew it was time for them **to be gathered** in their pastures so they could feed. Maybe more than Jacob's concern for the welfare of the gathered flocks was his desire to meet Rachel alone.

The shepherds informed Jacob that the stone covering on the well was too heavy for them to lift by themselves (see 29:8). The conversation between Jacob and the shepherds was still in progress when Rachel arrived. Immediately upon seeing Rachel, Jacob went over to the heavy stone and rolled it from the well by himself. Could there be better evidence for "love at first sight"? Just Rachel's appearance was enough to get his adrenaline flowing. He was enabled to lift more than normal. However, God was in everything that was happening as well. So overcome with the way God had led him, Jacob both kissed Rachel (the Hebrew suggests he gave her a kiss on the hand as a respectful salutation) and wept in appreciation to God who had so faithfully fulfilled this part of His promises.

When Jacob informed her of his relationship to both her father and to Rebekah, Rachel immediately ran back home to tell her father (see 29:12) who, in typical Eastern fashion, wasted no time running to meet Jacob and take him to their home (see 29:13).

## 3. JACOB MEETS HIS MATCH (29:13-30)

After Jacob told Laban who he was and offered news of his family, Laban responded, **You are my own flesh and blood.** That statement was more than the simple recognition of blood relationship between the two men. It was also in the context of a covenant that was to be made between the two men that would govern their relationship for the next twenty years, though at the moment the time duration was not comprehended. Laban was saying, "You have guest rights here, Jacob." After Laban had been informed of all that had happened to Jacob to make it necessary for him to be there—arriving virtually without money and needing a job—Laban's **flesh and blood** statement made Jacob know by verbal affirmation that he was fully accepted for any desired relationship.

Some of the information Jacob volunteered had to have related to his assigned quest for a suitable wife, and his affinity toward Rachel made it normal for him to stay for a time and to work for his room and board so as not to impose on his host. The arrangement was mutually beneficial for both men. Jacob got better acquainted with the family, especially with Rachel, and Laban had an opportunity to check out Jacob's work ethic. Laban appreciated Jacob's contribution over the month's period enough to give him continued employment and permit Jacob to set his own wage (see 29:15).

The purpose for this was clearly that Jacob had arrived virtually empty-handed. Abraham's servant had not needed to work to obtain Rebekah for Isaac. He had arrived with ten camel loads of dowry for Laban (24:10). In ancient times, one gave a dowry as a financial consideration for the loss of a daughter. Jacob had brought no money for a bride's price; his only option was to work it out.

At that point, Jacob had met and gotten to know both of Laban's daughters, Leah and Rachel. Leah had **weak eyes.** A better translation would be "tender eyes." Some early Jewish authorities thought the phrase indicated "beautiful eyes" but, even so, Rachel **was lovely in form, and beautiful** (29:17). Jacob focused his amorous attention on Rachel. He might have offered seven months labor, but if he had, Laban might well have exploded with, "You think my daughter is worth no more than that!" But **seven years** of labor **in return for your younger daughter Rachel** (29:18) was ample payment in Laban's mind for his daughter. Might not a biblical definition of love be found here? To Jacob, seven years **seemed like only a few days** (29:20). **Seven years** of labor was really a high price to pay for a bride, but it showed Jacob's high regard for her.

After seven years passed, Jacob was ready for his "salary" to be paid to him. He did not yet realize it, but his past actions were going to haunt him. As he had deceived, so he was about to be deceived. The point when Laban made his decision to deceive his future son-in-law is not clear, but by the time of the wedding, Laban's plans were clearly set.

From our knowledge of current cultural practices, the idea of marrying off an older daughter before a younger one does not seem to have been known outside of what is recorded in Genesis 29:26. This idea, then, would have been Laban's calculated way to insure Jacob's continued employment for another seven years.

In 29:21, Jacob made more than a request of Laban. In Hebrew, his words read something like, "Now then, let me have my wife!" Jacob referred to Rachel as his **wife.** This indicates that a couple engaged to be married was already considered man and wife, even though the marriage was only in the engagement stage and had not yet been consummated.[2]

Laban's response of silence to Jacob's request indicates that his deceptive plan was well under way. He could not reply with something like, "All right, I will give Rachel to you," for he had no intention of doing it. Instead, he invited **all the people of the place** (29:22), presumably most of the townspeople, for a wedding feast. Certainly both Leah and Rachel had known of their father's plan, but secrecy was required. Leah was dressed in her veiled best, and Jacob easily assumed she was Rachel. The bridal feast lasted seven days. Customarily the bride and groom consummated their marriage on the first night. The only light available for tents in that day was from flickering olive oil lamps, which did not give more than enough light to keep one from stumbling over objects. For his part, Jacob had no cause to believe that a bride switch had been made. Apparently, few words were spoken that night, so not until morning was the ruse discovered.

The next morning, after Jacob had discovered the deceit, he went straight to Laban and angrily demanded an explanation for the intentional trickery. As they had agreed, Jacob reminded Laban, **I served you for Rachel, didn't I?** (29:25). If indeed there was a custom of marrying the eldest first, Jacob should have been informed of such a practice, but Laban's main intent was to entrap Jacob in another seven years of labor. Had Jacob returned Leah after their time together, he would have brought shame on himself as well as Laban. Their marriage had been consummated. She was legally his wife. Laban knew how Jacob would react, so his plan had been neatly calculated to quiet Jacob by telling him

217

he could have Rachel also, but only after the seven-day period of festivities was over, making it clear to Jacob that he would have to work another seven years (see 29:27).

Perhaps Jacob's memory of what he had done to his blind father pierced his mind and made him unable to reply to Laban; instead he simply accepted Laban's offer. God had chosen Jacob to carry on the covenant relationship with Him, but that did not permit him to escape God's justice. Recall the proverb earlier stated: "He who digs a hole for another may fall in himself."

Jacob finally married the woman he loved, and because of the high social status of Laban's clan, each daughter was given a servant girl to work as a maid or special attendant (see 29:24, 29).

Marrying two daughters at the same time, as Laban caused Jacob to do, was later considered against the law as stated in Leviticus 18:18. Paul, too, admonished, "Since there is so much immorality, each man should have his own wife, and each woman her own husband" (1 Corinthians 7:2).

## 4. JACOB HAS HIS FAMILY (29:31–30:24)

Jacob favored Rachel over Leah, since Leah was not of his choosing. To Jacob, Leah represented her father's cruel deception. Yet the Lord did not approve of Jacob's slighting his first wife, so He allowed Leah to bear children, while **Rachel was barren** (Gen. 29:31).[3]

Leah named her firstborn **Reuben** (21:32). The actual meaning is "See, a son." Leah knew of the similarity of sound between the Hebrew words that mean "seen" and "misery." The fuller meaning is "God has looked upon [my] misery." Leah recognized God's hand in her ability to bear a son, which thus compensated her for Jacob's neglect. Her fond hope that **my husband will love me now** was unfortunately not the case (29:32). Not long after, her second son arrived. Leah sensed she still was not loved.[4] In naming this son **Simeon** ("The Lord has heard"), Leah reflected on Jacob's failure to accept her even after she gave birth to Reuben, for the continuation of the thought is "That I am [still] unloved (literally, "hated."). For her this was a happy moment. In spite of the unhappy circumstance of her life, God helped her cope by giving her another son. With Reuben, "God saw"; with Simeon, "God heard." She felt that God had still not forgotten her in her distress.

Malachi quoted God at the beginning of his book (see Malachi 1:2-3), using the same comparative expression ("loved"—"hated") with respect to Esau and Jacob, and especially of the outcome of the path the descendants of each man chose to follow. Each brother and his descendants had input to their own destinies. Esau and his descendants chose to live lives that led to an "inheritance to the desert jackals" (Malachi 1:3). On the other hand, Jacob and his descendants always had a remnant that merited God's "love" (or "loved more") category, though indeed there were times they tested God's love by their actions. Paul quotes the Malachi passage in Romans 9:13. God had gifted both Esau and Jacob while they were still in their mother's womb, not as a son doomed to be hated ("loved less") and a son destined to be loved ("loved more"), but with propensities in both sons that could, by sin's dominance, be led astray. Each son's destiny was a mixture of unmerited grace and merited favor connecting his name with the verb meaning "has heard."

Still yearning for more attention, when the third son arrived Leah hoped that **at last my husband will become attached to me.** The name **Levi** sounds like the Hebrew word for "attached." Why Jacob continued to cohabit with Leah when he loved her less is not stated. She was mothering the sons he wanted, yet this still was not endearing her to her husband. The name of her fourth son, **Judah,** was a title not related to a loveless relationship, but expressing "praise" to the Lord for His mercy in allowing her to bear children. This might indicate that Leah realized she could never obtain what she might consider her fair share of Jacob's love, so she praised God for His part in giving her sons. The last phrase of Genesis 29 states that **she stopped having children** (29:35). That statement's thrust may be that Jacob simply stopped having sexual relations with Leah until she petitioned him in 30:16.

God showed his care for Leah. He gave her the children that all women wanted in that day, and without which she would have been far more miserable. As well, her third son became the father of the Levites and priests, and it was from her fourth son that David, the successive kings of Judah, and ultimately the Messiah would come.

With the birth of each son, probably one for each of the first four years of Jacob's marriage to Leah, Rachel came to envy her sister to the point that she was ready to die, or so she told Jacob (see 30:1). She knew her lack of fertility was not because of her husband, who had already fathered sons. In the Bible, children were considered a special gift from God. Rachel's desperate retort was out of place. She should have uttered a prayer rather than a protest. Jacob's angry answer let Rachel know that he believed it was God who had intervened and caused her barrenness. Jacob did not recognize that God was responding to Jacob's inattention to Leah and that God knew Rachel wanted children for the wrong reason.

Desperate to have a child by any means possible, Rachel presented her maid Bilhah to Jacob, saying literally, "She can bear children for me" (30:3). As with Sarah earlier who gave her maid Hagar to Abraham (see 16:1-2), Rachel thought she could adopt the child of her maid. Rachel would rear this child as her own. Both Sarah and Rachel were guilty of taking matters into their own hands rather than waiting on God to act.

Sarah had been quite unhappy with the birth of Ishmael, largely because of the attitude of Hagar, and blamed Abraham for doing what she had told him to do (see 16:4-5). Rachel, on the other hand, rejoiced at the birth of Bilhah's son, and felt that through this baby God had vindicated her (see 30:6). She named him **Dan** (meaning "judged me") to indicate judgment by God in her favor. She had prayed to God and said in 30:6, **[He] has listened to my plea.** Perhaps at long last Rachel realized her complaining had not served her well. She finally turned to God in a request for a child, and God permitted Dan's birth through her maid.

Soon after the birth of Dan, Bilhah gave birth to her second son, whom Rachel named **Naphtali** (30:8). Rachel chose this name, for she had wrestled with God about Leah and had prevailed. The word meaning "mighty wrestling" (see 30:8) indicated an intensification on Rachel's part over the earlier "voice" God heard from her before the birth of Dan. **Naphtali** reflects her presumed victory over her sister.

But jealousy in the family does not die easily. Leah matched Rachel's actions by giving her maidservant Zilpah to Jacob. Zilpah then gave birth to his seventh son, **Gad,** a name meaning "good fortune"—again Leah's appraisal at the birth of the child. The name **Asher** was given to the eighth son of Jacob, second to Zilpah. This name means "with my happiness."

The competition for Jacob's attention through the birth of the eight sons so far was not abated. We are allowed to learn of greater manipulation to gain fertility on the part of Leah and Rachel.

The days of **wheat harvest** (30:14) in Israel were March or April. At that time of the year, the oldest child—Reuben, son of Leah—went out in the field and discovered a yellow fruit that grew near the ground and had the appearance of a tomato. These were given the name of "love apples," translated in this passage as **mandrakes** (30:14). These were believed to increase fertility—at least Rachel believed they would help her. She haggled with Leah over them. Genesis 30:22 reveals that the fruit had little to do with Rachel's ability to give birth to a son; it was rather God's doing.

Leah gave birth to her fifth son, whom she named **Issachar,** a word that sounds like the Hebrew word for "reward." With this name, Leah referred to the fact that this son was her payment for having given her maid to Jacob. Later a sixth son was born to Leah. The name he received was **Zebulun,** for Leah believed that this son, a "valuable gift," would cause her husband to **treat me with honor** (30:20).

Genesis 30:21 is almost parenthetical in its description of the birth of a daughter, **Dinah.** The text gives no background to the meaning of this name, as it had with all the sons, maybe because she was a daughter or because the meaning—"vindication"—was rather obvious to the first readers. Normally, daughters were not even mentioned, but in this case, the author was preparing readers for a subsequent event described in Genesis 34.

This section in Genesis closes with Rachel finally happy. She bore a son because **God remembered** her (30:22). The time span of misery for Rachel was likely the entire seven-year period of her marriage. Needless to say, she was glad her time had come. The name **Joseph** signified for her that **God has taken away my disgrace** (30:23), and she followed the baby's naming with a prayer for the future: **May the Lord add to me another son** (30:24). In time, God answered that prayer, but the next birth cost Rachel her life.

While God did not inspire the writers of the Old Testament to condemn multiple marriages, their writings certainly show the disasters that resulted from them. Jacob would live to regret his demotion of Leah and her sons to secondary status. He also would grieve for making Joseph his favorite son. God always responds to a faithful and obedient heart. But when looking at the fallible people of Genesis, we see that His will is accomplished in spite of their sinfulness and not always because of their goodness. His grace is made available not on the basis of human merit but rather on the basis of His overriding mercy.

## 5. JACOB AND HIS "BARGAIN" (30:25-43)

The birth of Joseph coincided with the fourteenth year of labor Jacob had completed as a bride price for both Leah and Rachel (see Genesis 29:30). Jacob had hoped to complete his agreed-upon amount of labor in half that time (see 29:18). It was doubled because of Laban's trickery. In expressing his desire to leave for home, Jacob did not make demands but rather asked permission to leave: **Send me on my way . . . to my own homeland** (30:25). Yet it was a straightforward request without even a "please." The words could have been spoken tersely. But Laban had come to realize that Jacob's departure would leave a huge hole in his operation, and, furthermore, he had recognized how much **the LORD has blessed me because of you** (30:27). The New International Version quotes Laban as saying, "**I have learned [this] by divination.**" Since God had prospered him, it is less likely that Laban had resorted to a magical omen. He could plainly see what God had done through Jacob's labors. Perhaps a better translation of Laban's words would be, "I have observed the signs, and the Lord has blessed me because of you."

Laban used both courtesy and cunning in replying to Jacob. He was most polite in ignoring Jacob's request to leave. Laban knew his present status was largely the result of Jacob's fourteen years of labor. So he offered, **Name your wages, and I will pay them** (30:28).

Jacob reminded Laban of the tremendous increase in animals that had occurred during the years Jacob has been in charge and how **the LORD has blessed you wherever I have been** (30:30). "But," Jacob continues, "I am also interested in doing **something for my own household.**" Laban quickly responded, **What shall I give you?** (30:31). The reply indicated that he had no plans to give Jacob anything if he left. It would have been normal to give Jacob a parting gift; this was not in Laban's mind. Even after another six years of labor, Laban still claimed livestock belonging to Jacob by previous agreement: "[Your] flocks are my flocks. All you see is mine" (31:43). Only if Jacob stayed and continued to work would Laban offer him wages. Such a situation left Jacob with no choice but to stay, for he could not make it back home if he left with nothing.

At that point, Jacob appears to have learned that he had caused many of his own problems. They had come as punishments for what he had done in the past. It must be understood that God was not the source of the punishment. It was an automatic result of his deviousness. God never holds grudges after He forgives, but sin usually has its own repercussions. Jeremiah underscored this principle on three different occasions when he wrote, "Your own conduct and actions have brought this upon you" (Jer. 4:18). "Your wickedness will punish you; your backsliding will rebuke you" (Jer. 2:19). "Am I the one they are provoking? declares the LORD. Are they not rather harming themselves, to their own shame?" (Jer. 7:19).

Jacob chose to continue working for Laban and at a very modest wage. Their agreement was as follows: Jacob would go through the flock and separate out all the variegated or irregularly colored sheep and goats; he would take for his wages all the multicolored animals. In addition, any dual-colored animals born in the future would be Jacob's wages as well. Indeed, it appeared Jacob had learned his lesson. He had to have known that, on average, every fifth sheep or goat born would be variegated in color. To receive only twenty percent of the offspring would be less than normal wages for a shepherd in that day.

Laban readily agreed, obviously thinking his herds would grow four times faster in the future than those of Jacob. And to craftily insure Jacob's wages would begin at nothing, before Jacob could go out into the field and claim his irregularly colored animals, Laban went there first and, after removing them, left them **in the care of his sons** (30:35). Then **he put a three-day journey between himself and Jacob** (30:36). This is the first indication that Laban had sons. It is probable that they had been born after Jacob had arrived, and thus their ages were thirteen years or younger. Among social customs known to have existed during this time when fathers had no sons, a landless man who wanted to become a son-in-law was adopted so as to be able to render services in payment for the expected bride price.[5] How it relates to this incident is that usually there was a stipulation that if subsequent brothers to the daughter were born, they would take precedence over the adopted son-in-law. We will see an even greater significance of this in 31:19.

There was nothing Jacob could do about Laban's deceptive tactics. Jacob had made a verbal, binding agreement to remove all the variegated-in-color animals that he found in the field as his wages, but when he went there, none were to be found. By then, Laban had set a distance of as much as sixty miles between them. Realizing his verbal arrangement had been carried out, Jacob kept his agreement **to tend the rest of Laban's flocks** (30:36), which now were made up of only pure white sheep and pure black goats.

Jacob's concern, now that he had been outsmarted again, was how he could increase his pay in animals. His only hope was to get solid color animals to have spotted offspring. Jacob was an experienced shepherd, for he had kept sheep since childhood. He took **fresh-cut branches from poplar, almond and plane trees,** peeled them in such a way as to expose **the white inner wood,** and put them **in all the watering troughs** of the animals so he could influence the mating of the flocks (30:37-38). While Jacob may have been a party to breeding methods that escape modern nonfarming readers, it is quite clear in the next chapter of Genesis, as the Lord revealed to Jacob in a dream (see 31:10-12), that the Lord himself saw that Jacob was rewarded.

Jacob was keen enough to realize that by crossbreeding the animals the way he did (see 30:37-40), according to the laws of heredity, he would increase his flocks twenty-five percent over what would otherwise have occurred without his selective breeding procedures. In addition, 30:41-42 describes how Jacob's breeding method was applied in such a way as to ensure that the stronger offspring would be his, while the weaker would be Laban's. Jacob did not use deception as Laban had done; he simply applied his keen knowledge of animal husbandry and trusted the Lord to help him outwit Laban.

Both Jacob and the author of Genesis knew that in reality God was fulfilling the promises that He had given Jacob at Bethel (see 28:13-15). This serves as a vivid illustration that God is not hindered by crafty deceivers, that He sees justice is done, and that His promises come to pass regardless of all attempts to hinder Him.

## ENDNOTES

[1] Howard F. Vos, *Genesis and Archaeology* (Grand Rapids, Michigan: Zondervan Publishing House, 1985), footnote p. 93.

[2] Compare the New Testament example of Joseph and Mary (Matthew 1:18; Luke 1:27).

[3] Except in the book of Job, one is hard pressed to find elsewhere in the Old Testament the understanding between God's directive actions and His permissive will. This may have been more the influence of the pagan idea that the "gods" caused everything. There can be no doubt that God influenced Rachel's infertility, but had a modern gynecologist given her a physical, he or she likely could have given a medical explanation as to why she was barren. Even Job, who could not know that God had allowed Satan to cause his loss of wealth, afterwards attributed the event to God's taking it away (see Job 1:21). This explanation does not put God in a position of being unfair in causing Rachel's barrenness for something Jacob was doing in slighting Leah. Rachel's barrenness and later Leah's were somewhat emotionally as well as physically influenced. God, able to do all things, did relieve the barrenness when He deemed it worthy.

Jacob favored Rachel, which caused his inattention to Leah, but she found solace in God. In rather quick fashion, she became the mother to Jacob's first four sons.

[4] The actual Hebrew rendering is that Rachel was "loved" while Leah was "hated." These words were a literary Hebraism to show relationships within love. These "love" and "hate" words here are a typical Hebrew expression of that time to compare not the extremes as they reflect in today's usage but a relationship *within* the limits of "love." They were meant to reveal a love of Rachel that was partially taken from what should have been given to Leah, the inevitable result of multiple mates.

[5] D. Winton Thomas, *Archaeology and Old Testament Study* (London: Oxford University Press, 1967), p. 74.

# 23

# THE GREAT ESCAPE

## Genesis 31:1-55

We do not know how Jacob was made aware of the brooding of the sons of Laban as to what had happened in the ensuing six years, but their assessment was that **Jacob has taken everything our father owned** (Gen. 31:1). While this was an overstatement, it showed Jacob that there were dark clouds gathering around him. If the sons were preteen-agers when Laban separated the flocks (see 30:35), at this point they were in their late teens and beginning to think about the impact all this would have on their inheritance. In spite of the legitimacy of what Jacob had done, it was evident to him that Laban, too, had an entirely different attitude. It must have soured significantly when Laban realized that all his deceptive craftiness was coming to naught, and yet his hands were tied by the verbal agreement he had made (see 30:34).

## 1. JACOB DECIDES TO LEAVE (31:1-21)

After he had wrest from his father the blessing intended for Esau, Jacob had had to flee to escape harm at the hands of Esau. When he had arrived at Bethel, he had reached a place of desperation. There, God had appeared to him. At this much later point, when Jacob faced trouble again, the Lord reappeared to him with instructions. These words were exactly what Jacob wanted to hear: **Go back to the land of your fathers and to your relatives, and I will be with you** (31:3). Jacob wasted no time in responding.

He called Rachel and Leah to **come out to the fields where his flocks were** pasturing. This might well indicate that Jacob did not want his conversation to be overheard by any servant loyal to Laban. Not only was it a critical time for Jacob to leave, but because of the situation he could not seek Laban's permission to leave, lest it end in Jacob's demise.

Aware that the loyalty of either wife—especially Leah, who had been at best neglected by Jacob—could be leaning toward their father, Jacob went to some length to convince them of the necessity for them to return to his homeland.[1] He began by saying something they could both agree to: **Your father's attitude toward me is not what it was before** (31:5). In effect, Jacob was saying that what had happened was not his fault. At the same time, he was not criticizing Laban, but notice all the way through his speech that Jacob always referred to Laban as **your father** (31:5-7, 9). In what Jacob said, there was a contrast between "their father" and **the God of my father,** whom he says, **has been with me** (31:5).

Jacob reminded his wives of how hard he had worked for their father, **with all my strength** (31:6). He told them of how their father had cheated (more accurately, "made a fool of") him, **changing my wages ten times** (31:7). And, he added, how it was really God who had acted for him— **taken away your father's livestock and has given them to me** (31:9). Jacob followed with the dream he had had **in breeding season** (31:10), telling Rachel and Leah that the angel of the Lord had revealed to him how God had ensured that his flocks grew in proportion to Laban's. Following this, Jacob informed them of the divine messenger's command to immediately return **to [his] native land** (31:13).

Astutely, Jacob said nothing about Laban's sinister plan to force Jacob to work an additional seven years and to marry both women, for that could have revived painful memories, especially for Leah. Jacob had to have Leah's support as much as Rachel's. Jacob also did not mention why he had come to this region: the deadly designs of Esau. This could have made both women more fearful of his plan to return. Yet all his carefully planned arguments were unnecessary to both wives. They supported Jacob fully, for Laban had treated them **as foreigners** (31:15). Their question, **Do we still have any share in the inheritance of our father's estate** (31:14), seems also to imply that since their brothers had been born, they were expecting to receive no inheritance. And furthermore, they added, the dowry that Jacob had worked out years before was supposed to have come to them. Instead of giving it to them, they said, their father had **used up what was paid for us.** While this information is new to the readers, it may not have been new to Jacob. Laban's chicanery had been indiscriminate. His daughters had suffered from it, too.

Having gained the full support of his wives, Jacob hurriedly placed them on camels, put his herds at the front of the group, and collected everything else he had accumulated over twenty years, readying his departure. He had chosen the right time, for **Laban had gone to shear his sheep** (31:19), apparently traveling a three-days' journey to accomplish that task (31:22). Genesis 31:19 indicates that before the entourage left, **Rachel stole her father's household gods.** She acted alone. Neither Jacob nor Leah knew what Rachel had done.

# 2. LABAN PURSUES HIS "GODS" (31:22-32)

From the clay tablets found in Mesopotamia, one learns that it was common for a father of (only) daughters to adopt a son-in-law who would then at the father's death inherit his estate. However, if sons were born into the family subsequently, they took precedence over the earlier adoption.[2] This might explain Rachel's strategy in taking the household gods before leaving her home, for it can be found in the tablets that these gods represented the title deeds to the family property. Rachel must have reasoned something like this: "It is not fair! My husband was to inherit our father's property until my brothers were born. It really belongs to him. I will take these title deeds for Jacob."

Laban made a Herculean effort to halt Jacob before he made it back to his homeland (Jacob had a three-day start; see 31:22) and caught him in seven days (see 31:23).[3] The lost gods were Laban's most important concern.[4] The text gives no indication that these were actually used by Laban or were venerated by Rachel for the purpose of worship, though if they were, this might explain Laban's devious dealings with both daughters and Jacob for the preceding twenty years. His respect of the Lord may have been shaky at best.

Laban wanted to hurt Jacob as soon as he caught him, as Laban's words make clear, **I have the power to harm you** (31:29), but he added that God disturbed his sleep **last night,** telling him to **be careful not to say anything to Jacob, either good or bad.**

Laban accused Jacob of a long list of crimes, deception, kidnapping as in wartime, secrecy, and betrayal in not even allowing him the normal parting festivities and good-bye kisses. Then one can almost feel the explosion in Laban's loaded question, **But why did you steal my gods?** (31:30). If these gods represented title deeds to property, Laban saw a theft of enormous proportions. The ownership of his entire estate was in jeopardy. He was sure his gods were in the possession of someone in Jacob's company, but he lacked more specific knowledge. Perhaps the servant who had run to inform him of Jacob's departure had also discovered that Laban's gods had vanished from their usual location. Laban really believed he owned all of Jacob's herds, but as yet Laban had said nothing about them. He wanted his gods above all else.

Jacob also recognized the enormity of the disappearance of the gods, for he affirmed that **if you find anyone who has your gods, he shall not live** (31:32). He did not know Rachel had them, so he had actually pronounced a death penalty on his beloved wife! Sure that no one had them, Jacob gave Laban permission to search for **anything of yours here with me;** and if he found it, he could **take it.**

## 3. JACOB AND LABAN ARGUE (31:33-42)

After Laban searched diligently through the tents of Jacob, Leah, and the two maidservants, **he entered Rachel's tent** (31:33). Rachel had taken them and secured them **inside her camel's saddle** upon which she was sitting. She watched her father rummage through everything in the tent. Then, as soon as he turned toward her, probably glancing at the saddle, she told him she could not stand because "I'm having my period" (31:35). As she had hoped, that was enough to prevent Laban from going through her saddlebags.

After this frenzied search had produced nothing, Jacob's anger exploded with the words, **What is my crime? What have you found that belongs to your household? Put it here in front of your relatives and mine, and let them judge between the two of us** (31:36-37). Jacob was so convinced of his innocence that he asked for **[our] relatives** to act as a third party to pass judgment upon both of them. Then, before Laban could reply, Jacob began describing all he had done for Laban, even to the extent of bearing the loss of his animals when their loss was not his fault. As Jacob had earlier told his wives, he now told Laban in front of everyone, **You changed my wages ten times** (31:41). Jacob concluded his speech with an accusation—which Laban knew all to well to be true—that had it not been for God's intervention, Laban would have sent him **away empty-handed** (31:42). To drive the point home, Jacob told him it was the same God that **last night . . . rebuked you.**

## 4. JACOB AND LABAN MAKE A COVENANT (31:43-55)

Laban had met his match. He was trapped. He knew he had to surrender his daughters, his grandchildren, and all the flocks Jacob claimed, which he said really belonged to him. In fact, Laban said,

**All you see is mine** (Gen. 31:43). But he knew he had lost it all when he admitted, **Yet what can I do . . . ?** But a solution to his most vexing problem, the loss of his gods, came to his mind. He suggested, **Let's make a covenant . . . and let it serve as a witness between us** (31:44).

One can feel the tension in Jacob's lack of response to Laban. Instead Jacob took action. He set up a stone as a pillar. He then told his relatives to make a stone heap around the base of the **pillar.** Numerous stone pillars have been found throughout Israel. From such evidence "it is clear that the erection of such pillars was a common practice in those times. These pillars were erected to commemorate important events, such as a divine manifestation (28:18) or a military victory, as well as to solemnize a vow (as here), or to keep alive the memory of some ancestor or other notable person."[5]

Laban and Jacob shared a covenant meal together to serve the purpose of sealing their agreement. Laban's native language was Aramaic, so he named the pillar **Jegar Sahadutha** (31:47), meaning "witness heap." Jacob, though bilingual, used his native Hebrew in calling it **Galeed,** which had the same meaning. Perhaps he intentionally used Hebrew instead of the Aramaic he had likely been speaking for the previous twenty years. This may have been one way that Jacob was signaling the severing of any further connection with Laban.

The greatest concern on Laban's mind was that the title deeds to his property were no longer in his possession. For that reason, he established, **This heap is a witness, and this pillar is a witness, that I will not go past this heap to your side to harm you and that you will not go past this heap and pillar to my side to harm me** (31:52). Laban was not concerned about possible physical harm coming from Jacob. He knew that, with those gods, Jacob held the potential for the greater harm, which was underscored by the fact that Jacob was the only one to take the oath (see 31:53b). Jacob did not find this oath difficult, for he had no designs on Laban's estate.

Much has been conjectured as to what Jacob meant by the phrase **Fear of Isaac,** used not only here in the Bible but also in Genesis 31:42 (and in the original Hebrew only in 31:53.) Isaac was too nonaggressive throughout his entire life to inspire fear in anyone. The best translation seems to be that Jacob was taking the oath **in the name of** the One God of Isaac who inspired dread.

The meal in 31:54 was likely the same meal mentioned in 31:46. Genesis 31:54 also describes a sacrifice, an essential component of the covenant made. The meat would have included the animal they had just sacrificed. This encounter cleared the air for both Jacob and Laban. Each had guaranteed respect for the other's family and land. This allowed a night of sleeping in peace and a parting the next morning with the normal kissing and blessing of Laban's daughters and grandchildren, after which Laban began his trek back home.

<h2 style="text-align:center">ENDNOTES</h2>

[1]Jacob needed to be assured that neither wife would be reluctant to go with him. Rachel had been passed over by her father so Leah would be his pay for the first seven years of labor (see 29:21-26). She also had blamed Jacob at one point for her own barrenness (see 30:1-2). Leah had felt always second in importance to Rachel.

[2]G. Ernest Wright, *Biblical Archaeology*, rev. ed. (Philadelphia: Westminster Press, 1962), p. 44. Other documents, such as the Emar texts, also affirm the connection between household gods and the estates of heirs.

[3]The seven days are intended to mean something like "extended period," for the distance between the city of Haran and the hill country of Gilead, where Laban finally caught up with Jacob, is on a straight line, 350 miles apart. Laban could not have covered a distance of seventy miles a day.

[4]See Genesis 31:25-30. Laban concluded his long speech with "but why did you steal my gods?"

[5]Gonzalo Baez-Camargo, *Archaeological Commentary on the Bible* (New York: Doubleday and Co., Inc., 1981), p. 21.

# Part Ten

# FOCUS ON THE NEW JACOB

## Genesis 32:1–37:1

Samuel Johnson (1709–1784), an English lexicographer, essayist, and poet, once said, "Wickedness is always easier than virtue, for it takes the short cut to everything."[1] This quote describes the early years of Jacob's life. He let his craftiness control his actions, causing him to achieve—by his own manipulation alone—what God, in His time and in His way, would have given him. Had Jacob been more patient, he would have avoided much of the misery, sorrow, and uncertainty of his interaction with both Esau and Laban. Jacob learned the hard way, over the twenty years in Laban's country, that something inside him made him choose wrong routes over right roads. He discovered something inside him that seemed to fight God rather than cooperate with Him. Fortunately, God still had been watching over Jacob during all those years.

As Jacob started again toward home after Laban's departure, he worried how Esau might still view his deceptive acts against him twenty years before. Jacob had his guesses. "Does he still harbor a murderous hatred toward me? Will he seek and find me wherever I go? Might he take out his vengeance on members of my family and let me suffer the grief of it for the rest of my life?" Jacob knew he needed God in the worst way, and God knew it, too.

### ENDNOTE

[1]Rhoda Thomas Tripp, *The International Thesaurus of Quotations* (New York: Thomas Y. Crowell Publishers, 1970), item 1048, p. 12.

231

# 24

# JACOB'S NEW NATURE

## Genesis 32:1–33:17

Verse 1 of Genesis 32 continues rather soon after 31:55. Laban returned to his home; **Jacob went on his way** toward Canaan, but was met by **angels of God** (32:1). God was aware of the turmoil of Jacob's soul and undoubtedly had sent the angels. They said nothing. Jacob recognized them and immediately named the place **Mahanaim,** meaning "two camps." Why did Jacob choose this name? The appearance of the heavenly visitors was meant to reassure Jacob that God was still with him. The angels knew he was headed for another most trying experience. Since the phrase "two camps" normally would have a military connotation, it could be that Jacob saw two armies of angels, and he recognized their purpose and good intentions on his behalf.

### 1. JACOB WITH GOD (32:1-32)

Jacob's immediate concern as he continued his movement south was how Esau would take his brother's return after a twenty-year absence. Jacob probably thought that Esau had neither forgotten nor forgiven him for his duplicity. He could not wait until they met face-to-face, so he sent **messengers ahead of him to his brother Esau [in] Edom** (32:3). Jacob wanted the messengers to know he was not coming to Esau as **master,** but as if Jacob were Esau's **servant,** for he told the messengers, **"This is what you are to say to my master Esau: 'Your servant Jacob says'"** (32:4).

Jacob also wanted Esau to know that although Jacob had been given the leadership blessing from his father that had been intended for Esau, and though the birthright Jacob had bought from Esau allowed Jacob a double portion of inheritance, Jacob actually had left with no animals at all. And Jacob wanted it known that he was not returning to claim his share, for he had his own **cattle and donkeys, sheep and goats, menservants and maidservants.** As Jacob returned, his intent was to **find favor** (literally, "grace") **in [Esau's] eyes** (32:5). Jacob spoke out of fear induced by a guilty conscience and wanted to find some way to correct his position with Esau. He hinted further that his lengthy stay away was because **I have been staying with Laban and have remained there until now** (32:4). More correctly, Jacob had been "working for" not "staying with" Laban. Jacob's remaining there so long was less his choice than Laban's requirement.

Several days passed before the messengers returned. Jacob must have spent many anxious hours fearing the worst but praying for the best. He may well have read the messengers' demeanor as they came into sight. Their message was not going to be as Jacob had hoped. Rather than a report of Esau's glad reception of his brother, Esau was on his way with **four hundred men** (32:6). Jacob must have known how his brave grandfather used only 318 men to defeat four kings and their armies, but that gave him little courage at this moment.

Jacob did not plan to meet force with force but planned simply to survive with as many of his people as possible. Every person and animal was put into one of two groups with the idea that **if Esau comes and attacks one group, the group that is left may escape** (32:8). After Jacob acted expediently with all that he had, he then prayed quite an exemplary prayer. He began and ended with God, and in the middle he quoted God's promise to him, noting how the Lord had fulfilled that promise. God had taken Jacob from ownership of only a shepherd's staff twenty years ago to the place where his family and possessions now formed two large groups. When Jacob claimed he was **undeserving,** he literally said to the Lord, "I am little" (32:10). The word **undeserving** is normally used of one who lacks credentials and is completely dependent on another. This word aptly described Jacob's situation! He could not claim anything with Esau, and he really could depend on no one but God himself.

Jacob planned (32:7-8), prayed (32:9-12), then planned more (32:13-21), prayed again (32:22-32), and planned still more (33:1-3). While Jacob's own activity was elaborate, he should not be condemned for lacking faith—for God approves of planning that does not substitute for dependence on Him.

Jacob could not know how quickly the "army" of Esau would approach. He spent the entire night waiting and preparing. He separated 550 of his animals. Jacob may have been attempting to give Esau the extra half of the inheritance Esau would have received in the birthright transaction, even though Jacob had left home without even the animals that would have been his as the younger son's inheritance.

Jacob demonstrated his fear for his life by sending everything to precede him: animals first, in five separate groups, led by servants who would offer the flocks to Esau as Jacob's gifts. Jacob hoped the gifts would **pacify** Esau (32:20). Next went groups of Jacob's family and other servants, each of whom affirmed that the animals were **gifts** Jacob was **sending** (32:18, 20). Finally Jacob would go later at quite a distance, for **he himself spent the night in the camp** (32:21), staying on the north side of the Jabbok River.

Suddenly, after everyone else had left, without a warning to Jacob, **a man** appeared in the darkness and they wrestled until morning (32:24). Could Jacob have thought he was wrestling against Esau for his life? Had Jacob known his visitor was divine, he might not have entered a wrestling match. After some time, when Jacob was about to win at least a draw, his visitor **touched the socket of Jacob's hip,** dislocating it. At that point, the heavenly visitor spoke: **Let me go, for it is daybreak** (32:26). The writer subsequently identified the visiting wrestler as God (see 32:28). Why would God engage in such a match? It indeed showed Jacob's tenacity in the engagement, but there was no way God would let him win. God felt concern that at daybreak Jacob would look into His face. Could Jacob have survived that experience?

Whatever Jacob may have assumed during the time of his struggle with the **man,** he came to realize that his opponent was more than human. In his desperation, Jacob refused to let go **unless you bless me.** God then asked, **What is your name?** (32:27). Why would God need to ask? So that Jacob would reveal his deceitful and grasping nature that began at birth and had plagued him ever since. In speaking his name, Jacob would confess that he had cheated Esau. Had he not suffered enough for that sin? Oh yes, but God wanted him to deal with the cause behind all of his deceptive ways—his old sinful character. God wanted to change Jacob, so He could change his future destiny. In the Hebrew culture, a character change merited a name change (see 17:5, 15). God changed Jacob's name to **Israel** (32:28). No longer would others know Jacob as "one who takes by the heel" (25:26). From that point on, they would see him (by the sound of his new name) as "you have struggled with God and succeeded" (and prophetically, "now you succeed with people").[1] Jacob's new name told him that something deeply spiritual had happened inside him; God was remedying his carnal character flaws.

W. Robertson Nicoll pictures graphically the struggle that took place:

> All this self-confidence culminates now, and in one final and sensible struggle, his Jacob-nature, his natural propensity to wrest what he desired and win what he aims at, from the most unwilling opponent, does its very utmost and does it in vain. His steady straining, his dexterous feints, his quick gusts of vehement assault, make no impression on this combatant and move him not one foot off the ground. Time after time his crafty nature puts out all its various resources, now letting his grasp relax and feigning defeat, and then with gathered strength hurling himself on the stranger, but all in vain.[2]

When Jacob sensed he was struggling with someone divine, he must have wondered, "Is this really God or some angel? I must know." **Please tell me your name** (32:29), he said. The reply, **Why do you ask my name,** probably had the sense of "Jacob, don't you know who I am? I just told you!" (32:28). After Jacob learned the visitor's identity, God blessed him and immediately left.

Believing that in the semidarkness he had seen **God face to face, and yet [his] life was spared** (32:30), Jacob named the place Penial, meaning "the face of God." The Hebrew words make it clear that the sun had not risen, so Jacob had not visually identified God by His face, for "no one has ever seen God" (John 1:18).

As the sun rose, Jacob passed the spot where he had wrestled, and limped as he did. His change-of-character limp would always remind him of this encounter with God. God's people remembered Jacob's limp **to this day** (the day of the author's writing). And observant Jews still **do not eat the tendon attached to the socket of the hip** (32:32) because of that incident.

## 2. JACOB WITH ESAU (33:1-17)

Very soon after Jacob's wrestling ordeal at Penial, and as he caught up to his family, he lifted his head to the horizon and saw in the distance **Esau, coming with his four hundred men** (33:1). Jacob's heart must have frozen, but his mind quickly assessed what he should do. He organized the maidservants with their sons; they were to lead. Then he planned for Leah and her children to follow, and finally, last of all, would follow Rachel and Joseph.

But notice the change! As Esau approached, Jacob walked in front of all three groups. The day before, Jacob carefully had ensured that he would be last to meet Esau. He had wanted his servants, wives, and children all to precede him (see 32:17-21). His fear had dominated his strategy. This day, after his wrestling match with God, he was motivated by a new confidence, and he bravely walked alone toward his brother (although still uncertain that he would live through the confrontation). He stood as only one man against four hundred but as one man newly filled with God's power!

With his new confidence, there was an accompanying contrition. He bowed down seven times, apparently taking a few steps between each bow as he approached Esau. This was a common practice for a vassal meeting his overlord. Jacob took this position even though Isaac's blessing had included these words: "May your mother's sons bow down before you" (27:29). Jacob's humility may have indicated more than recognizing Esau's elder-brother status. Perhaps Jacob hoped Esau would see Jacob's acts as an apology.

If Esau had come to exact vengeance, he had been now totally disarmed. Besides Jacob's multiple bows, Esau would have noticed his brother's limp. Surprised at all the changes in Jacob, Esau dropped any murderous ideas he may have had. Esau ran to **meet Jacob and embraced him; he threw his arms around his neck and kissed him.** Apparently, without either saying a word, **they wept** together (33:4).

When Esau saw Jacob's children coming in groups, he asked, **Who are these with you?** (33:5). Jacob replied with no hint of former craftiness or deceit, but with deferential words. Calling himself **your servant** (33:5) and Esau **my lord** (33:8), Jacob referred to the children as those **God has graciously given** (33:5). Esau's question surely included the identity of the four women, but Jacob adroitly did not mention them. Did he fear that Esau's knowledge of their relationship to Jacob might make Esau more readily recall his purpose for leaving the family twenty years before, which had prevented Esau from exacting what Esau then thought was fair vengeance? Probably, so Jacob chose not to resurrect any of that.

Jacob's servants had already told Esau that Jacob wanted to give him the flocks that led the entourage. Even so, Esau asked Jacob their purpose (see 33:8). Was he testing Jacob, looking for Jacob's earlier deceptive tactics? Whatever the reason for the question, Jacob repeated his offer: They were **gifts** (see 32:18, 20-21); they were **to find favor in your eyes, my lord** (34:8).

Esau appreciated his brother's generosity and returned the favor. Esau announced that he already had **plenty** and that Jacob should keep the animals for himself. But Jacob saw **favor in his [brother's] eyes** as more important than 550 animals. He told Esau to **please accept [them], for God has been gracious to me, [and without them] I have all I need** (33:11). Because of Jacob's insistence, Esau accepted the generous gift.

Esau's next words may have alarmed Jacob: **Let us be on our way; I'll accompany you** (33:12). Was Esau suggesting that they go to Seir (Esau's home) or across the Jordan to their former home? If to Seir, then Jacob could go only for a visit lest he disobey God's command to return home, for he had been told, "Go back to the land of your fathers and to your relatives" (31:3). And Esau said nothing about a mere visit.

Esau might have felt true concern for Jacob's safety, and yet Jacob did not know exactly what his brother was thinking. Jacob's rationale for declining the invitation was reasonable: **The children are tender** (33:13). His oldest child could not have been more than twelve years of age, and Joseph, the youngest, was probably not more than a year old. Also, undoubtedly, during the long trek from Haran, several animals had given birth to young. To go with Esau would make it too hard for everyone.

Esau persisted, offering to leave some of his men behind to travel at a slower speed (see 33:15). **But why do that?** Jacob asked. Then Jacob told Esau that all he wanted was to **find favor in the eyes of my lord** (33:15). Esau finally accepted Jacob's reasoning and started his return to Seir. This encounter included the final recorded conversation between these men. They later did come together at Isaac's funeral, and it appears that the meeting was amiable (see 35:29).

Jacob gave the impression that he would follow along more slowly on his way after Esau had left, but instead Jacob traveled north and west to get to Succoth, even re-crossing the Jabbok River. Yet he seemed to feel no fear, for he settled there for a time, making **shelters for his livestock** (33:17). By the time of the next chapter of Genesis, his children had aged markedly. Perhaps, during that time, Jacob did visit Esau in Seir, but the Genesis account does not indicate this.

Jacob must have felt greatly relieved at the reconciliation between him and Esau. However, he did not want to enter too close an association where painful memories would resurface. He may have surmised that Esau's spiritual barometer measured many degrees lower than his own, and also Seir was not Jacob's "homeland" (31:3). Canaan was where he had been born, had grown to adulthood, and by divine direction was to return. Jacob was simply following a higher calling.

## ENDNOTES

[1]The translation is from the Greek Septuagint.
[2]W. Robertson Nicoll, *The Expositor's Bible,* vol. 1 (New York: Doran), p. 80.

# JACOB'S NEW PROBLEMS

## Genesis 33:18–37:1

Nearly thirty-three years have passed since Jacob fled from Canaan. Jacob likely felt relieved at his escape from danger with respect to his meeting Esau. But he almost immediately entered another situation fraught with potential harm for his whole clan and especially his daughter Dinah, who was defiled by a royal son of the ruler of Shechem. Jacob had apparently hoped to stay in the vicinity of Shechem for a time, attested by his purchase of land (see 33:19), but it would not happen. However long Jacob had hoped to stay, his naïve and venturous daughter, Dinah, thwarted his plans (see 34:1-2). Her violation brought out the brutal, bloodthirsty nature of her brothers, probably accentuated by Jacob's reluctance to take action (see 34:5). Jacob was motivated more by what his sons' actions would do to *him* than he was about the honor of his own daughter (see 34:30). "He (Jacob) may have limped away from Peniel as 'Israel,' but this episode illustrates there remained features of the old 'Jacob.'"[1]

Fortunately for Jacob, God did not forsake him. He instructed Jacob to return to Bethel, where God had appeared to him on his flight from Esau (see 35:1). In order to find repair, Jacob began to take firmer charge of his family, ordering them to divest themselves of any hindrances to an unfettered worship of God. At Bethel, Jacob heard God promise him the **land I gave to Abraham and Isaac** (35:12). This strong affirmation let Jacob know that God was still with him, however much Jacob may have felt he did not deserve it, and God had been faithful in bringing him back to Canaan as He had promised (see 28:15).

241

# 1. JACOB AT SHECHEM (33:18–34:31)

There is not even a hint as to how long Jacob remained at Succoth, but he finally arrived at Shechem, a city about twenty-five miles to the west, where he camped. Why this city? He likely knew that this had been the initial stop Abraham had made so many years before when he had first arrived. Jacob may have known of the altar Abraham had built there, though it likely was not still standing, for Jacob built one of his own (see 33:20). Jacob named the altar Elohe Israel, meaning "God, the God of Israel" and, for Jacob as he used his new name, meaning "God, even my God."

Before Jacob built the altar, he deemed it necessary to purchase land, for which he paid **one hundred pieces of money** ("Kesitahs" in Hebrew). The value of this weight in comparison to the shekel, which was mentioned in connection with Abraham and elsewhere in the Old Testament, is unknown. Therefore, the size of the land Jacob purchased is also unknown. But it appears that Jacob wished to obtain enough land in which to settle, as well as to build his altar to the Lord.

When, twenty years before, Jacob had built an altar at Bethel, Jacob had promised that if God would be with him then the Lord would be his God (see 28:20-21). With the name of this new altar, Jacob was recalling that pledge and affirming that the Lord was, indeed, his God.

Dinah, the only daughter mentioned among the many sons of Jacob, was the daughter of Leah. She was born after Leah had borne her six sons. Dinah was likely as young as six or seven when the extended family left Haran. By the time of this incident, she had become an older teenager or perhaps even a bit older.

The writer introduced the **ruler of the area,** named **Hamor,** who had named his son after the city **Shechem.** We are told that **Shechem took [Dinah] and violated her** (34:2). Then we get the impression that Jacob did not show much concern about what had happened, for we read, **When Jacob heard . . . he kept quiet** (34:5). This helps to explain Simeon and Levi's reaction of **grief and fury** (34:7) and their devious determination to render vengeance on not only the guilty party but also all the men of the town. As additional information, the writer may be indicating that Dinah, in modern parlance, was "asking for it" in that she **went out to visit the women of the land** (34:1). Early Jewish authors considered this comment in the text condemnatory in that it suggests the young girl's indiscretion and carelessness. She certainly rowed her boat too close to strong countercurrents.

Since new waters always seem more inviting, Prince Shechem saw, lusted, and—accustomed to having what he wanted, even if it was beyond conventional reach—forced himself on Dinah. To his credit, he **loved** her, for in the Hebrew we read that "his soul stuck to Dinah." So, in spite of having shamed her, he wanted to observe proper procedures to marry her. Yet the young man showed his immature, impetuous nature as he told his father, **Get me this girl as my wife** (34:4). There was no "please," just a blunt, brusque imperative: "Get me what I want." Also, despite exhibiting tenderness toward Dinah after he had violated her, he referred to her literally as "this child." This derogatory remark shows that Shechem could easily put on different faces, one to Dinah after he had raped her (34:3), another when it came to the household of his father—"most honored" (34:19)—and yet quite another to his father privately (34:4). Probably this last face was his real one, showing a brash and brazen ego. We could say he was a "good actor."

While the next fifteen verses in Genesis 34 reveal what appear on the surface as polite negotiations, they show first that Simeon and Levi could put on an act, too (see 34:13), and second that Dinah was being held virtually a prisoner in Shechem's house (see 34:26). That she was being detained against her will does not in any sense justify what Simeon and Levi did, but it does offer some basis for their devious strategy. They were negotiating under duress. Another important factor to understand is that if this proposed marriage had succeeded, it would have opened the door to a more widespread practice of intermarriage (see 34:9) with the people of the land.

As **the ruler of that area** (34:2), Hamor took his son to mediate with Jacob and his sons. He began the negotiation (see 34:8-10), but rather quickly Shechem took over (see 34:11-12). Shechem's determination to have Dinah was underscored when he told Jacob and his sons that he was willing to pay whatever amount they required.

We cannot know if the sons of Jacob had a concern about circumcision as a religious rite. The plan of Simeon and Levi to require it of all the town's men was intended mostly to put them at a disadvantage so the brothers could attack them during their great discomfort after surgery, **three days later** (34:25). Jacob's sons knew the pain would peak then. They thought there was some possibility that the town's men would balk at the idea, for they planned an alternative: **But if,** they said to Hamor and his son, **you will not agree to be circumcised, we'll take our sister and go** (34:17). This was a veiled threat, to be sure and, regarding the freeing of their sister, one that might well have involved armed conflict.

When the sons of Jacob presented the plan (see 34:15), **their proposal seemed good to Hamor and his son** (34:18), and **they lost no time in doing what they said** (34:19). But how could they get the men of the town to consent to the plan? The two rulers went **to the gate of their city to** convince the others that the plan was a good one (34:20). Hamor and Shechem argued, **We can marry their daughters and they can marry ours** (34:21), which of course Simeon and Levi had promised. The statement was calculated to be more acceptable to the town's men, in that they would believe they would benefit in this way.

But Hamor and Shechem presented another advantage that would appeal to everyone: **Won't their livestock, their property and all their other animals become ours?** (34:23). The father and son appealed to both their lust and their greed. The arguments were accepted by the town's men, and **every male . . . was circumcised** (34:24). Nothing happened until the day (34:25) when the angry Simeon and Levi wielded their swords on the unsuspecting, unarmed, and physically handicapped men of the town. While Simeon and Levi cannot be justified for what they did, the words Hamor and Shechem spoke described a real danger for Jacob's family. Jacob and his family could have lost everything. The end result of all this brought about what God wanted to happen, but again, God had a better way of gaining the goal. Human mechanization can never substitute for divine preference.

Usually the eldest son was expected to be more responsible since, in the absence of the father, he would be in charge. Reuben, the eldest, did not participate in the ensuing carnage, nor did the younger eight sons. Dinah's other four (full) brothers would have had good reason to be participants. But Simeon and Levi alone wielded their swords. All eleven did not hesitate to participate in the looting, however (34:27). The taking of booty in warfare was common, so all the sons may have approved the act as revenge for what had happened to Dinah and for her ongoing captivity. Though Jacob was greatly disturbed, fearing that what had happened would unite the other **people living in the land** against him (34:30), the sons quieted his objections with a question: **Should he have treated our sister like a prostitute?**

We note that Simeon and Levi did not refer to Dinah as "your daughter," but they rather emphasized their own **sister** relationship to her. Tensions in the family by the children of each mother continued after this incident, so possibly Simeon and Levi may have felt that if Dinah had been Rachel's daughter, surely Jacob would have shown more concern. The biting remark of Dinah's brothers, that Dinah's marriage to an uncircumcised man **would be a disgrace to us** (34:14), was likely directed at Jacob's actions as much as to those of Prince Shechem.

# 2. JACOB AT BETHEL AGAIN (35:1-15)

Perhaps with concern for Jacob's safety as well as the need for spiritual repair after the killing and looting of the town, God told Jacob to **go up to Bethel and settle there, and build an altar there** (35:1). The Lord reminded Jacob of having met him there years before when he was fleeing from Esau. Before this occasion, there is no record in Genesis of God's giving instruction for an altar to be built; there was a special need for one after what had happened at Shechem.

Before Jacob told his family of his plans, he commanded them all to **get rid of the foreign gods you have with you, and purify yourselves . . .** (35:2). He further told them to change their clothes, their outer garments. This command related to the battle with Hamor and his company. To what foreign gods did Jacob refer? Perhaps his sons had collected idols in the Shechemite plunder. Another possibility is that Jacob had discovered the household gods taken by Rachel when they all had fled from Haran (see 31:19). In either case, the little figurines might have intrigued Jacob's family enough to want to keep them. There is no record that they had had time to worship them, but curiosity and fascination can be fast tracks to veneration. The idols had to go.

No reason is given as to why they all disposed of their earrings. While Jacob had not requested this, he buried the earrings with the figurines under **the oak at Shechem** (35:4). In subsequent Old Testament stories, gold from such jewelry was used to make idolatrous objects, once with Aaron's golden calf (see Exodus 32) and another time with Gideon's golden ephod (see Judges 8). The association of idols and earrings in this Genesis passage might be for one of two reasons. First is the possibility that the gods they had taken were of the same precious metal, causing the association and the elimination of both the foreign objects of worship and the metal with which they easily could be cast. Second is the possibility that the earrings were part of the loot that had been taken. Maybe even the outer garments Jacob's family members were told to change had formerly been those of the Shechemites. Jacob did not want his household to appear before God at Bethel with any stolen items.

Jacob's fears of the surrounding Canaanites may have been well founded, for God saw it necessary to strike terror in the hearts of the Canaanites to prevent them from pursuing Jacob's family (see 35:5). A lesson Jacob's family likely grasped later was that ready obedience has quick, though sometimes unexpected, results.

After a twenty-mile trip south, Jacob's family arrived at **Luz** (35:6). Jacob had stopped near this city twenty years earlier when he was on his way to Haran. God had given him a dream with angels ascending and descending on a ladder (see 28:10-17). The Lord appeared atop the ladder and spoke to reassure Jacob that though he was leaving the land of his birth as a fugitive, "I [the Lord] will bring you back to this land. I will not leave you until I have done what I have promised you" (28:15). Jacob had named the place Bethel to memorialize that spectacular meeting with the Lord (see 28:19). The author used **Luz,** the original name of the location, but he added, **that is, Bethel** (35:6).

Jacob hastened to build the altar commanded by the Lord. When it was completed, he named it **El Bethel** in remembrance of God's earlier appearance. The Hebrew word **El** denotes God himself. Thus, **El Bethel** indicates "God of Bethel" or "God of the house of God."

Almost parenthetically, mention is made of Rebekah's nurse having died, and for the first time her name is given—Deborah. She had been buried under an oak tree nearby, which had been named Allon Bacuth, meaning "oak of weeping." No mention is made of Rebekah's death, lending to the idea that she had died while Jacob was in Paddan Aram. For emphasis, Jacob's name change to Israel is retold, without reason given for the change. The writer assumed that his readers already knew the reason.

At that point, God spoke to Jacob once again. God repeated many previous promises, but added a commitment: **Kings will come forth from your body** (35:11). God had promised this to Abraham (see 17:6), but not to Jacob. Could it be that, before his Penial experience, Jacob was in no condition to receive this word? As it had been with Abraham (see 17:22), so here. Both times when God had completed His revelation, He **went up from him** (35:13). In whatever form God chose to reveal himself, His presence left Jacob rising. As Jacob had done before at the same place (see 28:18), he set up a pillar and poured oil on it, but this time he added to the solemnity by also pouring a drink offering on the pillar.

# 3. JACOB SUFFERS LOSS (35:16-29)

Shortly after Jacob's worship at Bethel, the family moved farther south, heading toward Hebron, some thirty miles away. Ephrath, an early name for Bethlehem, seems to have been their next intended stop. It was the halfway point between Bethel and Hebron. At this point, the writer offers the information that Rachel was carrying her second son. When she had found out she was pregnant, she must have rejoiced to know that her prayer at Joseph's birth had been answered (see 30:24). The writer gives no description of her joyous days; little did she know how abruptly her life would end.

Jacob's family was still **some distance from Ephrath** (35:16) when Rachel began intense labor pains in delivering her second son. The experience was so severe that she finally gave birth at the expense of her own life. After having been informed of the birth, and before breathing her last breath, Rachel named her son **Ben-Oni,** meaning "son of my misfortune."

Jacob did not want to be reminded of Rachel's tragic death every time he called his young son's name, so he changed it to **Benjamin,** meaning "the son of my right hand." Jacob likely associated his right hand with the ideas of "good fortune" and "strength," similar to today's idea of "the right hand of fellowship." He wanted to reverse Rachel's dying thought and replace it with his finding strength through his new son. Jacob's experience of losing his wife at the birth of Benjamin likely endeared him more to his youngest son.

The traditional spot for Rachel's burial is presently one mile north of Bethlehem. Generally, scholars suggest she more likely died north of Jerusalem, or at least eight miles north of Bethlehem. As far as the Scriptural description goes—**some distance from Ephrath**—the traditional spot would seem just as valid as one farther away.

Jacob memorialized the grave of Rachel by setting up a pillar, which the writer said was there **to this day** (35:20), meaning the day he chronicled the material. If Moses was making the notation, he was emphasizing that the pillar still stood hundreds of years later.

With no desire to linger at the site of mourning, Jacob moved south to **Migdal Eder.** The meaning of the place's name is "tower of the flock." It was mentioned as if the place was a well-known spot at the time of writing, perhaps a place frequented by shepherds. There would have been many of these towers scattered around the country. Micah mentions it (Micah 4:8), maybe in his mind the same one, in a messianic context of Jerusalem and Bethlehem. This could be the place designated by Jeremiah (see Jeremiah 31:15).[2] Since only these three Bible passages mention this place, it is impossible to precisely identify the spot, but it must have served Jacob during his time of grief.

A most unfortunate incident occurred that brought more grief to Jacob. It may seem to the reader that an unbridled sexual urge motivated Reuben to sleep with his stepmother, Bilhah. Scripture quickly passes by the event to avoid going into sensational details. But when one understands the undercurrents of the culture, the incident takes on a whole new meaning.

Reuben was Jacob's oldest child (born to Leah). He might well have had two reasons for what he did. First, he wanted to prevent Bilhah from taking Rachel's place as the favorite wife, as might otherwise have been expected since Bilhah had been Rachel's maid. Reuben may have felt lingering resentment that Jacob had not favored Leah, his own mother. Reuben also had wanted to assert authority over his father. Much later, a crafty Ahithophel advised Absalom to do a similar thing with David's wives, whom Absalom had left in Jerusalem as his first official act after taking power: "Then all Israel will hear . . . and the hands of everyone with you will be strengthened" (2 Samuel 16:21). Reuben sought to lay a major claim to Jacob's estate, to succeed him as the family patriarch.

Was such a rationale pleasing to God? Certainly not! In the Law given on Mt. Sinai, such an act was forbidden, meriting God's curse (see Deuteronomy 27:20) and even the death penalty (see Leviticus 20:11). Jacob appears to have done nothing about Reuben's act against him, as Jacob had reacted after the violation of Dinah (see Genesis 34:5). Jacob's lack of response might suggest that his authority over his eldest son was beginning to wane. However, later on his deathbed Jacob found courage to turn the traditional blessing of the firstborn into a curse (see 49:3-4).

After giving a summary of Jacob's sons and their mothers, the writer describes how Jacob finally arrived at the place **where Abraham and Isaac had stayed** (35:27), a place known then as Kiriath Arba. The author's last mention of Isaac related to events twenty years prior when Isaac lived in Beersheba (see 28:10). At some intervening point, perhaps after the death of Rebekah, Isaac had left there to settle at Kiriath Arba. There he did not feel alone but rather sensed the closeness of God as in the past (see 13:18; also Genesis 15, 17–18). Of possible importance, too, is that his father, Abraham, had purchased his first plot of land there when he needed a burial place for Sarah (see Genesis 23).

The author gave a notation of the years Isaac lived, then described his funeral, attended by both Jacob and Esau. Perhaps the funeral was mentioned to underscore that though the sons were once time zones apart in their relationship, they had been reconciled just after Jacob's Penial experience (see Genesis 33). And though they no longer lived where they could be in frequent contact, the peace between them held.

A phrase of interest with respect to Isaac's burial is **and [he] was gathered to his people.** The patriarchs lived during a time known to archaeologists as the Middle Bronze Age (roughly 2000 B.C. to 1500 B.C.). Archaeological digs offer much information on burial practices during that time. Cave burials were common and generally in the same cave where the ancestors of earlier generations had been buried. When a new member of the extended clan died, the bones of previous burials—which had been given a central place—were often pushed aside, out of the way, to make a place for the body of the latest member.

The traditional burial site for Abraham, Isaac, and Jacob, with their three wives, Sarah, Rebekah, and Leah, is in Hebron in a cave underneath a building subsequently built by King Herod, just before the time of Christ.

Good had resulted at the funeral of Abraham in that the estranged Ishmael and Isaac were reconciled and attended the event together (see 25:9). Likewise, Esau and Jacob underscore their reconciliation by together laying Isaac to rest (see 35:29).

## 4. THE FAMILY OF ESAU (36:1–37:1)

It is difficult for readers today to wade through long genealogical lists like the ones found in Genesis 36, one of the longest chapters in the entire book of Genesis. Today, with mobility and distant settlement of immediate and extended, family members, it is hard to keep track of even aunts and uncles, let alone cousins and more distant family members. But not "keeping track" so often renders us with a sense of rootlessness. Ancient people maintained stronger family ties. Family trees are extensive in the Bible, where at times names found nowhere else are chronicled. Generally speaking, the listings of Esau's and, to a greater extent, Ishmael's descendants have nothing to do with the flow of covenant promises (after all, all these descendants were born to pagan wives). Yet, the author wanted to show bridges that tied the past to the future.

The eight kings of Edom (see 36:31-39) seem totally superfluous, but since they came through the descendants of Esau, their names may indicate the first fulfillment of the promise made to Abraham of kings ultimately coming from him (see 17:16), a promise subsequently given to Jacob (see 35:11). Also detailed in that promise was the fulfillment of the prophecy of "two nations" given to Rebekah (see 25:23-26). By their spread in time, these kings appear to go beyond the times of the patriarchs,[3] so that Genesis 36 had to have been a later addition, at some point inserted here.

Genesis 37 easily continues where chapter 35 ends. An intriguing suggestion is that after King David had conquered Edom, state archives became available to scribes who felt compelled to include them at the end of information given about Esau.

Verse 1 of Genesis 37 relates to the close of Esau's lineage begun in chapter 36. It also ties chapter 37 to the end of chapter 35, returning to Jacob and preparing readers for the remainder of Jacob's life.

### ENDNOTES

[1]Bill T. Arnold, *Encountering the Book of Genesis* (Grand Rapids, Michigan: Baker Book House, 1998), p. 137.

[2]Jeremiah's mention of Rachel gives the impression that in the hours before her death she suffered more than physical pain alone. She may have wept for the pain of her children and their yet-to-be offspring, all the way to the death of the Bethlehem infants on the orders of King Herod (see Matthew 2:18).

[3]The last king named may be the Hadad that is mentioned as having led a revolt against Solomon (see 1 Kings 11:14-22).

# Part Eleven

# FOCUS ON JOSEPH

## Genesis 37:2–39:23

This section in Genesis begins with the introduction **This is the account of Jacob** (37:2). We recognize that the author had been giving Jacob's account since chapter 27. This introduction, then, might seem to fit better back there. But the author placed it here to show that his primary interest was not in Jacob but rather in Jacob's sons. Even though his emphasis was on Joseph, the rest of Jacob's sons remained important players without whom the Joseph story could not be told. Then, too, without all that was chronicled in these chapters, Jacob's final blessing could not be fully understood (49:1-28). Note also that chapter 50 tells of Jacob's burial.

Jacob was the third of the three patriarchs, the fathers of the faith. With Abraham and Isaac, all other relatives were eliminated from the messianic line. They alone and their immediate descendants were selected. With Jacob, all born to him were included in the family of God's blessing.

When God chose Abraham, He directed him to leave his relatives. With the exception of Lot, Abraham obeyed (see 12:4). The relatives are given additional attention in Scripture when they intersect with Isaac in the selection of Rebekah for his wife (see Genesis 24). They intersect again with Jacob during his twenty-year stay in Haran. Otherwise, they pass from the pages of Scripture. God's main interest was on Abraham, Isaac, and Jacob, excluding extended family members. Afterward, all the descendants of Jacob were included in the chosen race.

Although Joseph receives primary attention through the remainder of Genesis, the messianic line did not pass through him, but rather through Judah. Wonder could be expressed as to why Judah isn't given more attention.  One reason could be that he took the leadership role in getting rid of Joseph (see 37:26), but perhaps another more important one is found in Genesis 38 when Judah begins his venture among the Canaanites.

Joseph had an uncertain beginning.  To his brothers, he seemed a spoiled and arrogant brat, full of boasting.  In the end, he rose to become the top man in Egypt next to the Pharaoh.  In the beginning, he was the one nearly destroyed by his brothers, but eventually he became the means of their salvation and the salvation of uncounted others.  In the words of Gordon Wenhem, "The story of Joseph shows how God's secret providence is behind the darkest deeds of men and works to their ultimate good."[1]

It is striking that, with Joseph, God seems to have moved offstage. Not once did God speak directly or play a direct role in Joseph's fortunes. But "the divine intention underlies the web of events in this drama of conflict among brothers."[2]

### ENDNOTES

[1]Gordon J. Wenhem, *Genesis 16–50,* Word Biblical Commentary, vol. 2 (Dallas: Word Books Publishers, 1994), p. 357.

[2]Christian E. Hauer and William A. Young, *An Introduction to the Bible* (Upper Saddle River, New Jersey: Prentice Hall, 1998), p. 74.

# 26

# JOSEPH: FROM STATUS TO SLAVERY

## Genesis 37:2-36

Joseph, by now a teenager, worked with his older stepbrothers (those born to the servant wives, Bilhah and Zilpah) as a shepherd. Leah's sons were the oldest, but Jacob regarded them like sons of these slave wives. He highly regarded Joseph and Benjamin. They were Rachel's sons. Perhaps Joseph worked with his brothers to keep an eye on them for his father. Or maybe Joseph wanted this assignment to find things out that he could tell Jacob to maintain his own special status with his father.

Jacob had treated Joseph with more favor than all the other sons. This was the situation when the events of Genesis 37 opened. So the brothers' hatred had had years to fester before this time. It exploded in chapter 37 and resulted in Joseph's becoming a slave.

## 1. JEALOUSY OF THE BROTHERS (37:2-11)

The Hebrew description of Joseph's words given to his father—translated **bad report** (Gen. 37:2)—suggests that Joseph slanted the information he gave Jacob, stretching the truth at best, or possibly flat out lying.

Jacob did nothing to hide his preference for Joseph, and he emphasized it by giving Joseph a badge of favoritism, **a richly ornamented robe** (37:3). Evidently, Jacob transferred the love he had had for Rachel to Benjamin and especially Joseph since he was the older of the two. How sad that Jacob did not recognize how a robe would make a bad situation worse.

(From this point, both titles "Jacob" and "Israel" are used for the father, but "Jacob" is the most frequently found.[1] If a pattern is found, it may be in that when Jacob is seen as the spiritual leader of the clan, "Israel" is preferred, but when he is referred to in his human weakness, "Jacob" is used.

The King James Version refers to the garment as one of "many colors," carried over in the New American Standard Bible as "varicolored." This picture comes from both the early Latin and Greek translations of Genesis. The words **richly ornamented** found in the New International Version were influenced by the only other biblical use of the Hebrew word (see 2 Samuel 13:18) where it describes the robe of a princess. A tomb painting, found 170 miles south of Cairo at a place called Beni Hasán, shows a group of people, thirty-seven in all, who lived during the time of Abraham, coming to Egypt for the purpose of obtaining food. The men and women shown in the painting wear multicolored garments. A few wear all-white clothes. This might lend weight to the translation, "varicolored."

The hatred of the brothers toward Joseph was now to the point that they could not speak one word of kindness about him or to him (see Genesis 37:4). Then Joseph, lacking sensitivity, or determined to maintain a place of superiority over his brothers, described to them a dream he had had. He told of a harvest time when his brothers' sheaves bowed down to his sheaves. Joseph did not ask for the dream, but instead of keeping it to himself as he might have, he shared it with his brothers who already hated him. During this time, dreams were thought to give divine revelations of coming events, as, of course, this dream did. The anger of Joseph's brothers rose to the boiling point. Later Joseph had a second dream, where eleven stars, plus the sun and moon, bowed down to him. Still seemingly oblivious to their reaction, he told them this dream. He might as well have thrown gasoline on a glowing fire.

Joseph told his father of the dreams. Jacob finally registered surprise, interpreting himself and Rachel as the sun and the moon, and his sons as the stars (see 37:10). Belatedly, he rebuked Joseph but then did nothing more to douse the spreading flames (see 37:11).

## 2. JOSEPH'S DEATH PLOTTED (37:12-24)

Shepherds of that day traveled great distances when necessary to find pasturage for their flocks. On this occasion, the sons of Jacob had to go to Shechem, a distance of over fifty miles from their home. This raises some questions. Why would the shepherd brothers all go so far away without Joseph going with them? And why would Jacob not have cautioned the ten sons to avoid Shechem (the site of Dinah's violation; see Genesis 34)? Would not the local populace have sought revenge on the brothers? And why would the sons need to travel even farther north to the Valley of Dothan (see 37:17)? Did Jacob not know of the hatred the sons felt toward Joseph? When they were all so far from home, did he not foresee the possibility that they might harm him? No answers are satisfactory for any of these questions.

Joseph must have traveled at least three days to reach Shechem. He was sure that his brothers were there somewhere. A local man found Joseph not on the road passing through the region but **wandering around in the fields** (37:15). When the man asked what Joseph was looking for, Joseph told him and asked if the man had seen his brothers. The brothers were known well enough, for the man was aware not only that they had been there but that they had gone on to Dothan—information he had heard them say to each other (see 37:17).

As Joseph approached Dothan, his brothers recognized him even before he saw them (perhaps because of his varicolored coat?). The brothers knew how far away from home they were. It was the appropriate time to plan a solution to their problem of this **dreamer** (37:19). Apparently several possibilities were discussed. One of the brothers voiced a plan that seemed to have been generally accepted, after which someone must have queried, "What shall we tell Dad?" They decided a ferocious animal story would convince Jacob that Joseph had died a tragic death. The brothers wanted to kill Joseph and throw his body in the abandoned cistern afterward.

Why was Reuben the one who tried to stop the evil act? Perhaps he had missed the first discussion. Perhaps he had been a short distance away when he, too, saw Joseph; perhaps he had started toward the other brothers, arriving just as the agreement was reached. In the absence of the father, the eldest son was to be in charge.[2] Since Reuben was the oldest, he knew Jacob would blame him most if Joseph died. Reuben immediately tried to alter the plan. If the brothers threw Joseph into the well without harming him, Reuben could return later, rescue Joseph, and take him safely home (see 37:22).

Reuben's argument, spoken from his position of authority, worked. Joseph was seized, and after being stripped of his colorful garment, he was dropped in a dry and abandoned cistern. (The cistern was probably not the normal one that filled whenever it rained, but one hewn out where water could be stored on occasion when needed, and thus it was completely dry.)

The brothers' hard hearts and cold calculation were emphasized by their sitting down for a meal afterward, perhaps just far enough away from the well so as to avoid hearing Joseph's cries for help. For some reason, Reuben went away again, this time far enough to be unaware of a change of plans. The other brothers sold Joseph to an Ishmaelite caravan. These Ishmaelites are also called **Midianite** in 37:28, suggesting that the terms were interchangeable. They had come from their home across the Jordan River in Gilead on their way to Egypt with their load of **spices, balm, and myrrh** (37:25), items the Egyptians highly desired.

## 3. JOSEPH SOLD INTO SLAVERY (37:25-36)

The most opportunistic of the brothers seemed to be Judah. He was quick to suggest selling Joseph as a slave. He certainly must have approved killing him earlier. He might have known that spilled blood "cries from the ground" (Gen. 4:10), but in any case he swayed his brothers to his scheme. His main motivation was money. He pointed out that nothing could be gained if they killed Joseph (see 37:26). Instead, he said, **Let's sell him to the Ishmaelites** (37:27).

If there were dissenters among the brothers, the opportunity to make money—while getting rid of Joseph without staining their hands with his blood—must have convinced them. They all agreed to the new plan. The caravan halted, negotiations were conducted, Joseph was brought up from the well, twenty shekels of silver were weighed out, the slave sale exchange was made, and Joseph was loaded on a camel. Finally, the caravan moved away and later disappeared from sight.

The twenty-shekel price was the going price for a slave of Joseph's age. The roughly eight-ounce amount at current market value would today be worth a little over one hundred dollars. But at that time (when a standard wage was eight shekels a year) twenty shekels, evenly divided among all nine brothers,[3] assuming Reuben refused his share, would have been considered a nice "bonus."

Where was Reuben all that time? Perhaps the author did not know, but when Reuben returned, he went straight to the cistern, then panicked. He followed the ancient grief customs and **tore his clothes** (37:29). Running to the other brothers, he found out what they had done and lamented, **Where can I turn now?** (37:30). In that reply, Reuben knew he would be held responsible by Jacob for what had happened. He must have been relieved a bit to learn that at least Joseph was alive.

The brothers finished their plan. You can almost hear it develop. One said, "If we kill one of the goats and soak his garment in its blood, we won't have to lie to our father. He will draw his own conclusion." They agreed to this plan. The Hebrew original, "they sent and it was brought" (37:32), suggests that the brothers may have sent a servant on ahead to their father so as to avoid the moment Jacob first glimpsed the blood-soaked coat. In any case, the brothers returned to Hebron, all brazenly acting ignorant of what had happened. Jacob recognized the coat immediately and made the assumption for which the brothers had hoped.

Jacob tore his clothes, donned sackcloth, and spent many days in that condition of mourning. He would not be consoled when **all his sons and daughters came to comfort him** (37:35).[4] He stated that he would mourn for the rest of his life, all the way **down to the grave.** He continued to weep (see 37:35), and in unrelieved grief a deep scar was cut that lasted for more than twenty years.

Though none of the family knew what happened to Joseph, the writer tells his readers that Joseph did reach Egypt. The brothers felt sure they had rid themselves of their problem. But the undying grief of Jacob kept them from completely forgetting Joseph.

As the author intended, and as he was inspired by God, we are given a rather complete account of the lives of the patriarchs and certainly some of their most traumatic situations, some of which were beyond their control and others which were of their own making. Throughout the accounts, we have God always close at hand, ready with a message, a vision, a covenant, a reassurance, a direction, and numerous promises to show that He was working "in all things . . . for the good of those who love him" (Romans 8:28).

### ENDNOTES

[1]"Jacob" is found thirty-six times; "Israel" twenty-six times.

[2]Joseph recognized Reuben's leadership position when he selected Simeon, the second oldest son, to be kept in Egypt while the others returned to their homeland (see 42:24). It was Reuben who informed Jacob that they would have to take Benjamin with them when they returned and who took full responsibility for Benjamin's safety (see 42:37). The seating arrangement Joseph made for his brothers reflected the normal seating procedure of eldest to youngest (see 43:33).

[3]In the days when the Judges served, a young man Micah employed a traveling Levite as his personal priest for the sum of ten shekels a year, including room and board, which was of somewhat greater value than payment for a slave (see Judges 17:10).

[4]This is the first mention of Jacob's having more than one daughter. Either other daughters had been born after the death of Rachel and are only mentioned here, or there had been other daughters born besides Dinah and only she is mentioned because of the tragedy that befell her.

# JOSEPH AND JUDAH COMPARED

## Genesis 38:1–39:23

enesis 38 appears as an unwarranted interruption, and if it had not been included, the story of Joseph would be better related. So why did the Lord inspire it as a part of Scripture? At the time Genesis appeared, the birth of the Messiah was still centuries away. Judah, not Joseph, would be the ancestor of the Promised One. Perhaps God wanted later readers like us to know how lawlessly this ancestor of His Son regarded his responsibility to the future.

What was the message for the readers in Old Testament times? Genesis 37 had concluded with Joseph's entering the house of Potiphar as a slave. Since the intent in the rest of Genesis is to chronicle the events of the life of Jacob and all twelve of the sons, even though much of it centers on what was happening to Joseph, what Judah did before Joseph's rise to power was considered most important information. Note John Sailhamer's insight here:

> As so often before in Genesis, the narrative begins with the mention of three sons (cf. the three sons of Adam, Noah, and Terah). Two of the sons died because of the evil they did, and now the seed of Judah was put in jeopardy. Who would prolong the seed? The point of this . . . information is to show that the continuation of the house of Judah lay in Judah's hands. The narrative which follows will show that Judah does nothing to further the seed of his own household. It would take the "righteousness" of the woman Tamar (38:26) to preserve the seed of Judah. As in chapter 20, where the seed of Abraham was protected by the "righteous" (20:4) Abimelech (as also in 26:9-11), here it is the woman Tamar, not Judah the patriarch, who is ultimately responsible for the survival of the seed of the house of Judah.[1]

The first lesson that vividly stands out is that *deception leads to no advantage*. Somewhat in parallel presentations, Judah had to identify the **seal and cord and staff** that were his (38:25), as Jacob had to identify **his son's tunic** (37:33). Jacob deceived Isaac, and in turn was deceived by his ten sons. Judah deceived Jacob (see 37:26), and later Judah's own daughter-in-law deceived him (see 38:14-16)

The second lesson underscored is that *injustice will ultimately encounter justice*. All the brothers had to admit that they were being punished for what they had done to Joseph (see 42:21), but Judah was first to admit to Joseph that **God [had] uncovered your servants' guilt** (44:16). Judah had been unjust to his daughter-in-law, first withholding his son from her and then wanting her to be put to death for becoming pregnant, not realizing that she could prove he was the father. He had to admit, **She is more righteous than I, since I wouldn't give her to my son Shelah** (38:26).

The third lesson suggested is that *shallow living leads to emotional hardness*. The reaction of Jacob at seeing Joseph's blood-soaked tunic is contrasted with the reaction of Judah at the news of the death of two of his sons. Jacob's unabated grief, he said, would last until he died (see 37:35). With the passing of Judah's two sons, there seems to be no mourning at all. The callousness of Judah's conscience that had made him regard Joseph as some cheap commodity later infected his feelings until he became emotionally hardened about his own sons.

And had it not been for the sovereignty of God's turning events to His eternal purpose by working through Joseph—the one from whom Judah himself had tried to profit—mixed marriages, as in the past, would again have threatened the very existence of the chosen people. God may have preferred, for His people, slavery in Egypt rather than apostasy in Canaan.

# 1. JUDAH IN CANAANITE LAND (38:1-30)

Soon after Joseph was sold to the desert traders (**at that time** [38:1]), Judah decided to go **down** to Adullam. The direction was north-northwest. It is possible that the author was thinking more of *down* in altitude, but the whole chapter also speaks to a moral decline for Judah. He may eventually have realized this to be the case, for when we return to events related to Joseph in Genesis 39 through 50, we will learn that Judah had returned to Jacob's home. (Compare the use of *down* with Jonah, who went "down" to Joppa, "down" into the boat, "down" into the sea, and "down" into the big fish. The direction for him proved to be one of moving away from God's design for him. In comparing the status of Joseph as we left him in Genesis 37 and Judah as we find him in Genesis 38, the words of Saint Augustine come to mind: "He that is good is free, though he is a slave; he that is evil is a slave, though he be a king."[2]

Since the wives of all three patriarchs had come from among their own people (see 11:29; 24:4; 29:23, 28), and since other family members who intermarried with other races brought grief to their family (see 16:4; 21:9; 27:46), it seems unlikely that Jacob would have approved of Judah's actions in this chapter.

One may wonder, who was **Hirah,** the man whom Judah met (38:1)? Perhaps he was a stranger, another shepherd who chanced to cross Judah's path. He may well have been instrumental in Judah's meeting and marrying the daughter of a man named Shua, a Canaanite. This woman gave birth in quick succession to her first two sons (see 38:3-4). The development and growth of those sons is also passed over quickly.[3]

It is uncertain why Judah **got a wife** for the eldest son (38:6). Taking into consideration all that had happened in the twenty years that transpired in Genesis 38, it is likely that Er was married earlier than was customary, perhaps in his middle teens. His life was so wicked that God was somehow instrumental in his death. Perhaps that wickedness had revealed itself quite early, and part of Judah's motivation to arrange his marriage was in hopes of his reformation. Er's unexplained death shortly after his marriage to Tamar left her a very young widow.

The concept of Levirate marriage, described in Deuteronomy 25:5-10,[4] seems to have been observed to some degree during the time of Genesis. As reflected in Deuteronomy, the law was limited to "if [or when] brothers are living together" (25:5). In other words, the law covered a time when a childless widow could not easily find another suitable companion outside the clan, and if she left the family, she might easily end up as a prostitute. This marriage custom would provide a suitable husband for a widow, making her departure unnecessary. The conventional morality of the time of Judah required a responsibility on the part of the father-in-law, who had other sons, to provide another husband for the widow, since a man had a fundamental duty to father children.

Upon the death of Er, Judah told Onan to **fulfill your duty to . . . produce offspring for your brother** (38:8). Onan did act as husband but, uncharacteristically for that time, selfishly refused to be the father of children that would not be considered his. Though in his relations with Tamar he apparently made her think he was trying to do his duty, he carefully did not allow her to be impregnated, discharging his seed on the ground. What was **wicked in the Lord's sight** (38:10) was that this oldest surviving son of Judah had an utter disregard for what was considered his fundamental duty assigned by his father. Though Judah could not know it at this time, all of his own actions had relationship to the messianic line that was to come through him. He was the bearer of the Messianic Seed that would ultimately bring forth the Son of God. Onan's death was his punishment for what was presumed his callous disregard for assigned duty.

Judah's third son, Shelah, was considered too young to marry, otherwise Judah's suggestion to Tamar, **Live as a widow . . . until my son Shelah grows up** (38:11) would have been pointless. Judah likely had a real fear that Shelah would lose his life, too. Perhaps he even thought Tamar bore some responsibility for the two sons' deaths. As suggested, Tamar returned to her father's house, hopefully waiting for her chance to be married to this youngest son of Judah, for she would have been considered engaged to him. All the while, she was required to wear the clothes that would immediately identify her as a widow (see 38:14, 19). Enough time had passed for Shelah to come of age. Tamar became aware that Judah's pledge to her (see 38:11) was either forgotten or, more likely, had all been an intentional ruse.

In time, Judah's wife died. He had his period of mourning, after which he and Hirah went to a town not very far away to shear sheep. A very desperate Tamar, who had made no move as long as Judah's wife lived, but who knew she should have been married to Shelah by that time (see 38:14), decided to act. She was told of Judah's whereabouts. She decided on a strategy of pretending to be a woman of the street. Perhaps she realized that if something wasn't done soon, that would be her only other option. She may also have been aware of Judah's vulnerability so soon after the loss of his wife (see 38:12).

She took off the garments that marked her as a widow and put on the garb of a shrine prostitute. She sat by the side of the road where she knew Judah would soon appear, and when he passed, he requested a night with her (see 38:16). Judah could not recognize her since her face was fully veiled.[5]

That this was an unplanned stop on his trip is proven by the fact that Judah had nothing to pay for her services. She requested remuneration. He offered to send her a young goat from his flock later (see 38:17). Tamar's immediate reaction was that she could not depend on what he said. She had good reason not to trust him. She wanted something as a pledge that he would keep his promise. He wanted to know what she desired. She requested his signet **seal** (the instrument he used to sign his name on clay) and his **staff** (38:18). He complied.

The many prostitutes who were connected with fertility rites and usually frequented "high places" were literally called "holy women" in pagan terminology. It is likely they tried not to become pregnant, though sometimes this happened. This can be surmised from fertility figurines that have been found. Tamar had planned carefully to make sure she would get pregnant.

Tamar learned that Judah was going to the nearby town of **Timnah to shear his sheep** (38:13). Sheep shearing was a festival time, as was harvest time. Pagans believed that their gods, by means of rain — their semen — fertilized the earth. So these special agricultural occasions were places where sexual activity might make the fertility god happy and more prone to give rain. All kinds of orgiastic activities took place at threshing floors (see Hosea 9:1 for a much later example) in hopes of helping to produce bumper crops (see Hosea 4:13-14). Judah believed that Tamar was just such a **shrine prostitute** (38:21). This whole incident reveals how far Judah had fallen away from God. He had become as pagan as the Canaanites among whom he lived.

After the encounter with Judah, Tamar returned to her role as a spurned widow. Judah wanted to reclaim his signet seal and staff, so he sent Hirah with the goat to exchange for his personal items. The presumed shrine prostitute was nowhere to be found. When Hirah asked local people concerning her whereabouts, he was told that no such woman had been there at all. When Judah was told this fact, he did not want to become a **laughingstock** (38:23) by a further search for his seal and staff. He believed he had done his duty to the woman and forgot the occasion.

**About three months later** (38:24), when Tamar's pregnancy was publicly known, Judah was told of her condition and that she was **guilty of prostitution** (38:24). Since she was considered the same as married to Shelah, Judah wanted her punished by execution. When Tamar was brought out, she sent a message to Judah that she had incriminating evidence: The one responsible for her pregnancy was the owner of a **seal and cord and staff** in her possession (38:25). Judah was trapped. He might claim the staff to be one only similar to his, but his personal seal was unique. It was as valuable as a driver's license is today; it was as incriminating as a photograph. His public reaction was, **She is more righteous** ("right" is better) **than I** (38:26). He then admitted that his inaction with respect to his youngest son had driven her to entrap him. He had learned his lesson the hard way. The relationship between them ended.

In his confession, Judah was saying, "Tamar was more concerned to perpetuate my line of descendants than I was." And though neither could know what his or her part was to be in the line of messianic forebears, in effect Judah was also saying, "Tamar was more concerned about my place in the divine plan for the world than I was."

It is not difficult to see the similarities between Judah and King David (see 2 Samuel 12). Both were in the messianic line; both committed the sin of illicit sex leading to an illegitimate birth; both tried to cover up their sin; both expressed a desire that the guilty should pay with his or her life; and, in the end, both admitted their guilt publicly. David's reaction was more complete, for Psalm 51 is a direct result of his plea for forgiveness, and Psalm 32 appears to be his reaction to the release he felt after God had cleared his record. Unfortunately, there is no such record of Judah's confession and forgiveness.

Comparing the closing verses of Genesis 38—the birth of Tamar's twin boys—with the genealogy of Jesus in Matthew 1, one can see that the "Seed" first mentioned in Genesis 3:15 came through Judah, then through the younger of Tamar's sons, Perez. As seamy as the events of Genesis 38 may be, they show that Judah was little concerned about the responsibility of what he was doing with his seed, and it became necessary for a pagan Canaanite woman to preserve it. There are some similarities between this story and a later one when God used a Moabite woman named Ruth, at the time when Moabites were hated,[6] to further the messianic line.

In Old Testament times, great emphasis was placed on the order of birth. The oldest or firstborn child was given a special place in the family, even in the event of twins, as noted with Jacob and **Esau.** The same concern can be seen with the birth of Tamar's twins (see 38:28-30). Zerah started to be born first, but then pulled back his arm. He was later born after his brother Perez. The midwife hastily tied a scarlet thread on Zerah's wrist before he drew it back, and even though he was delivered after his brother, he was considered the firstborn.

## 2. JOSEPH IN POTIPHAR'S HOUSE (39:1-23)

Genesis 37 ended with Joseph's having been sold. Chapter 39 continues the story with his having been purchased by **one of Pharaoh's officers** (39:1), a man by the name of Potiphar. There were without doubt hundreds of other men who could have purchased Joseph. He might have become a slave to a little-known sheik of the desert where the Midianite caravan stopped for water or supplies. Joseph's potential value might well have been seen by some caravaneers coming from some other place altogether who might have offered more money to his owners. The reason that all these possibilities did not occur is underscored in the opening sentence of 39:2: **The LORD was with Joseph and he prospered.**

We are given no view into the window of Joseph's mind during the days or weeks between the close of chapter 37 and the beginning of chapter 39, but there is a discernable difference in the picture of Joseph before and his picture after. The brash attitude and arrogant demeanor that invited his brothers' hatred (see 37:4) were gone. The blood-soaked varicolored tunic was no longer available to stress his honored position, and no father was near to give special favors. Everything that he had been able to call his own was gone. He had fallen from favored son to shackled slave in a matter of hours. He had become only human flesh to be sold.

No prayer to God during his long trek to Egypt was recorded in our Bible, but who would deny that one was said? Joseph was dramatically changed. He knew God had chosen him and was with him. And no matter how fully he comprehended that before he began his enslavement, he did so more completely by the time he arrived in Egypt. In whom else had he to trust but God? To whom else could he go?

When Joseph entered Potiphar's house, he was a dramatically changed young man. He made no demands for special status; he worked to earn it. He demonstrated every day his loyalty, his reliability, and his dependability. While God was favoring him, he was favoring God. There is no better combination.

Joseph's value to Potiphar was immediately recognized, and Joseph was assigned responsibilities **in the house** of this high official. Only slaves deemed of superior ability and trust received in-house responsibilities. Potiphar recognized quickly that there was a connection between Joseph's quality and the God he served. Joseph achieved **success in everything he did** (39:3). There is no quicker road to maximum achievement than for a person to feel he must answer to God for everything he says and does. Joseph chose not to walk the path of assimilation so as to be more accepted by the Egyptians, for he was aware that God knew all about him.

By a daily trust in God and His accompanying blessing, together with Joseph's own dependability and reliability, Joseph moved from house slave to personal assistant to house manager to the head of operations of the plantation in quick succession. Potiphar saw that, because of Joseph, the Lord was blessing everything Potiphar had **both in the house and in**

**the field** (39:5). He had to worry about nothing more than the food he ate (see 39:6). The God-given personal qualities that would ultimately be necessary for Joseph to obtain the status of second-in-command only to the Pharaoh, to bring the whole country of Egypt and surrounding areas through a major crisis, were being honed while Joseph served as a slave. The best way to the top is to begin at the bottom and live by an integrity that God will cause others of importance to notice.

This is not to say that one of integrity will not be abused by the world or even suffer persecution at the hands of those intent on evil's triumph. According to the psalmist, the one who does "not walk in the counsel of the wicked or stand in the way of sinners or sit in the seat of mockers," but delights in, and meditates regularly on, the law of the Lord will be "like a tree . . . which yields its fruit in season [and] . . . Whatever he does prospers" (Ps. 1:1-4).

As for all Joseph's good works and favored blessing of God, another with mischievous and evil intent also took notice. Joseph's physical quality and moral excellence, seen daily by a virtually abandoned wife, was bound to appeal, tantalize, allure, and finally lead her to an attempt at seduction (see 39:7). Potiphar's wife saw in Joseph a chance to try to lift herself up by pulling him down.

Likely Joseph had observed the increased attention being paid to him, the lingering look, the prolonged smile, the profuse compliments, the generous flattery, the ever more tender touch. As much as possible, these were likely being discouraged by Joseph, but as they increased he knew where they were headed. His mind may have gone over and over what he would say and do. Finally came the open invitation: **Come to bed with me** (39:7).[7]

What had held Joseph steady at his high moral level now found voice. After describing the many responsibilities entrusted to him, he said, **My master has held nothing from me except you, because you are his wife.** Joseph drew that line firmly for himself. Joseph knew that to take part in a sexual relationship with Potiphar's wife, even though both were consenting adults, would be a **sin against God** (39:9). Since God defined the limits, Joseph felt that to cross them was to sin against Him.

Sex is indeed a blessed-by-God tool, but unbridling it outside of marriage makes what God intended to be a tool—to express relationship and blessing with a spouse—become a weapon to damage character, destroy relationships, and ultimately steal one's maximum happiness. Unlike many other sins, such as murder and theft, illicit sex leaves no apparent physical evidence. Because it is more easily hidden, once the boundaries are crossed, one is encouraged to continue participating in it. Then all kinds of secret trysts are arranged, causing two people to pretend something is not happening, so that they begin to live a lie, develop a hypocritical lifestyle, and end up speaking a lie to protect themselves.

Joseph's protests did not stop the advances of Potiphar's wife. She simply changed her tactics. The literal Hebrew of 39:10 indicates that she was inviting him day after day to just sit beside her, to come close, to keep her company. Apparently her idea was, "If I cannot storm him, I can excite him." She wanted to get him into a compromising situation where she could more easily break his resolve. She did not know Joseph as well as she thought she did, nor could she apprehend his close walk with God.

That the plan of Potiphar's wife failed is emphasized by the description of Joseph attending to his duties as usual on the day of her strongest attack (see 39:11), a day when no other servants were inside the house. Gentle and provocative invitations had failed. She resorted to greater force this time, using his cloak and perhaps her body to force him down on the bed.[8] Joseph was able to wiggle free, but only by leaving his garment in her firm grasp. He quickly fled from the house. She then screamed (see 39:14).

Potiphar's wife was first frustrated at Joseph's rejection, then angered that nothing had succeeded to break his will. She knew that questions by servants who would have witnessed Joseph's hurried exodus from the house would quickly surface: "Why would the property manager, the epitome of control and confidence, be in such a hurry?" With quick thinking, the spurned wife concocted a false but believable story that reversed what had just happened. Joseph was the aggressor, not she, she said. She immediately called the household servants, those who would be aware that something unusual had happened. Before they arrived, she carefully arranged Joseph's garment **beside** her (39:15). When they arrived, she told them that Joseph had intended to **sleep with [her],** but when she screamed he fled after he had partially disrobed. They were convinced. She carefully left the garment beside her until her husband returned (see 39:16). She repeated her story, also duping him into believing it to be true (see 39:19). She primarily blamed Joseph, of course, but she implicated her husband, too, by saying, **That Hebrew slave you brought . . .** (39:17). In other words, "This would not have happened to me if you had not hired him."

Two possibilities present themselves. That Potiphar believed his wife's story suggests she had been effectively hiding her desires for Joseph from her husband for many months, for he asked no more details nor had any more questions. He was sure that his trusted manager had betrayed his confidence and trust, so he **burned with anger** (39:19). The other possibility is that Potiphar was not totally convinced of his wife's explanation. Potiphar sent Joseph to prison; he could have ordered him to be killed. Potiphar may have done what he did to confine Joseph until Potiphar could make a more thorough investigation of his wife's claims. If this latter interpretation is correct, Potiphar was not able, after his search, to completely vindicate Joseph, so Joseph remained incarcerated.[9]

The prison warden quickly recognized Joseph's superb managerial skills, again accented by his dedication to God, and soon the warden made Joseph **responsible for all that was done there** (39:22). Tremper Longman notes, "Genesis 39 is a concrete illustration of God's overruling the evil of other people, using it instead to bring about a great rescue, a salvation."[10] Joseph had much success **because the LORD was with [him] and gave him success in whatever he did** (39:23).

Judah had failed repeatedly; he had made a downward slide essentially to live at the level of the pagan Canaanites because the Lord was not with him. Judah had begun well, but because of his neglect of a close relationship to the Lord, he could go nowhere but down. Judah had suggested to his brothers the selling of Joseph, then soon after, he moved into the midst of pagan people. He rather quickly cohabited with a pagan Canaanite girl, and ended up sleeping with one he thought was a cult prostitute. His life spiraled precipitously down.

But Joseph offers a different story. He began badly, a bit arrogant, presumptuous, and prone to stimulate hatred in his family. These flaws nearly caused his untimely death. But from the time he was seized by his brothers, was put into an abandoned cistern to die, and then spent long hours on a camel as a slave to be sold, he must have had serious conversations with the Lord. He had nowhere to go but up. He emerged from it all gifted, charming, responsible, and efficient.

Where Judah easily succumbed to the slightest temptation, Joseph resisted allurements and won. Could there be a greater illustration of the difference God can make in one's life?

**ENDNOTES**

[1]John H. Sailhamer, *The Pentateuch As Narrative* (Grand Rapids, Michigan: Zondervan Publishing House, 1992), p. 209.

[2]George Seldes, *The Great Thoughts* (New York: Ballantine Books, 1985), p. 23.

³For all that is chronicled in this chapter to have taken place before returning to Joseph's life in Egypt, the births of Er and Onan had to have been very soon after the union, and very close together. Shelah came some time later.

⁴At the time God gave the Law that Deuteronomy contains, the marriage of the widow by the oldest surviving brother was not mandatory but recommended in order that sons could be born to the deceased brother's name. Onan could choose not to marry her. But if he made that choice, she could take him before the elders at the town gate, and if he continued to refuse to marry her, she could take off one of his sandals and spit in his face.

⁵Since there is no evidence that cult prostitutes wore veils, it is probable that this phrase refers to a heavy cosmetic covering on her face.

⁶The assumption is made that the events of Ruth took place during the time of the judge Ehud when the Moabites were the hated oppressors (see Judges 3:12-30).

⁷According to the literature of ancient Egypt, women were considered cruel liars, frivolous, and unfaithful. One archaeological discovery called "The Tale of the Two Brothers" is very similar to this story in Genesis. It may well have come about as a result of Joseph's experience, but if so, it was somewhat distorted, for in it cows talk. But the older brother's wife tried to seduce the younger brother with, "Come, let us pass an hour [together]; lie us lie down." (See *Egypt and the Bible* by Pierre Montet (Philadelphia: Fortress Press, 1968), pp. 78–80.)

⁸The Hebrew verb behind "caught" implies force.

⁹C.F. Keil and F. Delitzsch, *The Pentateuch,* The Commentary on the Old Testament (Grand Rapids, Michigan: Wm. B. Eerdmans Publishing Co., 1949), pp. 345–46.

¹⁰Tremper Longman III, *Making Sense of the Old Testament* (Grand Rapids, Michigan: Baker Book House, 1998), p. 36.

# Part Twelve

# JOSEPH: FROM PRISON TO PALACE

## Genesis 40:1–45:28

Genesis 39 records how Joseph arrived at the absolute bottom in his life: in a prison as an alien in a foreign country, with little else but his faith in God. But by the time the chapter ends, Joseph's faith and expertise and God's blessing had teamed together to start Joseph on his slow yet steady climb to the top.

The time reference at the beginning of the chapter—**Some time later**—gives only a hint as to how long Joseph was a prisoner, but the phrase suggests an extended period after Joseph's initial entry into his **dungeon** (40:15). This cave-like room was likely close by the palace (see 40:3), maybe at basement level, which made it appear to him as a **dungeon.**

At the beginning of Genesis 40, Joseph was still about as low as he could go. Though the warden had placed him "in charge of all those held in the prison" (39:22), Joseph received a new assignment to "attend" two of Pharaoh's high officials who were newly imprisoned. Though Joseph may not have immediately recognized it, God was in the assignment. When the cupbearer **forgot him** (40:23), Joseph may have thought God too had forgotten him, but He had not.

# 28

# JOSEPH: FROM SLAVERY TO STATUS

## Genesis 40:1–41:57

J oseph may have spent many sleepless nights wondering how his earlier dreams (see Genesis 37:5-9) would ever come true. Did God give him other dreams to help him through these most difficult years? If God did, it seems likely that we would have been told about them in the Scripture. During those years, about all Joseph had to go on was his faith that God was still with him and would somehow, sometime, cause him to be freed. But Joseph must have faced many temptations to doubt. "Might there not be a 'subtle serpent' around who will suggest to Joseph: 'Did not God say your brothers will bow before you? Is this how your God treats you in return for your obedience to Him?' All of the temptations are there, the temptation to be angry, bitter, resentful, cynical, self-pitying."[1]

### 1. JOSEPH INTERPRETS DREAMS (40:1–41:36)

What set the stage for Joseph's exoneration and promotion was the imprisonment of two servants of the ruling Pharaoh—the **cupbearer** and the **baker** (40:1). Since both men surely had their assignments in royal food service, it seems reasonable that they were being blamed and imprisoned for something that had happened to Pharaoh as a result of what he had eaten or drunk. The **cupbearer** and **baker** ended up in the same detention center as Joseph. As providence would have it, they were assigned to Joseph's care.

These two men had a high status while in prison, perhaps higher than any other prisoners, which helps to explain why Joseph's assignment was to attend them (see 40:4). This situation persisted for **some time,** again another extended period. What changed the situation from the usual day-to-day events of prisoners were dreams that the two royal servants had in the same night. Joseph, assigned at night to a different place, noticed their dejection when he came to work the next morning. He sought to know the reason for their discontent and was told about their dreams. The men felt that they had portended something. They feared that there was no one to interpret their dreams.

In antiquity, there was a widely held belief that dreams put one into the realm of the gods, but that dreams needed some one to tell their meaning. There were also specialists who were thought to have the ability to determine if dreams signaled good or bad omens. Partly because of this widespread high regard for an assumed connection to dreams and the future, God used significant people like Joseph to interpret dreams so as to prove that God ruled over everything.

Having a dream was not unusual, but the dreams of the **cupbearer** and **baker** caused them to be dejected (see 40:6), likely because they did not know the interpretation. When Joseph went to their cell the next morning, he immediately saw their sullen melancholy and asked its cause (see 40:7). Joseph's response is impressive. He could have said, "I can interpret your dreams for you." That would have been prideful and self-promoting. Instead, he immediately witnessed of his God as the one to whom **interpretations belong** (40:8). He was letting them know that the authority of any of the professional interpreters in Egypt had to be based on their own ideas; Joseph's God alone could tell the meaning of dreams.

There is no record of Joseph's having successfully interpreted dreams before this point. Yes, he had dreamed two dreams that foretold future events (see 37:5-11), but not yet having witnessed the fulfillment of either of them so as to verify what they presaged, his confidence was the result of his implicit faith in God. Joseph spoke to the men: **Tell me your dreams** (40:8). The chief cupbearer volunteered first. He told Joseph about seeing a vine of **three branches** which in quick fashion budded, then blossomed, then produced grapes (40:9-10). The cupbearer saw himself squeeze juice from the fruit into Pharaoh's cup, which he put in the king's hand. Joseph's interpretation came immediately. The number three represented the three days that would transpire before the cupbearer would be restored to his former position (see 40:13). So sure was Joseph of the interpretation that he begged the cupbearer to remember him to Pharaoh when he was freed, letting Pharaoh know of the injustices that Joseph had endured that had made him a prisoner.

It was likely that the dream of the baker was ominous enough that he hesitated to reveal his dream but, encouraged by the favorable interpretation of the cupbearer's dream, the baker related his to Joseph also. It involved the baker's carrying on his head three baskets full of baked goods intended for Pharaoh.

Of interest is the fact that there are at present many drawings and paintings, even small models, from Egypt which show servants with baskets of bread being carried on their heads. It apparently was a very common sight. As the baker's dream continued, the bread in the top one of the three baskets was being eaten by birds. Again Joseph's interpretation was immediate, but the news this time was foreboding. The dream presaged that within three days the butler would die by being hanged on a tree, and that the birds would **eat away your flesh** (40:19).

Both dreams referred to the birthday of the Pharaoh and the celebration to honor it. Both men were released for the occasion. True exactly to Joseph's interpretation, the cupbearer was reassigned to his former position, but hanging punished the baker. Pharaoh must have ordered an investigation of the two men and determined who had been responsible for the incident causing them to be imprisoned.

The cupbearer was so caught up in his vindication that he promptly forgot Joseph. Joseph spent an additional two years in prison with no change in his circumstances. Only Joseph's faith could have sustained him during that period. Why did it take so long? Why did not God inspire Pharaoh's dreams sooner so Joseph would have his golden opportunity? It can be assumed that the additional two years of Joseph's imprisonment were necessary to prepare for his elevation at the critical time—just before the coming period of abundance followed by the extended famine. God works in all things for his children's good (see Romans 8:28).

Finally, Pharaoh's dreams came. Two successive dreams of the Pharaoh initiated events that would dramatically change Joseph's status. The first dream involved the Nile. Standing beside it, Pharaoh observed seven obese cows coming out of it. (On hot days when heat and flies annoy, cattle love to avoid both by standing mostly submerged in the water of the Nile.) Pharaoh saw the seven fat cows emerge from the water and stand grazing on the shore. Behind them came seven very lean cows that, being famished, consumed the fat cows. That dream stirred the Pharaoh enough to awaken him.

Pharaoh soon fell asleep again and experienced a second dream that gave a similar message with seven heads of healthy grain being swallowed by scorched and perishing grain. Deeply troubled the next morning about his dreams, Pharaoh sought an interpretation from all the **magicians and wise men** of Egypt, **but no one could interpret them for him** (40:8). Suddenly the light of memory flashed on in the mind of the chief cupbearer. He recalled the similarity of his own situation in having had a dream and recalled **a young Hebrew** who could interpret this dream (40:12).

Pharaoh lost no time in sending for Joseph. When Joseph appeared, the king told him he had heard of Joseph's ability to interpret dreams. Again Joseph could have taken the credit for the earlier correct interpretations of the two servants of Pharaoh. It was a beautiful and tempting opportunity to boast about his abilities. Instead he said, **I cannot do it, but God will** . . . (41:16). Had Joseph looked at the situation from a purely human perspective, taking at least some of the credit, Pharaoh might have respected him more highly. But Joseph was more interested in giving all the credit to God. For Joseph to honor God was as natural to him as breathing.

After being told the two dreams, Joseph gave an interpretation. He told the Pharaoh that both dreams revealed the same facts about the future. Soon God would bring about seven years of great abundance; then He would follow with seven years of famine (see 40:29-30). After the interpretation, Joseph offered advice seemingly based on his hard-earned, God-given, superb managerial skills. He did not say, "God told me to tell you this." Having developed his expertise while working for Potiphar and polishing it while in prison, Joseph quickly saw what should be done (see 40:33).

## 2. JOSEPH MADE PRIME MINISTER (41:37-57)

Pharaoh's first reaction was to ask his officials if anyone could be found to put Joseph's plan into effect, and then added **one in whom is the spirit of God** (41:38). The original word used for God here is *Elohim,* a plural noun that, in a pagan mouth like Pharaoh's, would possibly have meant "the spirit of the gods." Pharaoh may not have fully recognized Joseph's God.[2] However, Pharaoh was at least aware of the divine assistance God had given to Joseph and the high moral level that resulted from his obedience to this God.

Before the officials could even answer Pharaoh's question, the king realized that Joseph was just the type of man that was needed. Pharaoh announced, **I hereby put you in charge of the whole land of Egypt** (41:41). Pharaoh was no doubt impressed with Joseph's interpretation. But what motivated Pharaoh's decision to reward Joseph was Joseph's desire to solve the problem that would develop. It is always good to have someone point out a potential problem, but it is even more valuable for one to indicate a possible solution.

Pharaoh followed his announcement with the removal of his signet ring, placing it on the finger of Joseph (see 41:42). Stamp seals were often worn as rings because of the ease with which an impression in clay could be made. The wearer simply doubled his hand into a fist and pressed the seal in moist clay. Royal seals have been found that mention not only a king but also the court official who acted for him. In addition, Egyptian records indicate that at times the elevation of a foreigner to high position did occur. One inscription tells of a man named Antef who was elevated to prime minister and calls him "functionary of the signet [ring] . . . Chief of Chiefs . . . alone in the multitude, he bears the word to men; he declares all affairs in . . . Egypt; he speaks of all matters in the place of the secret counsel."[3]

Whatever clothes Joseph wore—probably prison garb—were replaced with **robes of fine linen** (41:42). Then a gold chain was placed around the neck of Joseph. Such a chain was a symbol of government power easily viewed by all, which would have insured immediate recognition of Joseph and a proper response to him on the part of the people and visiting foreigners, regardless of their station. Tomb paintings and written descriptions let us know that each Pharaoh did have a person working immediately under him to whom was given the title "Bearer of the Seal of the King of Lower Egypt." This **gold chain,** a costly gift, indicated that one of the responsibilities of this Prime Minister was the control of food distribution.[4]

During the time that all of this was happening to Joseph, not once did Joseph object or give an exclamation of surprise. He was silent, a reaction born of confidence in his ability to fulfill the office being given to him. He knew he could decrease the severity of the problem that would hit that entire region in seven years if rather immediate steps were taken. Others without his divinely given insight would not have moved with the same confidence or readily accepted the necessary responsibility. Joseph stood ready to assume his new duties immediately.

What a dramatic route Joseph had taken to arrive at that place! He had begun in his father's house hated by nearly all his brothers. He was elevated in the house of Potiphar, then was sent to the prison house, but now had come to occupy a royal house of the king. He was in charge of the whole land of Egypt (see 41:43). His had been a rocky journey, but one where God had watched over him carefully.

After Joseph's new assignment was made, he was given an Egyptian name and was married to the daughter of a priest (see 41:45). Neither the wife nor the new name is ever mentioned again. Given Joseph's new assignment and proper Egyptian protocol, these activities were considered necessary by both the author and Joseph. Joseph's chariot emphasized his second-in-command status, and runners who preceded him in places where people gathered shouted, **Make way!**

When Joseph's odyssey began, he was seventeen (see 37:2). At this point he was thirty. Most of his time spent in Egypt was full of heartbreak, setbacks, false arrest, and adversity. But Joseph held firmly to his faith in God while on that rocky road, and that led him to a high place of power and influence as Pharaoh's right-hand man.

Though we read virtually nothing of Joseph's immediate family life, during the seven years of plenty he fathered two sons who were named Manasseh and Ephraim (41:51-52). They became heads of two of the twelve tribes of the nation of Israel. When he named the firstborn, Manasseh, a Hebrew name, Joseph believed he was closing the door on his rocky past, for the name means "one who causes to forget." Ephraim, also a Hebrew name, was a name Joseph used to put a more positive spin on his experiences. God had made him become "fruitful in the land of suffering." Livingston, quoting Westermann, wrote, "If the name of Joseph's first son (Manasseh) focuses on a God who preserves, the name of Joseph's second son (Ephraim) focuses on a God who blesses."[5]

After seven years of bumper crops, the seven years of famine began (see 41:53-54). Famine was not limited to Egypt, for **there was famine in all the other lands** (41:54). For a time, Egypt was spared, but the famine soon spread there, too, forcing the people to cry to Pharaoh for food (see 41:55). Why did they not cry to Joseph? He had been quietly preparing for the crisis for many years, without fanfare or trumpeted headlines. The people simply did not understand why he had been accumulating grain.

The time arrived for Joseph to open the storehouses, for **famine had spread over the whole country** (41:56). Grain was sold as requests came in, and as the famine persisted past normal growing seasons, the news of Egypt's enormous stores of grain spread to the surrounding countries.

## ENDNOTES

[1]Victor P. Hamilton, *Handbook on the Pentateuch* (Grand Rapids, Michigan: Baker Book House, 1982), p. 132.

[2]The Egyptians venerated almost every god, for they did not want to offend any. A god might in some way contradict another, but they found ways to worship both of them. Respecting a new god posed no problem to them as long as they could retain the ones they already had.

[3]I.M. Price, O.R. Sellers, and E. Leslie Carlson, *The Monuments and the Old Testament* (Philadelphia: Judson Press, 1958), pp. 161–62.

[4]Gaalyah Cornfeld, *Archaeology of the Bible: Book by Book* (New York: Harper and Row, 1976), p. 27.

[5]Hamilton, p. 512.

# 29

# JOSEPH: REUNION WITH HIS BROTHERS

## Genesis 42:1-43:34

The major route that connected the continents of Africa, Europe, and Asia passed through the plains of Canaan, between the mountains and the sea. It was called "Way of the Sea" or "Way of the Land of the Philistines" (Exodus 13:17) in the Bible. Abraham went to Egypt and returned by it, tradesmen and travelers frequented it, and armies marched on it. By this route, news of the grain supplies easily reached Hebron, and no sooner had Jacob heard about them than he reprimanded his sons for not doing something to relieve their food shortage (see 42:1). He told them of the news that grain was available in Egypt and told them to go purchase some so they would not starve (see 42:2).

## 1. THE BROTHERS VISIT EGYPT (42:1-38)

Only ten sons made preparations to go. Since Jacob thought that Rachel's second son, Benjamin, was her only remaining son, Jacob refused to let him go. He feared harm might come to him. Could part of that fear have been accentuated because of the realization that it was when Joseph was with the ten, without their father, that misfortune had befallen him? Benjamin was made to stay home.

After a week of traveling over desert sand, the brothers arrived and were directed to Joseph, who controlled the distribution of grain to everyone. Joseph wanted close and strong control, lest in desperation some might forcefully try to steal grain. When the ten met him, there was not the slightest recognition of Joseph's identity, though he immediately knew theirs. Their assumption was that Joseph had died at some time during the last twenty years (see Genesis 42:32). Since it was a practice

281

for Egyptians to shave off their beards, Joseph would have had none. Though he could still speak Hebrew, he chose to use an interpreter (see 42:23) when speaking to them. In every way he looked and acted Egyptian. There was nothing to make his brothers suspect that the man to whom they spoke was Hebrew, let alone their long lost brother!

Their bowing **down to him with their faces to the ground** (42:6) brought to Joseph's mind those early dreams that had so angered his brothers but were now fulfilled. He pretended not to know them, and in a rough voice he demanded to know their place of origin (see 42:7). They told him and volunteered their purpose of coming to buy food.

Joseph's next reaction was to accuse them of coming to spy on Egypt (see 42:9). His motive was partially to keep his identity secret, and yet the accusation followed immediately upon his recollection of the dreams of their bowing **down to him with their faces to the ground** (42:6). In both dreams, bowing down to him was what the sheaves (see 37:7), and the sun, moon, and stars had done (see 37:9).

It would be revealing to know the thoughts that raced through Joseph's mind. Did he suddenly recall how his brothers had cruelly stripped off his varicolored coat, and did he feel the pain of being dropped into the abandoned cistern (see 37:24)? Did other bitter memories flood in? Or was Joseph overwhelmed with the joy of knowing his family was still alive and together? It had to have been difficult to contain his reactions, but he did it.

Joseph's idea was not to get even with his brothers but to help reinforce the heartlessness of their crime concerning him and bring it back to their minds in all its stark reality. They had not only betrayed Joseph but had cruelly deceived their own father. And those sins were still buried in their hearts.

Joseph undoubtedly wanted to know his brothers' present attitude toward what they had done. Did they regret it, or had they forgotten it completely? Had they come to the place where they no longer lived by deception, hiding the truth for personal gain? Had they embraced a more honest lifestyle? His numerous claims of their being spies (see 42:9, 12, 14-16, 20) were calculated to make them defenseless and see how they would react to being falsely accused. From his own experience, Joseph knew all too well how it felt to be falsely accused; they needed to know also. But it was just as important to Joseph to learn of the welfare of his father and the status of his brother, Benjamin. How had the ten brothers been treating him? The quickest route to answering all these questions was to falsely accuse them.

The brothers quickly responded to Joseph's accusation and defended their integrity. **No, my lord** (42:10). The information they volunteered was true (see 42:10-11). But had they abandoned dishonesty? They claimed they were **honest** (42:11). Joseph needed to know for sure; he continued the test. **No, you have come to see where our land is unprotected** (42:12). Their desire to convince Joseph of their honesty made them divulge information they did not need to volunteer, but it was exactly what Joseph wanted to hear: His father and brother were alive.

Joseph wanted his brothers to think the interrogation was insufficient to convince him of their truthfulness; he insisted on proving their statements by a test (see 42:15). They were to remain imprisoned in Egypt while one of them returned to Canaan to bring back the other brother of whom they spoke. Benjamin's appearance at the court of Egypt would verify the rest of their story (see 42:16). If Joseph's instructions were not followed, the ten would be convicted of spying, the punishment for which was death. They were given three days in custody to fully contemplate their options (see 42:17). The same Hebrew word for **put them in custody** was also used of Joseph's confinement. Perhaps for their own good, Joseph wanted them to taste for three days what he had endured for many years.

While the brothers were contemplating what they should do, Joseph was also thinking about what he had ordered. While the test was simply a way to see Benjamin and determine how he looked and was being treated, it appears he saw a loophole in his own logic. He wanted his brothers to think he still considered them to be spies, and the incarceration would emphasize the seriousness of the charge. Yet Benjamin's coming to Egypt would not give Joseph all the information he desired. He needed to know more about his brothers' present character and his father's present condition.

When the ten stood before Joseph again on the third day, he modified his request. He would continue to hold only one brother and would let the other nine return to get Benjamin. He could not let all return, for there was a chance Joseph would never see them again.

It would have been interesting to have been a party to their talking among themselves, obviously in Hebrew, thinking that Joseph could not understand them. The words one spoke captured the sentiments of the other nine—they were being punished for what they had done to Joseph (see 42:21). Reuben reminded them how he tried to stop their depraved plan, and he added, **You wouldn't listen** (42:22)! The way they had mistreated Joseph had entombed them in guilt. They automatically felt that their dilemma was a result of their being punished by God for what they had done.

Hearing them speak to each other caused Joseph to turn his head to keep them from seeing him weep (see 42:24). Recovering himself, he turned to have Simeon bound before their eyes. Why Simeon? He was the second oldest and, in Reuben's absence, should have tried to protect Joseph. They must have wondered how Joseph would know their ages. There is another consideration that would have been on Joseph's mind: "You willingly left me twenty years ago; will you be willing now to leave Simeon?"

Joseph was fully aware of not only who they were but of their serious economic condition. Their sacks were loaded with grain. The money they had used to pay for the grain was secretly replaced in their bags. Joseph also made sure they had **provisions for their journey** (42:25). One of the brothers discovered money in his sack on the trip home. It made them all tremble with the thought that God was further punishing them. The others discovered as they emptied their bags that all of the money they had paid was in their sacks.

Arriving home, they unfolded the whole story to Jacob, giving every detail, even the words spoken in conversation. Jacob's reaction was that as Joseph had been taken from him so he would never see Simeon again. Worse yet, **you want to take Benjamin . . . !** Jacob exclaimed (42:36). Jacob feared that Benjamin might disappear also.

Being the oldest, Reuben recognized immediately his place of responsibility in the family. He offered two of his own sons (he had four; see 46:9) to be put to death if Benjamin did not return from Egypt. Such an offer was of no interest to Jacob. **My son will not go down there with you** (42:38). Jacob feared that something might happen to Benjamin while on the journey. Did he fear that a wild animal would kill another son (see 37:33)?

## 2. THE BROTHERS RETURN (43:1-34)

The resolve of Jacob prevailed until the grain supply was nearly gone. He gathered his sons and instructed them to return to Egypt to **buy us a little more [grain]** (43:2). He said nothing about Benjamin. Did he forget the terms set down for purchasing more grain? Did he hope everyone had forgotten?

Judah was the one brave enough to tell Jacob they could not return to Egypt without Benjamin. That would be a useless trip, for Joseph would not even look at them if Benjamin did not accompany them (see 43:5). Judah was making quite clear to Jacob that he knew they would starve to death if they didn't go to Egypt, but the same result would happen if they went without Benjamin. Jacob then faulted them for having mentioned to Joseph that they had another brother. "How could we help it?" they replied. "We had to answer his questions" (see 43:7).

At that point, Judah affirmed that he would **guarantee [Benjamin's] safety** (43:9), and if he failed, he said, he would take the blame for the rest of his life. Jacob was now more swayed by their need than he was by Judah's affirmation. He had delayed making a decision for weeks. **If we had not delayed, we could have gone and returned twice** (43:10), Jacob was told. He knew he had no other choice but to send Benjamin. He instructed his sons to take back with them produce from the land as a gift (see 43:11) and also to take double the amount of silver since he thought the return of the silver they took previously was a mistake (see 43:12). Not until Jacob had given seven other orders to his sons (see 43:11-13) did he finally include the last command: **Take your brother also** (43:13). By that time Jacob realized that his reluctance to let Benjamin go with them back to Egypt was putting all of the family, including Benjamin, in grave jeopardy of starvation. It is as though he waited until absolutely necessary to allow them to take Benjamin. While consenting to what was necessary, Jacob knew he had no control over events that would transpire, and especially over his youngest son's welfare, so he offered a prayer that **God Almighty [would] grant [them] mercy** so that all of them, including Simeon and Benjamin, would return together (43:14). Yet Jacob showed concern that the worst might happen when he concluded his statement with, literally, "If I lose my children, then I lose them."

The trip was a **hurried** one (43:15). As soon as the brothers arrived, they went directly to Joseph, who, **when [he] saw Benjamin** with them, instructed the one in charge of his house to prepare a sumptuous meal for his brothers. Not aware of Joseph's intent for this special invitation, they feared the worst. They assumed it was a lure to trap and punish them for the silver they had found in their bags. They were sure they would be made slaves (see 43:18). Before even entering the house, they sought to remove the suspicion by telling Joseph's steward how they had found the silver, and that they had brought it back with additional payment for more grain (see 40:20-22).

The reply of the steward, **It's all right. Don't be afraid. Your God . . . has given you treasure in your sacks** (43:23), was met with stunned silence. It is as surprising to us as it would have been to any reader even in that day. The Egyptian steward of Joseph's house was the speaker. Had he been so influenced by Joseph that he had become a believer in Joseph's God? The idea is intriguing and probable. Believers never know how much of what they say and do in faithful allegiance to God impacts and influences unbelievers. Many with whom they communicate every day may be closer to conversion than they realize.

The brothers were mulling over the steward's statement when, soon after, Simeon was brought out to them (see 43:23). Their fear abated somewhat as they were treated more as honored guests than potential slaves. Nevertheless, the men prepared their gifts[1] to give to Joseph. When Joseph arrived, the brothers were waiting outside. They immediately **bowed down before him to the ground** (43:26), then silently followed him into the house where the gifts had been displayed. Following proper protocol, they did not speak until they were first addressed.

Joseph's opening remark showed a concern for their own well-being, followed by a query about their aged father: **Is he still living?** (43:27). Behind that question may well have been a fear that the lingering famine and the lengthy time that had transpired since their first trip had led to Jacob's death. Assuring Joseph that their father was indeed **alive and well** (43:28), the brothers again bowed low to pay Joseph honor.

Joseph then turned his attention to Benjamin. Being the youngest, and even though this was the first time Joseph had seen him in many years, Benjamin was not hard to identify. Still hiding his own identity, Joseph inquired, **Is this your youngest brother, the one you told me about?** (43:29). Knowing he was, Joseph could contain himself no longer. He hurriedly left the room to keep from breaking into tears in front of them (see 43:30). After he regained his composure and washed his face, he returned and ordered the food to be served (see 43:31).

Since it was not considered proper for an Egyptian to eat with foreigners, especially Hebrews, nor was it proper for a high official to eat with servants, the room likely held at least three tables to accommodate Joseph, his brothers, and the Egyptian servants. "The prejudice against eating together was probably not social (as in 46:34) but cultic, since foreigners would technically defile the food."[2] Aalders explains, "The custom that forbade Egyptians from eating with people from another country was based on a religious practice that did not permit Egyptians to eat the meat of certain animals that were commonly eaten by other peoples."[3] The arrangement of the banquet may have been Joseph's first step in showing forgiveness for his ill treatment. Whereas the meal the brothers had had near Dothan was denied Joseph (see 37:25), the meal Joseph now gave was one to which the brothers were guests. Another step Joseph had taken was to make sure each brother was seated in order by his age. Their **astonishment** grew, for they had no idea how their ages had been made known to this Grand Vizier of Egypt (43:33). Such would have been dificult or impossible to guess given the closeness of their ages. The Hebrew word for **astonishment** reveals a reaction to something unexpected yet rather unpleasant.[4]

Another intentional hint of Joseph's identity clearly came when he piled **five times as much [food] as anyone else** (43:34) on the plate of his only full brother. This may have been a planned move for Joseph to determine if the ten brothers would react with the same jealously that had been shown to him. The half brothers could do no more than look at each other. The banquet continued until all were filled.

### ENDNOTES

[1]The gifts, **best products of the land** (found only here in the Bible; see 43:11) included **balm, honey, spices, and myrrh.** The Midianite caravan that took Joseph to Egypt took with them the same products from Gilead (see 37:25), an area of Canaan just east of the Jordan River. We can assume that these items were highly desired by Egyptians.

[2]Derek Kidner, *Genesis,* Tyndale Old Testament Commentaries (Downers Grove, Illinois: InterVarsity Press, 1967), p. 204.

[3]G. Ch. Aalders, *Genesis,* vol. II (Paideia, St. Catharines, Ontario, Canada: Zondervan Publishing House, 1981), pp. 232–33.

[4]The astonishment may well have expressed the Egyptian reaction that this Grand Vizier was actually eating with these foreigners and showing them such deferential treatment.

# 30

# JOSEPH: IDENTITY REVEALED

## Genesis 44:1–45:28

The afternoon found the brothers occupied with preparations to leave. They likely retired early in the evening so they could get an early start for home the next day. Picture the brothers' amazement at the rocket-like odyssey they had traveled in such a short period of time, from the fear of losing their freedom to a life of slavery, to the honor of a private feast at the royal table. They must have enjoyed a pleasurable night's sleep. Little did they know of the test Joseph was preparing for them. They were going to be totally surprised when, pursued by Joseph's steward, they would be accused of the theft of Joseph's cup. When the cup was found in Benjamin's sack, it was Judah who rose to the occasion and was ready to sacrifice himself for his half brother and Joseph's full brother.

Joseph's disguise would have to fall. He would reveal his true identity to all of them. Plans were quickly made to return with ample vehicles to bring the entire clan to Egypt. Though it would be difficult to believe that his long lost son was still alive, Jacob would make preparations for their reunion.

## 1. JOSEPH'S FINAL CHECK OF HIS BROTHERS (44:1-34)

Joseph chose to test his brothers one last time. He put them through a pressure-packed experience of pretending Benjamin would have to be left in Egypt instead of returning home with them. He set up a situation where he could determine their attitude toward both Jacob and Benjamin. Would they be heartless enough to leave Benjamin and return to their father with the news that would certainly end his life? Would they have a "let the chips fall where they may" attitude? Or would they do everything possible to protect their father and Benjamin?

The preparations were made. Joseph's assistants filled the sacks with grain as expected, and again the silver meant for payment was returned in the sacks (see 44:1-2). Into Benjamin's sack was also placed the personal, symbolic-of-office cup of Joseph himself. Likely this cup had been placed temptingly to the brothers in a prominent place at the banquet so that everyone would recognize its importance and connection with Joseph. Often, high officials used a cup for **divination** (44:5; see Nehemiah 1:11). Into such cups, oil and water were poured. It was commonly believed that the movement of the two unlike liquids would give an official answers to hard questions.

Questions immediately come to mind: Why would Joseph use such a cup? Was it to satisfy proper Egyptian protocol? Had he shifted from knowing the future by dreams from God to one using a pagan procedure? Later law forbade any kind of divination or soothsaying (see Leviticus 19:26; Deuteronomy 18:10).

There are two possible solutions. First, linguistically it is possible to translate **uses for divination** as "be sure to notice." The passage would then be saying that Joseph would be sure to notice the missing cup. This translation is not conclusive, however. Second is the possibility that Joseph's cup was unlikely used for drinking and also for oil and water divination. A more probable solution to the problem is that a Grand Vizier would not be divining the future. That task would more likely have been delegated to magicians or soothsayers.

Joseph allowed the brothers to get a short distance from the city, perhaps out of sight (see 44:4). He then sent his steward immediately to follow and apprehend them for "stealing his cup" and securing it in one of their sacks. When the charge was made, the brothers protested. They reasoned, "Why would we do such a thing when we did not even keep the silver that someone had returned to our sacks the first time we came" (44:8)? They were confident of their innocence; one of them declared, **If any of your servants is found to have it, he will die; and the rest of us will become my lord's slaves** (44:9). The disclaimer was designed to put them to the strongest test. Would they come to the defense of Benjamin when he was accused of the theft, or would they show a remnant of the behavior that had resulted in Joseph's slavery?

So sure of their innocence, the brothers submitted themselves to a potential punishment of slavery or death. This offer indicated how confident they felt that none of them carried the sought-for cup in his sack. They thought they had nothing to hide. Each man quickly lowered his sack for inspection (see 44:11). The inspection was also designed to add to the drama; the sack of each of the brothers was opened in order of their ages. The cup was not found in any of the first ten sacks. But, horror of horrors, it was discovered in Benjamin's sack (see 44:12).

In the elaborate, typical mourning custom, the brothers **tore their clothes** (44:13), then reloaded their donkeys and returned to the city to appear before Joseph. He rhetorically asked them, **What is this you have done? Don't you know that a man like me can find things out by divination?** (44:15). The thrust of the second question was, "Don't you realize I do not need the cup to discover secrets? You may have thought that I needed that cup to find you guilty and that you could foil my ability if you took it. Think again!"

Judah spoke for the brothers (see 44:16). He suggested that all of them, including Benjamin, become Joseph's slaves. They had agreed to die if the cup were found. Judah knew his was a better option. What he said was designed to save the life of Benjamin, who was thought guilty. By what had been suggested, Benjamin should have died. But Judah was saying, "We are a group. If one is guilty, we all are guilty."

Judah was likely not assuming guilt for the cup's presence in Benjamin's bag, though a cursory reading suggests such: **How can we prove our innocence** (44:16)? Judah was more likely confessing to the crime for which he knew they were all guilty—their treatment of Joseph years before—when he said, **God has uncovered your servants' guilt.** This had been their reaction when they were imprisoned for three days on the first trip (see 42:21). At that time they had said it to each other, only among the guilty. Here Judah said it to Joseph, now an admission outside the circle of the guilty. More assured that they were being punished for their guilt, Judah told Joseph, **God has uncovered your servants' guilt. We are now your slaves—we ourselves and the one who was found to have the cup** (44:16).

Joseph knew the validity of such a confession, but he needed to know if it was made simply because they had been caught. The question he surely wanted to have answered was, "Are you truly sorry for what you have done?" He chose a test that would give him the answer. He first protested Judah's suggestion that he should hold the innocent for what the guilty had done. His steward had already made that clear to them (see 44:10). He then reiterated, **Only the man who was found to have the cup will become my slave. The rest of you, go back to your father in peace** (44:17). As nearly as possible, Joseph had recreated the situation he had faced with his brothers twenty-two years earlier. They had abandoned him; would they also leave Benjamin?

Judah rose to the occasion. He gave the lengthiest, most impassioned and persuasive speech to be found in Genesis. And in it he revealed the dramatic turn he personally had taken. The very burr that had caused his original evil response to Joseph—Jacob's favored love for Joseph— became the basis of his request for mercy (see 44:27-31). In his speech, Judah showed that deep love for Jacob had replaced jealous hatred for Joseph. Judah's statement, quoting Jacob—**my wife [Rachel] bore me two sons** (44:27)—reveals this vividly. Before, Judah would likely have responded, "Is not my mother, Leah, your wife, too? What about my brothers and me? Are we not also your sons?"

In Judah's former mind-set, the possibility of a few shekels gained from Joseph's slavery had callously ignited his mind (see 37:27). At this point, Judah offered the rest of his life in slavery to save Joseph's brother. Before, he crassly held Joseph's bloodied coat and sneered when he thought of how Jacob would react. Now he was ready to go to the limit to protect Jacob: **Let [me] remain here as my lord's slave in place of the boy. . . . How can I go back to my father if the boy is not with me?** (44:33-34). Before leaving for Egypt on the current trip, Judah had told Jacob he would personally bring Benjamin back, and if he could not do it, he would **bear the blame** for the rest of his life (43:9). Was Judah just being oratorical? Or did he mean it? He meant it with his very life; he would willingly be a **slave** for Joseph if Joseph would only allow Benjamin to go home to their father. With his impassioned speech, Judah inferred that if Joseph refused to allow Benjamin to return, then Joseph would bear some responsibility for the **misery that would come upon my father** (44:34).

The reader of the entire episode of Joseph's relation to his brothers during the two visits and before he revealed his identity to them (see Genesis 42–44) might have the impression that Joseph went a bit beyond simple quizzes to final exams. He put the brothers, Benjamin, and even his father through more than we would expect of one who had completely forgiven the evil done to him. The brothers may later have felt there was a tinge of revenge in all that Joseph had put them through. They would feel unsure that the forgiveness he expressed would prevail after Jacob's death, as is recorded in 50:15. And they would express this fear directly to Joseph, causing him to weep (see 50:17).

We must be careful that our forgiveness is not any less generous than the forgiveness God himself gives. Jesus spoke to this concern strongly when he told the parable of the king who forgave a servant such a debt that he would have had to work 165,000 years to repay it, at the standard wage of the time. In turn, this servant found a man who could not repay a debt to him of about three months' pay, and had the man imprisoned for it. The king heard of this, labeled his servant a "wicked servant," and sent him "to the jailers . . . until he should pay back all he owed" (Matthew 18:23-34). Jesus concluded His story with these words: "This is how my heavenly Father will treat each of you unless you forgive your brother from you heart" (Matt. 18:35). Forgiven people must forgive, hold no grudges, and seek no revenge

## 2. JOSEPH IDENTIFIES HIMSELF (45:1-28)

Joseph could no longer question his brothers' attitudes toward how they had treated him nor their concern for Benjamin and their father. He could not ask for more. No other test was needed. He could not have given one anyway. Ready to lose all composure again, this time in front of all his attendants, he ordered the attendants out. Then he cried uncontrollably, loudly enough to penetrate the walls so that the Egyptians heard it and immediately reported it to the household of Pharaoh (see Genesis 45:2).

Before the brothers could get over their shock at the loss of composure of the one they assumed to be their severe judge, Joseph tearfully identified himself: **I am Joseph** (45:3). He immediately asked, **Is my father still living?** He knew Jacob was alive, but his concern added to the validity of his self-identification. To the brothers' utter surprise was added sudden shock, which produced a paralyzing fear. Standing like zombies with their mouths gaping open, Joseph wanted the distance separating them eliminated. Warmly and tenderly he told them to **come close to me** (45:4). Seeing that they were still dumbfounded and disbelieving, Joseph underscored his true identity, this time adding something that would remove all doubt in their minds: "I am **the one you sold into Egypt.**"

Before their minds could process the new information, Joseph counseled them not to be angry with themselves for what they had done. While he passed over the part the brothers themselves and the Ishmaelites played in getting him to Egypt, he told them it was really God who **sent me ahead of you** (45:7). Then followed God's purpose more broadly — **to save your lives.** Just when during Joseph's experience might he have come to realize God's hand in what had happened? Perhaps little by little as his faith interpreted what was occurring. By this time, any lingering bitterness over the evil role his brothers had played in his experiences had been rooted out.

To make sure Joseph's brothers knew that he saw God's hand in all that had happened to him and that his forgiveness of them was complete, Joseph assured them, **It was not you who sent me here, but God** (45:8). And that, he added, was the argument he wanted them to use when they returned to **my father** (45:9). The use of **my** here is not intended to emphasize Jacob's greater love for Joseph than for the brothers. It was rather further proof of Joseph's identity: "Your father is also my father."

Joseph knew that, with his present responsibilities to the starving thousands in both Egypt and the surrounding countries, he could not return to Canaan even for a visit. He wanted his father, his brothers, and their extended families all to come to Egypt not only for a mere visit but to **live in the region of Goshen and be near me** (45:10). Obviously, Joseph's main purpose was to have his family close to him, but also to prevent their destitution if they remained longer in Canaan. This seems to be the main reason for his admonitions to his brothers to leave for home in a **hurry . . . don't delay** (45:9) and come **quickly** (45:13).

Seeking to remove any lingering doubt as to his true identity, he assured his brothers, **"You can see for yourselves** that I am indeed your brother"** (45:12). But would Jacob believe them? Knowing that Jacob was more likely to believe them if Benjamin would verify the fact, Joseph mentioned his only full brother. Then, closer blood attachment made him turn to Benjamin and, defenses no longer needed, throw his arms around him, causing Benjamin to return the affection similarly. They both wept (see 45:14).

Pharaoh was now apprised of all that had transpired. He told Joseph to do for his family just what he had proposed. Perhaps as the events were transpiring, Joseph had been discussing with Pharaoh the possibility of his bringing his family to Egypt and they had agreed on what area would be most suitable for them. They picked the **best of the land** (45:18): the Nile Delta where Goshen was located. While there was a dire need for rain in Egypt, the fresh waters of the Nile—especially in the Delta, having numerous canals—made the grass grow lush for the cattle, even without rain. The Nile generally provided water if needed for irrigation.

Pharaoh was determined to make the difficult migration as smooth as possible. He ordered Joseph's brothers to take **carts** back with them to ease the movement of children and wives (45:19). These carts would also help the aged Jacob to make the long trip. Joseph saw that Pharaoh's orders were carried out, and additionally he **gave them provisions for their journey** (45:21). Their clothes likely showed the wear of their arduous journey, so Joseph gave each brother new clothing (see 45:22). Might not the gift of clothing have been another way Joseph showed his forgiveness? These same brothers had stripped him of his valuable clothes; he was now "turning the other cheek" by providing new clothes for them.

For Benjamin, Joseph multiplied the new garments by five, and gave him additionally **three hundred shekels of silver.** Perhaps Joseph wanted to compensate his younger brother for the emotional trauma he had caused him (making him look guilty when he was totally innocent; see 44:12) in discovering his brothers' present attitudes. Of importance, too, is the fact that these two bore a special relationship to each other, through having the same mother, which their half brothers recognized. Their twenty-two-year separation and their mother's absence would fuse them more closely together.

Joseph wanted to show great generosity to his father. Twenty donkeys (probably in addition to the ones the brothers had brought with them) were loaded with expensive items (see 45:23), normally used only by the rich, along with grain, bread, and other provisions that would make their return trip easier. As his brothers left, Joseph had one parting admonition: **Don't quarrel on the way** (45:24). Was this said because of their previous inclination to do so? Or was Joseph fearful that, having been so blessed with goods, some might have been more reluctant to dislodge from their homeland? Could Joseph have been saying this in jest, more or less knowing that they would have a great future to which they could look forward? Perhaps the answer is best found in a mixture of all these.

The brothers' long trip is covered in one verse (see 45:25). They could hardly wait to get to Canaan to tell Jacob the good news. They were all richer, but the greater gain for all was release from the guilt that made them believe God was punishing them for their cruelty to Joseph. They must have felt like David, centuries later, who felt God's forgiveness for his sins of adultery and murder: "When I kept silent, my bones wasted away through my groaning all day long. . . . Then I acknowledged my sin to you . . . and you forgave the guilt of my sin" (Psalm 32:3-5).

As Joseph's brothers were approaching home, one can imagine them as they saw Jacob from a distance, with one of them shouting at the top of his lungs, **Joseph is still alive. . . . he is ruler of all Egypt** (45:26). To read that Jacob **was stunned** had to be inside the mark. Having believed for so many years that Joseph was dead, he would have had difficulty grasping the full realization of it. He had believed the sons when they were lying; he no doubt struggled to believe them when they told the truth. Though almost more than he could bear, he had believed the bad news. Could he believe the good?

Jacob needed only a little time to let the news penetrate his thinking. He listened to his sons tell him **everything Joseph had said to them** (45:27). Then when he saw the empty wagons that had been sent to take him and everyone to Goshen, his **spirit . . . revived** (45:27). In Scripture, such a phrase usually is reserved for the God-given, spiritual part of life—the soul.[1] Perhaps here it means to imply that Jacob was declining toward death, which may have been accentuated by the delay of his sons' return from Egypt and the increasing fear that something may have happened to Benjamin. Now Jacob not only had Benjamin back, but he learned that—wonder of wonders—a son thought dead was still alive and virtually ruling the great country of Egypt. Jacob was like a new man, but still one who knew his days were numbered: **I'm convinced! My son Joseph is still alive. I will go and see him before I die** (45:28).

## ENDNOTE

[1]See Genesis 2:7, 6:17, and 7:22 where it is translated "breath of life."

# Part Thirteen

# FROM CANAAN TO EGYPT

## Genesis 46:1–50:26

A t the time of the events this section of Genesis records, two long generations have passed since Abraham first went to Egypt. And coincidentally, that trek too was made necessary because of a famine. That had been a bad trip for Abraham, but the vital lessons he learned then aided him in his walk with the Lord.

When another famine occurred during the time of Isaac, God came to Isaac with a specific warning: "Do not go down to Egypt" (26:2). It may well be that, having known of his father's earlier trip there, Isaac gave such a move careful consideration. In time, Isaac fell into the same trap of passing off his wife as his sister to the Philistine king as his father had done with the Egyptian pharaoh. Fortunately for Isaac, the results were not as perilous for him as for Abraham. God saw to that.

But, years later during the time of Jacob and Joseph, a third famine arose, most likely more severe than the others.[1] This famine necessitated Jacob's contact with Egypt, albeit through his sons. God designed this famine to get His chosen people away from the grossly immoral religions of the Canaanites. Although in Egypt many more gods were worshiped, still there was a tolerance that would permit God's people to worship Him in relative peace for generations in Goshen. There they could develop their own faith without the fertility rites that were deemed necessary by the Canaanites, which involved "sacred prostitution."

### ENDNOTE

[1]Famines were apparently more common than what is mentioned in Scripture. They are only mentioned when they have some bearing on God's

great design. The book of Ruth reveals that a famine (see Ruth 1:1) caused Elimelech and Naomi to move to the land of Moab where, after Naomi lost her husband and two sons, she lived for ten years (see 1:4). This did not necessarily mean that the famine lasted that long, but it took years for her to hear how the Lord "had come to the aid of his people by providing food for them" (1:6). David also experienced a three-year famine (see 2 Samuel 21:1-14). Another famine occurred during Elisha's ministry (see 2 Kings 8:1). In the New Testament, Agabus prophesied a famine that came to pass in the days of Claudius (see Acts 11:28). The most significant famine was the one announced by Elijah that lasted for three and a half years (see Luke 4:25).

# 31

# JACOB'S FAMILY REUNITED

## Genesis 46:1-47:26

his section of Genesis opens with Jacob's entire clan ready for a move to Egypt to be reunited with Joseph. We learn how it came about that the tribes of Israel developed in Egypt. The migration would be difficult, but the author underscores the importance of the move with three important items in the text. First, God came to Jacob in a night vision to assure him that He would make of Jacob a great nation (see 46:3), but more importantly, God would go with him and be with him when **Joseph [would] close [Jacob's] eyes** (46:4). Second, the author included a list of the names of all Jacob's descendants that migrated with him (46:8-27). Third, the author provided a description of the famine, and its grip not alone on the countries around Egypt but on the Egyptians themselves. The nation of Israel would begin in struggle, in time would flourish in number, and eventually, because of their numbers, have their status reduced to slavery.

On God's timetable, when the people's misery merited it, when their cries were strong enough, and when their suffering was severe enough (see Exodus 3:7), God would lead them out of Egypt to their promised land.

## 1. JACOB MOVES TO EGYPT (46:1-47:12)

Prior to this third journey to Egypt, the sons had gone twice before to obtain grain. Jacob had sent them each time. It was time for him to go. He wanted to see Joseph, the son whom he had thought was dead for more than two decades. Though still in charge of the family, Jacob knew his physical capabilities had weakened to the point that he would soon die. However much he might have dreaded the move itself, just to lay eyes on his favorite son once again would have made the hardship seem worth it.

299

With such a large group of people and animals, around fifteen miles a day would have been as far as they could move. By the end of the second day, thirty miles from their starting point at Hebron, they had reached Beersheba. Jacob wanted to pause to worship and sacrifice **to the God of his father Isaac** (46:1). Possibly fear of the unknown had begun to set in. Jacob needed reassurance. But overriding whatever uncertainty he might have had about leaving his homeland and going to another country was, on one hand, the knowledge that his son, whom he had long thought dead, was alive, and on the other hand, that Jacob was on his way to see Joseph in person.

Jacob's father, Isaac, surely had told Jacob that this place was where God had met Isaac, too, at a crucial time in his life—a time when Isaac, too, had feared (see 26:23). After having had great difficulties with the Philistines, at this place Isaac had heard God identify himself as "the God of your father Abraham" (26:24). God had consoled him with the words, "Do not be afraid." It was just the message Isaac had needed.

It seems that a similar message came to Jacob after he went to sleep. God spoke to him in a night vision (see 46:2), calling him by name. God identified himself as **the God of your father** (46:3). He then followed with an instruction similar to what Jacob's father had been given: **Do not be afraid to go down to Egypt. . . . I will go down to Egypt with you** (46:3-4).

Did Jacob think this would be a trip to see, visit, and enjoy a reunion with Joseph, expecting in time to return home, even if his extended family stayed? This is not indicated. God let Jacob know that he and his family would become **a great nation** in Egypt (46:3). Then God told Jacob that he would return to his homeland. Jacob may not have grasped the full meaning of that promise, but, given his age, he may have. He realized from what the Lord told him that Joseph would be at his side when he died (see 46:4). Jacob's body would be returned to Canaan after his death. All of his descendants would return many years later in the Exodus.

At that time, families saw detailed genealogies as important. The author of Genesis gives the full list here. This material has little application to the present day, but we are informed that the total number of the clan was **seventy in all** (46:27). We note, though, that the names given indicate only the male descendants. Excluded are wives (see 46:26), daughters, and servants. It is likely that the total number was in the hundreds.

Had Judah gained prominence over his three older brothers, Reuben, Simeon, and Levi? He was now given a leadership position by Jacob to travel on ahead of the entourage **to get directions to Goshen** (46:28). It might be that since Judah had been instrumental in the separation of father and favorite son, Jacob wanted him to help with the reunion.

Judah alerted Joseph that the clan was coming. Joseph was so anxious to see his father that he did not stay at his house until his father arrived. Excitedly, he had his own chariot harnessed and headed for the group. Imagine the thoughts running through the heads of both father and son as they closed the distance that separated them. They met. No words were said. There were only open arms, hugs, and tears of inexpressible joy **for a long time** (46:29). Years of despair at ever seeing Joseph alive again were changed into a life-fulfilling climax. At the conclusion of it all, Jacob said to Joseph, **Now I am ready to die** (46:30). His death was not to come for another seventeen years (see 47:28), so rather than thinking he would expire soon, it was his way of expressing that the years of emptiness were dramatically and quickly eliminated. Nothing could happen to surpass that savored moment!

Joseph thought it necessary to prepare his family for their meeting with Pharaoh. He would go to Pharaoh first to make it clear that his family's occupation was tending animals. Egyptians liked animals for food, but they did not like to be close to them or even near people who tended them (see 46:34). Joseph wanted no hitches to develop. He may have feared that Pharaoh would seek to engage them in a different occupation and thus locate them in a place in Egypt other than Goshen, which would have been disruptive. So Joseph told his family that when Pharaoh asked them their occupation, they were to tell him that they had tended animals all their lives and that this was the same occupation their fathers had had. Joseph knew that such information would be enough to ensure their assignment to Goshen, the grazing area of Egypt.

When Joseph went to Pharaoh, he took with him five of his brothers. Which of the brothers he chose and why he chose them is not recorded. Joseph had worked for Pharaoh long enough to know that Pharaoh's leading question would relate to their occupation. Joseph had made sure that none of his brothers would answer something like, "What would you like for us to do? We are handy men; we can do most anything." But the brothers did not reply exactly as Joseph had instructed. He had told them to say they **tended livestock** (46:34), which is better translated "cattle breeders." They instead told Pharaoh they were **shepherds** (47:3). Both descriptions were true, but Joseph's description might have skirted an exact title for an occupation that was **detestable to the Egyptians** (46:34).

Notice also that the brothers did not answer merely, "We are shepherds." They prefaced that answer with humility: "We are **your servants.**" Twice more they repeated that fact. They wanted to make clear two things: (1) they were there to respect and serve Pharaoh ("You don't need to worry about us—we are not spies"); and (2) they were not asking for permanent residency. They had **come to live here awhile,** because the famine in Canaan had killed the crops their animals needed. In other words, they were saying, "We have not come either to undermine your government or to presume upon your generosity." The brothers then followed their answer with a request to settle in Goshen (see 46:4).

Having followed the proper protocol and having designated the particular part of Egypt where they wanted to settle—in the **best part of the land** (47:6)—they waited for Pharaoh's response. It came. They were to **live in Goshen.** Interestingly, this instruction was followed by Pharaoh's offering to place any of the brothers with **special ability** in charge of Pharaoh's own personal flocks as "royal shepherds." In that position, they would be "officers of the crown." While they would still not be considered Egyptian, they would receive added income from the government, be afforded additional legitimacy, and have official state protection. It may be that Joseph knew of this special need in Pharaoh's government, which could easily and efficiently be met by his brothers and which would have been part of the reason for the request to live in Goshen. God had told Jacob, **I will go down to Egypt with you** (46:4). Here is proof that He had kept His word.

At this point, Joseph wanted Pharaoh to meet his aged father. Jacob would have been recognized for his wisdom and lore. And the king would have been most anxious to get to know Jacob, since his son was leading Pharaoh's whole country through what must have been its most difficult crisis.

When the two met, Jacob both began and ended his visit to Pharaoh with a blessing (see 47:7, 10). Jacob's sons did not do this and probably could not have because of their "inexperience" compared to their aged father. Giving such a blessing would have been most out of place for them. The words of the blessing are not recorded, but one can well imagine what they were like. Perhaps Jacob said, "Lord, as this man has honored my son, so honor him. As he has been generous to us, so be generous to him. As you have given me long life, so may he have long life."

Pharaoh was prompted to ask Jacob his age, indicative of his respect for Jacob. Pharaoh learned that Jacob was **a hundred and thirty** (47:9).

That exceeded by twenty years the age to which most contemporary Egyptians would have aspired. That must have impressed Pharaoh, for in Egypt to live to the age of 110 was considered ideal. Jacob could not refrain from alluding to the years he had lived as **few and difficult** (47:9), probably indicating that his life had been made up of a few years of joy and many years of struggle.

Another idea of what was on Jacob's mind that spawned the **few and difficult** words could have been a belief, later to be inscripturated, that the one who honors his parents would "live long . . . in the land" (Deuteronomy 5:16). Jacob had not honored his father. His poor relationship with Isaac had caused him to live only a few years in the land of promise and many years out of it.

Joseph now oversaw the distribution of property to his father and brothers. They had hoped only for an area in which to **live . . . awhile** (47:4), but Joseph **settled** them and **gave them** deeds to **property** (47:11). They may have had in their minds that they would return to their own land; Joseph was thinking in more permanent terms.

## 2. JOSEPH EASES THE FAMINE (47:13-26)

The author's attention returned to the famine. It seems that some time passed since the settlement in Goshen and things had worsened, not only in Egypt but in Canaan as well. Joseph's keen analysis and management of the problem covered three stages as the famine worsened. First, **grain** was exchanged for silver bullion (47:14). When the people's silver was expended and they still lacked food, Joseph took their livestock in trade (see 47:15-17) for **food** (literally, "bread"). They gave away their possessions just to stay alive.

On a side note, 47:17 gives the first mention of horses in the Bible. Other sources show that horses began to appear in northern Asia about the beginning of the second millennium B.C. They appeared in Egypt by the eighteenth and seventeenth centuries B.C., probably introduced by invaders known as Hyksos, a people related ethnically to the Hebrews, who took over control of Egypt sometime between 1720 and 1700. This helps a bit in the dating of the lives of Jacob and Joseph.

**When that year was over** (47:18) and all silver and animals had come into the coffers of the Pharaoh, the Egyptian people appeared again before Joseph with a proposal of their own. They suggested that the government purchase their land, and then they could be employed by the government to work it. They asked for **seed so that we may live and not**

**die** (47:19). Joseph complied with their requests. Though the famine had reached its worst, perhaps Joseph could see the light at the end of the tunnel. Joseph acceded to their request with the purpose of planting the seed in the ground. It was not to be eaten (see 47:23). At the end of the famine, all people, livestock, and land were owned by the government, and the people were tenants who worked the land, tended the livestock, and farmed; they only had to return twenty percent of their yield to the government (see 47:24). The author of Genesis noted that the system was still in force as he wrote (see 47:26). The priests were exempt from this plan since they regularly received an allotment of food from the Pharaoh.

The people characterized themselves as **in bondage to Pharaoh** (47:19, 21, 25), technically "slaves of" Pharaoh. That word "slaves" loses its starkness with the realization that it was the responsibility of Pharaoh to maintain the food supply. A mere twenty-percent lease payment was very generous, especially considering today's practices in which a lessor and lessee may split the profit fifty-fifty. But the **bondage** of Old Testament times was really a self-indenturement—that is, when people became destitute, their labor was the road to recovery.

There is some similarity here to the economic system that was later to be instituted in Canaan when the tribes took over the land. A farmer in financial trouble first had the option of indenturing himself to a neighbor who was not to use him longer than six years. He was to regain his freedom in the seventh, or Sabbatical, year. If he chose not to receive freedom, he had to submit to having his ear pierced, probably to testify that he had the opportunity to accept freedom but instead chose servitude (see Exodus 21:2-11; Deuteronomy 15:1-18). A second option was permitted, in which a farmer could "sell" (more properly, "lease") his land, but only until the next Jubilee, which occurred every fiftieth year, when all land had to revert to the original owners and all property indebtedness had to be eliminated (see Leviticus 25:25-34). The third option was for one to become a slave (see Leviticus 25:39-54), but only until the year of Jubilee. (One such year would come in every man's working lifetime.)

Under the later Israelite system, the government did not become owner of the land at any time, for the whole system was based on God's ownership of it (see Leviticus 25:23). This later system offered advantages over the Egyptian plan. First, the people saw an end to their credit dilemma, and they knew the time would come when they would get their land back. Second, the people were encouraged to manage debt or, better yet, incur it only when absolutely necessary. Even then, they knew the return of their land to them would only be a matter of time. Gordon Wenhem notes, "Ancient slavery at its best was like tenured employment, whereas the free man was more like someone who is self-employed."[1]

## ENDNOTE

[1]Gordon J. Wenhem, *Genesis 16–50,* Word Biblical Commentary, vol. 2 (Dallas: Word Publishing, 1994), p. 449.

# FINAL DAYS

## Genesis 47:27–50:26

The author offers, in 47:27, a summary of what was happening to the descendants of Jacob. They settled down, purchased property, and were growing into a nation. He then described a period after the famine, defining the time by the approaching death of Jacob (47:29). The seventeen years of Jacob's time in Egypt were mostly passed in silence. The famine had become a memory, and a period of normalcy had begun with Joseph's position of authority more established. Near the end of his period in Egypt, Jacob realized his health was failing. He knew he was soon to die, and he had no desire to be buried in Egypt. Accordingly, he sent for Joseph so he could make known to him his hope for a final resting place in Canaan.

## 1. JACOB'S FINAL WISH (47:27-31)

When Joseph arrived, Jacob immediately gave voice to his fervent wish that he not be buried in Egypt, but rather with his father and grandfather (47:29-30). That was the custom in the patriarch age: "he was gathered to his people" (25:8). For Jacob, this had to mean Hebron.

While Jacob's burial place was important to him, there must also have been a firm belief that the nation (which his family was soon to become) could not have an unending future in Egypt, for it was never considered the "land of promise." The Promised Land was, rather, Canaan, and Jacob wanted to emphasize that fact with his burial site.

Naturally, Jacob had no way of insuring that his wish would be carried out, so he resorted to the most likely way of guaranteeing his wish—having Joseph put his hand under his thigh. This was the same ritual Abraham had requested of his servant as he promised to find a wife for Isaac (24:2). When one made such a solemn vow, especially when the one requesting might not live to see it fulfilled, the one making the vow put his hand under the other's thigh, as if to say, "I will answer to all your descendants if I fail." Though Joseph consented, Jacob had him **swear to** him that he would do it (47:31). In Jacob's mind, this additional act made Joseph responsible not only to Jacob and his descendants, but also to God to whom he would also have to answer if he failed. When Joseph complied with both requests, the much-relieved Jacob could only **[worship] as he leaned on . . . his staff** (47:31). Likely Jacob could walk only with the aid of his staff. He would have retired from shepherding years before. Jacob's physical powers were weakening.

## 2. JACOB'S FINAL BLESSING (48:1-22)

At some unknown time—**some time later** (Gen. 48:1)—Jacob was taken ill, probably the illness that led to his death. The author gives the impression that Jacob was now confined to his bed (see 48:2). Word was sent to Joseph, who considered the situation serious enough to take his two sons with him. As usual, sons were generally listed in the order of their births. The author lists Joseph's sons in this way in 48:1: **Manasseh and Ephraim.** Most societies honored the eldest son simply because he was the eldest (compare Isaac with respect to Esau). Generally, the eldest was honored with double inheritance and eventually, after the passing of the father, the leadership position of the family. Such a cultural custom did breed jealousy (compare Ishmael and Isaac); alienation (compare Sarah and Hagar); intrigue, deceit, and even hatred (compare Esau and Jacob). Needless to say, this custom could also interfere with God's plan. God considers the gifts and abilities with which a person is endowed. God wanted his leaders to possess leadership ability. When a leader was selected on the basis of age or height or both—such as with Samuel's near mistake of thinking that Jesse's oldest and tallest son, Eliab, was the one God had chosen to replace Saul (see 1 Samuel 16:6-7)—it usually missed the mark intended by God. We need only witness how many men God chose to be leaders who were not the eldest sons in their family.[1]

Apparently when Joseph got to Jacob, Jacob was unable to see clearly enough to recognize Joseph. When the announcement was made to Jacob of Joseph's arrival, it took great physical effort for Jacob to sit up in bed (see 48:2). It seems certain that this was his deathbed. But although his sight had dimmed and his hearing had diminished, Jacob had a clear memory of a signal event of God's appearance to him at Luz (Bethel) when he was in flight from Esau (see 35:9-15). Jacob told Joseph of the words God had given him there. God promised fruitfulness, the increase of Jacob's "seed," and land that would be **an everlasting possession to your descendants after you** (48:4).

That brought Jacob's sons to his mind, but in the case of Joseph (Jacob's firstborn of Rachel), Jacob also gave first consideration to Joseph's two sons, in effect elevating them to the level of his own sons. In referring to them, he turned around the normal order, naming the younger of the two brothers first, then comparing them to another pair, older but in the normal order: Reuben and Simeon (Simeon being the younger of the pair). It may well be that for posterity purposes, Jacob wanted Joseph to know that his two boys could consider Jacob their "father," too. This explains why, in the tribal allotments, only eleven sons received bordered geographical areas. Levi was allotted forty-eight cities distributed throughout the other tribal areas. But Joseph's allotment was divided between his sons, in effect giving him a double portion, and bringing the number of tribes to twelve.

For a moment Jacob overlooked (or failed to remember) the fact that Joseph was present when his mother had died, so Jacob reiterated the event, the place, and where he had buried her (see 48:7). Jacob looked at the blurred images of the two young sons of Joseph, who perhaps had stood silently nearby, and asked, **Who are these?** (49:8) Joseph identified them as the sons **God has given me** (48:9). Jacob then told Joseph to bring the sons closer to him, **so I may bless them.**

By Jacob's saying, **God has allowed me to see your children too** (48:11), Jacob did not mean that he had not seen the boys until that moment. It is more likely that he had often seen them in the seventeen years since his arrival. Jacob was thankful to God that he had enjoyed that blessing many times since he had first arrived.

Joseph then brought his sons near. They were grown men of nineteen or twenty years of age. They stood near Jacob's knees, and he kissed them. Joseph gently moved his sons away from their position in front of his father so as to enable him to bow **with his face to the ground** (48:12). What a beautiful picture! The ruler of Egypt, next to Pharaoh, bowing before an aged and dying shepherd father, for no other reason than that Jacob was his father.

Joseph was influenced by cultural norms. As he approached Jacob, he carefully put his left hand on Manasseh and his right hand on Ephraim. He knew as they walked forward again to receive the blessing Jacob wanted to give them, Jacob's right hand (the more important one in giving a blessing) would fall on the head of the older Manasseh, while the left would rest on the head of the younger Ephraim. But, to Joseph's surprise, his father crossed his arms to reverse Joseph's carefully arranged plan. Had God told Jacob to ignore the primogeniture custom? (Esau lost his position because of his light attitude concerning his place as oldest son [see 25:32]. Reuben's conduct with Bilhah after Rachel's death disqualified him from claiming the honor of assuming the leadership of the clan [see 35:22].) As far as we know, Manasseh had done nothing to lose his firstborn position. We have learned from clay tablets found at a site that used to be in northwest Syria, but is now in Turkey, named Alalakh, that fathers had a right to disregard the law of primogeniture and designate another son as "first born."[2] We can only assume that Jacob's reversal was more a reaction to their qualifications or that somehow Jacob was urged by God to make the switch. In the history of the twelve tribes, the tribe of Ephraim was always more prominent than the tribe of Manasseh.

The switch seems to have come after Jacob had started the blessing (see 48:15-16). Joseph was so displeased (the Hebrew word suggests "strong anger") that he not only interrupted his father but actually tried to move Jacob's right hand from the head of Ephraim and transfer it to Manasseh. Jacob refused and told Joseph that Ephraim would become greater. Jacob pointedly referred to Ephraim first before Manasseh (see 48:20), as he had when he had adopted them as his sons. Jacob concluded by saying, **May God make you** [anyone who is being blessed in the future] **like Ephraim and Manasseh.**

Jacob's final direction was given to Joseph concerning **the ridge land I took from the Amorites with my sword and my bow** (48:22). Shechem may have been his reference, for Jacob had purchased his first land there (see 33:18-20), but it was his two sons who actually took it by the sword. If not, the battle to which he referred in this passage appears to have taken place after what his sons did at Shechem and is not recorded in Genesis.

## 3. JACOB'S FINAL PROPHECY (49:1-28)

After adopting Joseph's two sons and giving them his final deathbed blessing, Jacob called all his other sons and told them to appear not one at a time but as a group. Interestingly, the author does not say anything like, "The word of the Lord came to Jacob, saying, 'Go speak to your sons.'" It is evident that Jacob spoke with inspired words about times yet to come, some very distant in the future. How fitting for him to prophesy at the end of his life, for that life began with a prophetic utterance (see

25:23). As God had enabled Joseph to determine coming events through dreams—his own, as well as others—now Jacob would exercise the same gift of seeing the future.

Jacob used the medium of Hebrew poetry with its typical parallelism or "thought rhythm." This was often the medium used by prophets; it seemed to help put emphasis on ideas in one way or another and added to the meaning of what they were saying. Jacob wanted each of the sons to give his full attention, because it was believed that what Jacob had to say would have much to do with their futures.

Jacob considered the sons of Leah first. He started with **Reuben,** his firstborn son. Jacob began by listing the advantages of having been born first at a time when this alone brought great honor, special status, and legal privileges, but Jacob then described Reuben's conduct:  as **turbulent as the waters** (49:4).  Perhaps Jacob never learned how Reuben had sought to save Joseph from being murdered. Though Reuben had succeeded, he could not stop Joseph from being sold. Reuben failed to take adequate, decisive action when he should have.

A similar hesitancy prevailed during the judgeship of Deborah. When other tribes rallied to her cause, the tribe of Reuben was indecisive. In her song, Deborah asked, "Why did you stay among the campfires?" Too much "searching of heart" kept them from being of any assistance in the battle against the Canaanites (Judges 5:16).

The bigger problem for Reuben personally, however, was his presumption in that he **went up onto your father's bed . . . and defiled it** (49:4; 35:22).  That incident had happened soon after the death of Rachel, when Reuben tried to take leadership in the family. He not only sought to preempt his father's leadership—laying claim to a significant part of his father's estate—but also engaged in underplot and intrigue by having relations with Bilhah to establish that he was filling the vacuum left at Rachel's death.

Whatever legitimacy Reuben may have thought gave him license to do what he did, Jacob now told him that he would **no longer excel** (49:4). The prophecy came true. There is no subsequent mention of primacy for Reuben's tribe among the tribes.  Reuben's descendants settled east of the Jordan River.  Not one of his descendents became a judge or a king, nor was there even a prophet. They slowly faded into oblivion.

Next, brothers 2 and 3—**Simeon and Levi**—were addressed together. Jacob's mind returned to their dastardly ruse of decimating the population of Shechem after the violation of Dinah (see 34:1-31).  Puzzling, though, is the reference to their having **hamstrung oxen** (49:6).  This speaks of a practice of cutting the rear tendons of animals to make the animals less useful. No mention is made of this in any earlier account. Since the use of parallelism—using literary terms to project certain ideas—was prominent, it may be that Jacob's reference to the ox is a reference to himself. Perhaps he felt that their acts **hamstrung** him in his efforts to make peace with the inhabitants so as to live in security among them.

As to the descendants of the two sons being "scattered," in time the tribe of Simeon lost separate identity, being absorbed into the tribe of Judah. Simeon was scattered indeed. The tribe of Levi was not given a land inheritance of its own; its people divided up and settled in forty-eight cities throughout the other tribes (see Joshua 21:41).

**Judah,** fourth son of Leah, next received attention from Jacob. Jacob began by mentioning praise coming to Judah from his brothers (see 49:8a). Jacob did not indicate the reason for this praise, unless he was referring to the future when Judah would beat his enemies (see 49:8b). The lion, so powerful, so brave, and so consistent symbolized Judah's potential for success. Though Judah had erred badly, his character would cause him to rule and lead, especially since his three older brothers had disqualified themselves for leadership.

That place of authority and greatness would remain with Judah. The **scepter** and **staff,** symbols of supremacy, **will not depart from Judah** (49:10). Then follows a most difficult phrase to translate. The New International Version reads, **until he comes to whom it belongs.** The King James Version renders it "until Shiloh come." Shiloh was where the Tabernacle was set up on a rather permanent basis after Joshua conquered the land, making Shiloh the religious center of the country. So the translation suggests that a reference to Shiloh was a prophecy of the coming religious system that, over centuries, led to Christ. This seems not likely to have been the intent, for the feminine noun "Shiloh" is coupled with the masculine verb **come**—not good Hebrew. One possibility is that Shiloh referred to an individual instead of a city.

Another possible translation is "until he [Judah] comes to Shiloh." Perhaps Shiloh, a city in the tribe of Ephraim (the leading tribe of the north), represented all of the northern tribes. If so, the prophecy could have pointed to the time when King David, from the tribe of Judah, would take over the reluctant ten tribes that had been loyal to the house of Saul (see 2 Samuel 5:1-5) and would rule over all twelve. If, then, the prophesy in a more complete sense referred to the dynasty of David, then it likely also pointed to a descendent of David, a king superior to David—none other than the Messiah himself, "the son of David, the son of Abraham" (Matthew 1:1).

Continuing with the information about the coming One given in Genesis 49:8-10, the next two statements could also apply to Him. The mention of a donkey (see 49:11) reminds readers today of the prophecy of Zechariah 9:9, which announces Jesus' Palm Sunday mount—a donkey. The mention of the donkey being tied **to the choicest branch,** along with **garments** washed in **wine** and **robes in the blood of grapes,** together speak of bountifulness and exceptional fruitfulness, a vivid reversal of the thorns and thistles punishment for the Fall and the resultant alienation from God. Luxuriant vines could be used to tether a donkey, and the product of the vine could be used to clean all kinds of soiled garments. Might not these words offer symbolic descriptions of Christ's rich ministry and His blood abundant enough to cleanse the whole world? The outward beauty of the coming Messiah is suggested by the reference to dark eyes and white teeth (see 49:12), two aspects of beauty highly desired by people in that area of the world.

The question can be raised as to how aware either Jacob or Judah would have been concerning these prophecies. Likely not very aware, if at all. The nature of prophecy is to reveal something that is yet to come. Prophecy is history waiting to happen. It is not uncommon that prophets spoke beyond their full comprehension, and yet they knew they were speaking the words God had told them to speak.

The words of Jacob given here proved to be an update of the coming of the "seed of woman" to be the bridge to reunite God and humankind. The seed had come through perilous times during Judah's earlier years, and at that most crucial time, God used a Canaanite woman to continue His grand design for the long awaited Seed to come (see Matthew 1:3). John the Revelator surely had read this passage, for it appears that God used it to inspire him to write, "The Lion of the tribe of Judah, the Root of David, has triumphed" (Revelation 5:5). Then John wrote of saints singing a new song: "And with your blood you purchased men for God from every tribe and language and people and nation" (Rev. 5:9).

Jacob turned his attention to **Zebulun.** Up to this point, he had spoken to and about each son in the order of his birth. Why did he jump over the next oldest son, Issachar? No adequate answer can be given for Jacob's changing the sequence.

Zebulun got only a few words (see Genesis 49:13). He was to live **by the seashore.** He did not and would not live *on* the shore, only *by* it. His tribe's border would extend to **Sidon**, then a major port where the Phoenicians lived. The name **Sidon** probably stood for the whole country of Phoenicia, and Zebulun's territory abutted it. In Moses' blessing in Deuteronomy 33:18-19, Zebulun is associated with Issachar, and both tribes are described as feasting "on the abundance of the seas." Though not actually located on the shoreline, they did benefit greatly from the trade and commerce connected with it.

By birth, Jesus was from the tribe of Judah, but he was reared in the tribe of Zebulun.

Jacob described **Issachar** as **a rawboned donkey** (49:14). A donkey was highly regarded in Canaan at the time. They were the minivans of the day, able to carry twice their weight. One that was **rawboned** would have been stronger than normal. His being content to lie **down between two saddlebags** may have been a description of him as protected by geography, enabling him to live a relaxed, comfortable life among the surrounding Canaanites. But this description may have also referred to a time when the tribe would ultimately have to submit to the rigors of **forced labor** (49:15). The Valley of Jezreel was located in the middle of their territory, and the main trade route for the three continents of Europe, Africa, and Asia passed through their midst. It may be that the prophecy looked to the time when their labor was required because of it.

**Dan** next got Jacob's attention. Dan was the first son of Rachel's maid, whose birth made Rachel feel "vindicated." Through Bilhah, Dan's actual mother, the stigma of childlessness had been eased for Rachel (see 30:4-6). Dan was given his name because of its meaning: "vindicated." It appears here that Jacob was saying the tribe of Dan would also be a vindicator for all the other tribes. For a fulfillment of this prophecy, readers could consider Samson, a Danite, who would help begin the deliverance from the menacing Philistines. Indeed, the image of a **viper** [Dan] **that bites the horse's heels** (the Philistines?) causing the rider to tumble backward (49:17) suggests the small overcoming the strong.

Jacob seems to suddenly blurt out the words that 49:18 records: **I look for your deliverance, O LORD.** How do these words fit in? Was there some compelling reason for him to say the words at that moment? Jacob had been uttering some difficult prophecies, but in the midst of it all he sounded forth his clarion faith that at some point in the future God would bring a salvation that was eternal.

This sudden change of tenor in Jacob's utterance reminds us of Jeremiah in what was probably the most difficult time in his life (see Jeremiah 20), when he had been kept in stocks all night for having said what God wanted said. Between asking God for vengeance upon his enemies and his cursing the day of his birth, he suddenly declared, "Sing to the Lord! . . . He rescues the life of the needy from the hands of the wicked" (Jer. 20:13).

Perhaps the mention of the name of Dan helped Jacob recall the need for "deliverance from" his own problems. But what were those problems? One suggestion is that Jacob saw the difficulties ahead for the tribes at that moment, so he briefly offered a quick request for their deliverance; he had depended on God's stepping in to vindicate him on many occasions when he had gotten himself into trouble. Another suggestion might be that Jacob, nearing death, felt a sudden stab of pain. Knowing he still wished to speak about his younger sons, he asked God to give him strength.

**Gad's** future would involve being **attacked by a band of raiders** (49:19a). Gad's tribal location after the Israelites arrived in Canaan was west of the Jordan, an area they had requested. This location was exposed on its southern flank to the Moabites and on the eastern side to the Ammonites. Yet Gad would **attack them** [their enemies] **at their heels** (49:19). The enemy would be successful in their counterattack. The Gadites were some of the most brave and loyal men to David during his years of trying to escape King Saul (1 Chronicles 12:8).

**Asher** came next. His destiny was bound up in **food . . . fit for a king** (Gen. 49:20). The area where Asher's descendants were to settle in Canaan was on the fertile strip of land along the Mediterranean Sea. It could be assumed that their close proximity to the Phoenicians and Canaanites made it lucrative for them to supply food to the courts of the kings of those people.

Of the sons of Jacob's wives other than Rachel, only **Naphtali** remained. This tribe's activity is largely unknown and receives little biblical mention. Along with the tribe of Zebulun, Naphtali raised ten thousand men to help Deborah and Barak defeat the armies of Sisera (see Judges 4:9-10). The place of the tribe of Naphtali in Canaan was one of the few places that showed no great incursions by the Canaanites. Perhaps the **doe** and **beautiful fawns** (Gen. 49:21) in some way show the ability and success in warfare (speed and unfetteredness?) of the tribe of Naphtali.

Judah next turned to **Joseph.** While Jacob gave to him the longest prophecy, it is often obscure and complex. Joseph was first compared to a fruitful vine, made more fruitful by its location **near a spring** (49:22). Jacob seemed to look back into the life of Joseph who was attacked by hostile **archers** (49:23). The most logical reference is to all those who previously tried to ruin him in one way or another—for example, his brothers, the Midianites, Potiphar and his wife, and perhaps the cupbearer. All of these foes were prevented from their designs by the blessings of the **Mighty One of Jacob** (49:24). In the midst of the blessing being given to Joseph, Jacob then looked to future blessings which would be **greater than the blessings of the ancient mountains,** which he desired would **rest on the head of Joseph . . . the prince among his brothers** (49:26).

Jacob's last blessing was reserved for his youngest son, **Benjamin.** Benjamin was compared to a wolf, devouring its prey in the morning, then in the evening taking what is left to its den to divide. Having become especially adept at warfare, the tribe of Benjamin won two battles in a civil war against all the other tribes, mainly because of its men's expertise in using slingshots with their left hands (see Judges 20:15-25). One judge, Ehud, came from them. He, too, was left-handed, and with that asset he brought about the death of the enemy Moabite king (see Judges 3:15-30). At a time when Israel most needed a king to fight the Philistines successfully, one of their number, Saul, was chosen. For some unexplained reason, many of the Benjaminite warrior relatives of King Saul joined David at Ziklag after they had been banished (see 1 Chronicles 12:1-2). Their military expertise was well established; they were known as "brave fighting men" (2 Chron. 14:8).

## 4. JACOB'S BURIAL (49:29-50:14)

Before Jacob breathed his last, he wanted to make sure that his final resting place would be where his wife, Leah, and his father, mother, grandfather, and grandmother were all buried—the cave of Machpelah, near Mamre. His mind was still clear; he recounted all the details of how his grandfather had bought the place. Jacob had earlier gained a pledge from Joseph that Jacob would not be buried in Egypt but with his fathers (see Genesis 47:29-31). It was so important to Jacob that he wanted all the family to know his wishes.

Having explained plans for his burial, the last of his energy now expended, Jacob quietly laid down, pulled his feet up into the bed, and took his last breath.

Joseph could restrain himself no longer. He had patiently waited, allowing Jacob to complete his blessings to each son. Then, as soon as Jacob expired, Joseph **threw himself upon his father and wept over him and kissed him** (50:1; the literal rendering is "fell on his father's face"). When Joseph had first greeted his father in Egypt, Joseph then "fell on his father's neck" (the literal rendering of 46:29). Joseph's greeting was one of joy; now Joseph fell upon his father in sorrow. No other son is mentioned as having grieved as much.

God had recognized the closeness between father and favorite son and had promised Jacob, just as he was leaving Beersheba, that "Joseph's own hand will close your eyes" (46:4). Contemporary customs gave that honor to one closest to the deceased.

Joseph ordered embalming procedures to begin immediately; this was necessary in a hot country to prevent decay as much as possible. The process was a long and elaborate one. It began by the removal of the internal organs that were the quickest to decay. They were placed in special jars, and the spaces left were filled with spices. The brain was then extracted. Afterward, the body was soaked in sodium nitrate, then wrapped in long, narrow strips of linen. The whole process is said to have taken **a full forty days** (50:3), after which the Egyptians mourned Jacob another thirty days.

Until this point, Joseph had had free access to Pharaoh. The text here states that he used Pharaoh's court to speak for Jacob. Why the change? Was there an Egyptian custom that prevented a mourner from approaching the king during the seventy-day mourning period? Or could it have been a hesitancy on Joseph's part to visit the king so soon after touching his dead father? Either is possible. But official permission had to be obtained quickly for Joseph to leave the country to bury his father. And since Joseph was so important to the Pharaoh, Joseph reassured Pharaoh, **"I will return"** (50:5).

Permission quickly came, more quickly since Pharaoh knew that Joseph would not use this as an occasion to leave Egypt for good. Had the Pharaoh feared that or had he not trusted Joseph's word, he would have ordered Joseph to stay. His trust in Joseph was complete.

To onlookers, the entourage must have had the appearance of a small army. It was described as **a very large company** (50:9). It included the high-ranking dignitaries of Pharaoh's court, plus elders of the whole country, Joseph and his brothers, and a military escort. It must have been a most elaborate and dignified state funeral, with pomp and ceremony second to none, one that normally would have been reserved for a king.

The place where they stopped, **the threshing floor of Atad,** located **near** (literally, "beyond") **the Jordan** River (50:10), raises a puzzling question. Why did they take that route? It was not the most direct from Egypt. In fact, it was a great distance out of the way. Some think that Jacob is referring to the route they had taken to get to Hebron, which would have been near Jericho. Of course, centuries later, the entire nation would follow the same route into Canaan. However, aware that no Canaanites were ever located on the east side of the Jordan River, some scholars believe the word translated **near** could mean "close to" rather than "beyond," and they locate Atad to be much nearer Hebron and on the west side of the Jordan.

Wherever Atad was located, the family stopped at **the threshing floor of Atad** for a loud and bitter lamenting period of seven days. During this time, the Canaanites became aware of the events. They **saw the mourning** (50:11), which suggests the tearing of garments, elaborate crying, perhaps the use of ashes and sackcloth, and fasting. They called the spot "Mourning of Egypt."

A final summary states that Jacob's sons had fulfilled the instructions of their father in conducting the actual burial in the cave where his forefathers were buried. The procession then made its way back to Egypt.

## 5. JOSEPH'S TOTAL FORGIVENESS (50:14-21)

As things in Egypt began to return to normal after Jacob's funeral, the brothers of Joseph started to worry about how Joseph would treat them without Jacob there to offer any protection. Though Joseph had made it clear to them that he felt no lingering animosity toward them, they still feared he might seek revenge. They worried that his love for Jacob had kept him from repaying them for their crime, despite his offers of forgiveness (see Genesis 45:5). The reason for their fear is quite clear. It had nothing to do with Joseph's action. It had everything to do with their continued awareness of their reprehensible actions. They had failed to acknowledge their guilt and had not yet asked for his forgiveness, so that unresolved guilt still tormented them.

At least the brothers realized their delinquency. The message they sent to Joseph informed him that before Jacob died he had instructed them to tell Joseph to forgive them for what they had done. The text contains no record of such an instruction, so perhaps they had invented the story. The text does not even describe Jacob's ever having received a full account of what they had done to Joseph. If Jacob had indeed instructed forgiveness, he would have spoken directly to Joseph rather than indirectly through his brothers.

It is to the credit of the brothers, though, that at long last they finally did request forgiveness. They sent a message to Joseph: **Now please**

**forgive the sins of the servants of the God of your father** (50:17). And before Joseph had a chance to reply, they appeared at his house. Joseph reacted by bursting into tears, just as he had done when he had revealed his true identity to them the first time (see 45:2). Those tears must have said, "What more can I do to show you I do indeed forgive you? Has everything I have said and done been to no avail?"

The brothers were now so ashamed that they **threw themselves down** (50:18) before Joseph. Joseph's response did not include the words "I forgive you." But these were not necessary. He had already forgiven them. He twice counseled them to forget their fears (see 50:19, 21) and let them know that vengeance belonged to God, not him. "And furthermore," Joseph told them, **You intended to harm me, but God intended it for good . . .** (50:19). Writer William Shakespeare might have been influenced by these words when, in "As You Like It," he penned, "Sweet are the uses of adversity, which like a toad, ugly and venomous, wears yet a precious jewel in its head."

Joseph finished the conversation by promising to continue to provide for them (see 50:21). In effect, he reassured them that their relationship with him would not change just because Jacob was gone. "I took care of you through the famine; I will continue to **provide for you and your children.**"

## 6. JOSEPH'S FINAL DAYS (50:22-26)

Very briefly, the author gives an overview of the remainder of Joseph's life: Joseph lived 110 years and enjoyed his grandchildren. Are the **brothers** (50:24) to whom he spoke before he died in his generation, or were they his brothers' children? The text does not say. All of his brothers but Benjamin were older than he was, and Scripture does not describe their deaths. But these **sons of Israel** (50:25) were made to swear by oath that they would take his bones with them when, with God's assistance, they returned to the land of promise.

Of significance is that when Jacob had made his request of his sons regarding his burial place (see 49:29-32), he had "instructed" or "ordered" them. Here Joseph made the **brothers . . . swear an oath.** Does the stronger phrase indicate that Joseph worried about their trustworthiness? Perhaps.

Like Jacob, Joseph's body was embalmed and placed in a coffin, likely an elaborate sarcophagus, as was customary for high-ranking Egyptian officials. Joseph's remains stayed there apparently in some very elaborate location west of the Nile (where Egyptian tombs all were located) for several hundred years. When the Hebrews moved out of Egypt in the Exodus, Moses saw to it that "the bones of Joseph" were taken with them (Exodus 13:19).

Joseph had not specified exactly where in the Promised Land he wanted to be buried, but under Joshua's leadership he was buried at Shechem on the property first acquired by Jacob when he returned from Haran (see 33:19; also Joshua 24:32). The deciding factor, besides its purchase by Joseph's father, was probably that the land was in the vicinity of the tribe of Manasseh, Joseph's oldest son.

Genesis begins the story of Adam in the Garden of Eden; it concludes with Joseph in an Egyptian coffin. But clearly this book of the Bible points far beyond itself. In Joseph's last words, he expressed his profound faith in the future: **God will surely come to your aid and take you up out of this land to the land he promised . . .** (50:24). The promise that God would come was repeated throughout the remainder of the Old Testament until God did come (in "the fulness of time" [Galatians 4:4 NASB]) in the form of the Divine Seed He had promised. The Gospels record the death of this Promised Seed but gloriously add the account of His resurrection. Then a climax builds throughout the New Testament to the end of Revelation, where the last words of Jesus are recorded: "I am coming soon." In all of the religious books of the world that chronicle the events of their leader and the adherents who follow, the Bible is the only book that does not close with a tomb.

## ENDNOTES

[1]For example, Abel, Isaac, Jacob, Joseph, Ephraim, Moses, Samuel, David, and Solomon. Not always selecting the eldest child may have been God's way of showing that selecting people for special service entirely on the basis of age would not always allow the right person for an assignment. A question that could arise is, did God more often endow second, third, or later born children with leadership qualities instead of firstborn children so as to show the faulted cultural bias of former days?

[2]D. Winton Thomas, *Archaeology and Old Testament Study* (London: Oxford University Press, 1967), p. 127.

# SELECT BIBLIOGRAPHY

This commentary has been written with the purpose of enabling the Christian in the pew to understand God's message in the book of Genesis. Below is a list of resources that may help the reader who wishes to do further study.

Aalders, G. Ch. *Genesis,* vol. II. Grand Rapids, Mich.: Zondervan Publishing House; St. Catharines, Ontario, Canada: Paideia, 1981.

Albright, William F. *The Archaeology of Palestine and the Bible.* Cambridge, Massachusetts: American Schools of Oriental Research, 1974.

Allis, Oswald T. *The Five Books of Moses.* Philadelphia: Presbyterian and Reformed, 1943.

*The Anchor Bible,* vol. 2. New York: Doubleday, 1992.

Archer, Gleason L. *A Survey of Old Testament Introduction,* 3rd ed. Chicago: Moody Press, 1994.

*Ariel,* Quarterly Review of the Arts and Sciences in Israel, no. 41, 1976.

Arnold, Bill T. *Encountering the Book of Genesis.* Grand Rapids, Michigan: Baker Book House, 1998.

Arnold, Bill T. and Bryan E. Beyer. *Encountering the Old Testament: A Christian Survey.* Grand Rapids, Michigan: Baker Book House, 1998.

Avi-Yonah, M. and Abraham Malamat, eds. *The World of the Bible.* New York: Educational Heritage, 1964.

Basset, F.W. "Noah's Nakedness and the Curse of Canaan. A Case of Incest?" *Vetus Testamentum* 21, 1971.

Baez-Camargo, Gonzalo. *Archaeological Commentary on the Bible,* New York: Doubleday and Company, Inc., 1986.

*Genesis,* Calvin's Commentaries, vol. 1. Grand Rapids, Michigan: Baker Book House, 1981.

Cornfeld, Gaalyah. *Archaeology of the Bible: Book by Book.* New York: Harper and Row, 1976.

*Encyclopedia Britannica,* vol. 10. Chicago, 1970.

Frick, Frank S. *A Journey Through the Hebrew Scriptures*. New York: Harcourt Brace College Publishers, 1995.

Gunkel, Herman. *Genesis ubersetz und erklart,* 9th ed. Gottinger, Germany: Vandenhoeck and Ruprecht, 1977.

Haines, Lee. *Genesis and Exodus,* The Wesleyan Bible Commentary. Grand Rapids, Michigan: Wm. B. Eerdmans Publishing Co., 1967.

Hamilton, Victor P. *Handbook of the Pentateuch*. Grand Rapids, Michigan: Baker Book House, 1982.

Hamilton, Victor P. *The Book of Genesis: Chapters 18–50,* New International Commentary on the Old Testament. Grand Rapids, Michigan: Wm. B. Eerdmans Publishing Co., 1990.

Harrison, Roland Kenneth. *Introduction to the Old Testament*. Grand Rapids, Michigan: Wm. B. Eerdmans Publishing Co., 1969.

Hertz, J.H. *The Pentateuch and Haftorahs,* vol. 1. New York: Oxford University Press, 1936.

Hicks, Peter. "A Very Special Book." In *The Complete Bible Study Tool Kit,* edited by John F. Balchin, David H. Field, Tremper Longman III. Downers Grove, Illinois: InterVarsity Press, 1991.

Hauer, Christian E. and William A. Young. *An Introduction to the Bible*. Upper Saddle River, New Jersey: Prentice Hall, 1998.

*The International Standard Bible Encyclopedia,* vol. 4. Grand Rapids, Michigan: Wm. B. Eerdmans Publishing Co., 1988.

*The Interpreter's Bible,* vol. 1. New York: Abingdon Press, 1952.

*The Interpreter's Dictionary of the Bible*. Nashville, Tennessee: Abingdon Press, 1962.

Jensen, Irving L. *Jensen's Survey of the Old Testament*. Chicago: Moody Press, 1975.

Kaiser, Walter, Jr. *Toward Old Testament Ethics*. Grand Rapids, Michigan: Zondervan Publishing House, 1983.

Keil, Carl Friedrich and Franz Delitzsch. *Commentary on the Old Testament*. Grand Rapids, Michigan: Wm. B. Eerdmans Publishing Co., 1978.

Kidner, Derek. *Genesis: An Introduction and Commentary,* Tyndale Old Testament Commentaries. Downers Grove, Illinois: InterVarsity Press, 1967.

*Genesis,* Lange's Commentary on the Holy Scriptures, vol. 1. Grand Rapids, Michigan: Zondervan Publishing House.

Lewis, C.S. *The Screwtape Letters*. New York: Macmillan Publishing Company, 1961.

Longman, Tremper, III. *Making Sense of the Old Testament*. Grand Rapids, Michigan: Baker Book House, 1998.

Matthew Henry Commentary, vol. 1. New York: Revell.

Montet, Pierre. *Egypt and the Bible*. Philadelphia: Fortress Press, 1968.

*The New Interpreter's Bible,* vol. 1. Nashville, Tennessee: Abingdon Press, 1994.

Nicoll, W. Robertson. *The Expositor's Bible,* vol. 1. New York: Doran.

Parrot, Andre. *The Tower of Babel*. New York: Philosophical Library, 1955.

Price, I.M., O.R. Sellers, and E. Leslie Carlson. *The Monuments and the Old Testament*. Philadelphia: Judson Press, 1958.

*The Pulpit Commentary,* vol. 1. Grand Rapids, Michigan: Wm. B. Eerdmans Publishing Co., 1978.

Rowley, Harold H. *The Growth of the Old Testament*. New York: Harper and Row, 1963.

Sailhamer, John H. *The Pentateuch as Narrative,* A Biblical-Theological Commentary. Grand Rapids, Michigan: Zondervan Publishing House, 1992.

Sarna, Nahum M. *Understanding Genesis*. New York: Schocken, 1970.

Seldes, George. *The Great Thoughts*. New York: Ballantine Books, 1985.

Speiser, Ephraim A. "The Wife-Sister Motif in the Patriarchal Narratives." *Biblical and Other Studies*. Altmann, A., ed. Garden City, New York: Doubleday, 1963.

Thomas, D. Winton. *Archaeology and Old Testament Study*. London: Oxford University Press, 1967.

Tripp, Rhoda Thomas. *The International Thesaurus of Quotations*. New York: Thomas Y. Crowell Publishers, 1970.

Tulock, John. *The Old Testament Story*. Englewood Cliffs: Prentice Hall, 1992.

Vawter, B. *On Genesis, A New Reading*. Garden City, New York: Doubleday, 1977.

Vos, Howard F. *Genesis and Archaeology*. Grand Rapids, Michigan: Zondervan Publishing House, 1985.

Wegner, Paul D. *The Journey from Texts to Translations*. Grand Rapids, Michigan: BridgePoint Books, 1999.

Wenhem, Gordon. *Genesis 1–15,* Word Biblical Commentary, vol. 1. Dallas, Texas: Word Publishing, 1994.

Wenhem, Gordon. *Genesis 16–50,* Word Biblical Commentary, vol. 2. Dallas, Texas: Word Publishing, 1994.

Wright, G. Ernest and David N. Freedman, eds. *The Biblical Archaeologist Reader,* vol. 1. Garden City, New York: Doubleday, 1961–64.

Wright, G. Ernest, *Biblical Archaeology,* rev. ed. Philadelphia: Westminster Press, 1962.

West, James King. *Introduction to the Old Testament*. New York: The Macmillan Co., 1971.

Young, Edward J. *An Introduction to the Old Testament*. Grand Rapids, Michigan: Wm. B. Eerdmans Publishing Co., 1960.